Becoming One

Becoming One

A Story of Triumph Over Multiple Personality Disorder

Sarah E. Olson

TRILOGY BOOKS

For information, address Trilogy Books, 50 S. DeLacey Avenue, Suite 201, Pasadena, CA 91105.

Cover design: J. Stevens Art & Design

Publisher's Cataloging in Publication

Olson, Sarah E.
Becoming one : a story of triumph over multiple personality disorder / Sarah E. Olson.
p. cm.
Includes index.
ISBN 0-9623879-8-3

1. Multiple personality--Case studies. 2. Child abuse. 3. Adult child abuse victims. I. Title.

RC569.5.M8057 1997 616.85'236
QBI96-40678

Library of Congress Catalog Card Number: 96-61720

Dedication

During years of sexual abuse and torture inflicted upon my sister and me by the husband of a family friend, my mother said repeatedly of me, "You know how she tells stories." Thirty years later, I had the extraordinary good fortune to meet Howard Asher. His genius and steadfast compassion journeyed with me each step through my private petrified forest. With patience, humor, and unwavering vitality, he transformed a lot of seemingly dead wood into a lavish country garden on a par with Giverny. He taught me that my stories are about the truth.

I also learned important truths about people, relationships, love, and trust. It is to Howard's great credit that I'm now in a loving, giving, supportive marriage to a man who, not surprisingly, mirrors many of Howard's qualities.

This book is dedicated to Howard, and to Dan, both of whom have demonstrated their love and commitment in myriad ways which still astonish me.

Acknowledgments

Just as life is enriched by people whose lives intersect with our chosen path, this book was enriched by a circle of compassionate individuals. I wish to express my love and appreciation to my friends Sandy, Hank, Jackie, Sue, Jamie, Rick, Keith, Chris, Kate, Hope, and Brian. They each encouraged me at moments when I was certain this project could not be completed. I also thank Jacob N. Segura and Leonard Korobkin of Beverly Hills, California for their legal talents and mitzvahs. And I am grateful to my immediate family for listening to this story unfold, and for staying with me even when it pointed toward them. As a survivor, I cannot ask for more.

Table of Contents

Foreword

I walked into the waiting room to greet my new patient. She was sitting in a wood frame chair in the far corner. Without saying a word, her face spoke volumes. She looked cautious, doubtful, uncertain, distrustful, apprehensive, and generally quite troubled. At the same time, her eyes indicated a character of strength, determination, and wisdom.

"Hi, I'm Howard Asher." I escorted her to my office and thus began my part in this 36 year old woman's journey back to life.

For most of her life, Sarah Olson had to live as many different people in one body. It is widely known as Multiple Personality Disorder (MPD). Clinically, this condition is now referred to as Dissociative Identity Disorder (DID), and belongs to a class of syndromes identified as dissociative disorders.

To the general public, DID is much like a sideshow oddity. Viewed with disbelief, people wonder if it's real, and its manifestations provoke fascination. Although genuinely intriguing, it fades from consciousness and people go about their lives.

But for those who suffer from dissociative disorders and exist as fragmented souls, going about one's life is a moment-by-moment challenge. In severe cases, ever-present is a hair-trigger potential for a life-threatening crisis. The resilience of these people and their coping powers are just impossible to imagine.

All indications are that dissociative disorders are caused by a steady pattern of childhood trauma. The nature of such trauma is any one or combination of mental, physical, and sexual abuse.

Sarah's courage and generosity to candidly share her remarkable experiences afford an invaluable understanding of the effects of severe child abuse and the psychological complexities of survival. Sarah provides important insights into the world of dissociation. She reveals how she existed and survived; and she shows us how she came back from hell to live again. Ultimately, Sarah's story is supremely triumphant. She has reclaimed her life, she is whole, and she is emotionally healthy.

Throughout this book, Sarah highlights the role psychotherapy played in her recovery. It is an intensely personal and intimate look inside the therapeutic process.

Effective psychotherapy requires that the patient and therapist form and maintain a partnership of equal responsibility. Their roles are certainly different, but their contribution to the process is equivalent. A positive transference must also exist. This simply means that patient and therapist regard one another favorably and with mutual respect.

For the patient, psychotherapy is a proactive endeavor to stop pain and take control of life. With the desire to help accomplish this, the process of psychotherapy for the therapist is like a high-wire act. It is the art of maintaining the perfect balance between two fundamentally contradictory truths, that all people are basically alike and that no person is like anybody else.

There really is no mystery about the essence of effective psychological treatment. Its constituents are plain talk, honesty, and commitment. The therapist's job is to gain understanding. The therapist does not have to know everything (which is impossible, anyway). He or she simply has to be genuinely curious so as to fuel the quest to understand. As this quest for understanding proceeds, the answers and resolutions automatically unfold. Emotional freedom and stability take hold.

While the process of psychotherapy must be conducted in an environment of safety and comfort, a successful outcome rarely occurs without risk. It is for this reason that a patient must feel a good rapport with the therapist and, above all, have complete trust in the therapist's abilities and concern for the patient's all-around welfare. Any misgivings about this should not be ignored! A competent and reputable therapist aware of such misgivings on the patient's part would not hesitate to recommend a referral to another therapist.

In this book, Sarah's written accounts beautifully illustrate the principles and dynamics of the therapeutic relationship. It is real and engaging.

Sarah's story is truly inspirational; it demonstrates that with perseverance and a dedication to honesty, life's most daunting challenges can be overcome.

Resources, such as clinical treatment, support groups, and many other resorts, are available to enhance anybody's natural gifts. However, one has to believe one is entitled to take his or her place in the world and create fulfillment for oneself and others. Sarah has done so. . . I hope we all do.

Howard Asher, M.S., M.F.C.C.
Woodland Hills, California
March, 1996

Introduction

"I grew up believing I had to be more clever than anyone else, or I wasn't going to make it."

— FIRST SESSION WITH HOWARD, JUNE 26, 1991

At age fifteen I required emergency appendectomy surgery.[1] As the anesthesia lost its hold on me in the recovery room, I tried to speak, pulling off my oxygen mask. The nurse replaced it, smiling, ignoring my garbled question. I reawakened in my room, my parents beside me, the pain's intensity rising in pace with my ability to focus. My first words were, "Where's Charlotte?" My mother said, "Don't worry about her now." With considerable effort, I persisted. "How is she?" My mother replied, "You're the one who's in the hospital. You're the one we're worried about." I asked again, "Where is she?"

My mother was a no-nonsense woman who demanded control of most situations, especially those involving me. She spoke in her "irritated" voice: "You'll see her later." I insisted that I see Charlotte immediately. In a low, angry voice, my mother said, "I will get her for you, but don't think for a minute that your behavior is acceptable because you're in the hospital." This voice was far more recognizable than the earlier noises of concern. Moments later, Charlotte stood by my bed, and smiled, "Hello, Sissy."

For 22 years, I replayed that scene in my mind, and asked: "Why did I care where or how Charlotte was? Why did it matter?" It was not until October 1991, when Charlotte and I compared notes, that I felt a strange "spinning" sensation in my head, as if something inside physically shifted, and I knew the answer. I was confused coming out of the anesthesia, and believed Ron, the man who molested and tortured us over many childhood years, had stabbed me. Since we were often together during these atrocities, I believed that if my parents did not produce Charlotte, she must be dead. But at fifteen I had no conscious memories of being abused, and five years had elapsed since Ron vanished from our lives. I quickly forgot again whatever I knew in that moment.

Throughout my life, ostensibly benign, random thoughts and events regularly occurred that created panic and confusion in me because I could not explain them. I asked forever, "Why?" Such was the power of these events, and of the fear dwelling continually just below consciousness, that Charlotte's and my memories of our years of torture were blocked for more than thirty years.

Until mid-1991, at age 36, I seldom concerned myself with issues of childhood sexual abuse. It was the year Marilyn Van Derber courageously disclosed the truth about Miss America's childhood. I tuned it out. I listened abstractly to daily accounts of children in peril, betrayed by everything familiar. Children for whom salvation was denied by the people they trusted most. I felt no connection to me.

But I was not happy. I began therapy with Howard Asher because I wanted to know why I was self-destructing with food when everything else in my life seemed to finally be coming together. All the "why's" of a lifetime tumbled out, to the point where Howard affectionately dubbed me "the endless why person." I opened my life up for examination in ways I'd never before experienced in therapy. Then my oldest sister, Linda, handed me the key for which I'd searched my entire life. She asked if it were possible that I had been present when Charlotte was molested. A door in my mind, groaning against the force of 30 years of constraint, was flung wide open.[2]

The view from this door was scary, surreal, foreign, and yet painfully familiar. I discovered a world where all the rules changed, and nothing happened the way it did in fairy tales. These little girls had terrible nightmares that strongly echoed the events of their days, but no one believed them or comforted their nights. Only in dreams were they occasionally rescued by the likes of Quickdraw McGraw. Degradation and pain were demonstrated more consistently than love, and life was reduced to basic survival for days while the adults put on their party faces and played cards.

No one ever wondered why or how two out of three children in our family came to behave in withdrawn and antisocial patterns, least of all, our parents. They reminded us often how lucky we were to be part of our family. Charlotte coped by sleeping constantly. I grew up angry. Linda, who escaped the abuse, distanced herself from Charlotte and me. We all got robbed.

As my therapy progressed, Howard and I uncovered intricately woven layers of family secrets and compelled unreality. My therapeutic process exposed issues of gross betrayal, credibility, denial, resentment, intense anger, misplaced loyalty, deception, and treachery. It opened wounds no one should be required to bear.

Howard recognized during our first session that my "friend" Sarah, (who lived somewhere inside me, and whom I freely described), evidenced a parallel life. He believed my childhood to be necessarily traumatic to support Sarah's continuous existence 30 years later. Eventually, we discovered a small village of other such friends — and a few unfriendly types — whose collective existence supported a diagnosis of Multiple Personality Disorder (MPD), subsequently reclassified under DSM-IV[3] as Dissociative Identity Disorder (DID).

DID is not a form of insanity, as sometimes popularly conceptualized. It is actually a brilliant coping mechanism relied upon in the most desperate of circumstances, and is nearly universally associated with severe trauma suffered by very young children. DID reveals — or perhaps more correctly, conceals — a highly creative, terrified young mind doing whatever needs to happen to survive in an untenable world. At age three, when first exposed to Ron's abuses, I began to split my self into compartments to protect and preserve some aspect of me that would survive untainted by my childhood experiences.

I was once a child of joy, but there was nothing hopeful or joyous about living in my childhood world. Everything about it made me feel crazy. When I complained about Ron's treatment, my mother claimed I was lying or having bad dreams. She was strongly motivated to promote another version of the truth. As a result, nobody listened to me. I was known for my tantrums, which cost me opportunities for rescue, but I did not know how else to attract attention.

I first considered suicide at age six. Thankfully, more parts of me insisted on survival than those that longed for oblivion. I survived, but as a child of rage. My mother was fond of screaming, "How did you get to be so mean and spiteful?" It was a really good question, but she never expected me to answer it.

Due to DID's unavoidable side effects, I endured a lifetime of bizarre circumstances, some of which I mistook for normal events. Some I felt certain confirmed my insanity, which I labored incessantly to conceal. This was especially true as a child, as I feared my mother could easily put me away. My stories about Ron's abuse threatened the look of her pseudo-perfect world — and "the look" was her obsession. It allowed her to rationalize anything, including her children's health and safety. An angry, crazy child represented a substantial embarrassment at places like church. But a child accusing her secret lover of monstrous acts was a tremendous liability, and I knew it. I did not feel safe to retrieve memories from early childhood until many years following my mother's death.

I grew up a child of the Fifties, which still retained an aura of innocence. This was a full generation before children's faces routinely appeared on milk cartons; before "incest" was said in public or "pregnant" allowed by TV censors; before McMartin rendered every day-care provider a potential suspect; before children were routinely videotaped and fingerprinted; before MTV and Madonna brought sexuality into our living rooms; before the pill and legal abortions gave us all choices; before anyone thought to take children seriously, with rights and advocates of their own.[4] My Fifties' childhood had all the hallmarks of that innocence and normalcy.

And we were outwardly model children. Whatever was wrong with my childhood was never apparent to anyone but me. Regardless of how articulate I became, I could never clarify, much less resolve, my constant depression and dread. That's a direct product of abuse, which invariably teaches unfortunate lessons to children. They learn that they exist at the whim of adults. They are of no consequence, either physically or emotionally. They are unlovable (because the people who are supposed to love them don't, which is somehow skewed into the child's flaw). They are worthless because they are treated like so much garbage, disposable and easily forgotten.

Even with the greatest motivation and therapy, adult survivors continue to have problems accepting that they are lovable, valuable, and contributing members of society. Those childhood lessons can be unlearned, presumably to complete eradication. Then a survivor sees or hears or touches something which triggers an ancient memory, and those feelings involuntarily overwhelm again. It is a rare survivor who manages to completely grow up and out of childhood, to the extent that it no longer negatively impacts adult life.

Some survivors say surviving is about existing. There is no joy, no sensuality, no real experience of love. Some cannot delight in how food tastes, or enjoy the rapture of a Mozart symphony. They don't know how. I believe surviving is really about thriving. It's about living the life you would have had if your abuse never occurred. It's about acknowledging the past, dealing with it, and persistence in reaching for attainable dreams.

My goal is to empower survivors, wherever they are on their journey of discovering the truth about their lives, to make conscious choices which no longer create new victim status. To accept themselves for all the talents and flaws they possess. To flourish in their present lives. It's not easily done. I certainly have to work very hard, sometimes minute by minute.

As a child, I wrote stories about cherished little girls who never had to wonder if they would live till morning. I grew up to become a paralegal — a ghostwriter for attorneys. This effectively guaranteed that no matter how brilliantly I wrote, I seldom received the credit. Why didn't I become a lawyer? While I've excelled at many things attempted in life, I've also done everything possible to deflect attention away from me. (This is a crazy-making dilemma.) I learned too well as a toddler that attention is a dangerous thing. What I want now is to no longer be afraid to proclaim who I am, and to feel at ease with legitimate attention. I am facilitating my own recovery here, and hope to be an example for others who still hesitate to live up to their own potential and dreams.

My case demonstrates that, with sufficient motivation and courage, the recovery process does not necessarily require double-digit years of therapy. That may be true for some cases, but I cannot believe I am the sole exception to the rule. Some therapists have a mindset which says, "You are a victim; you don't have to face the tough stuff if you don't want to now." Clients frequently and blindly relinquish control of their recovery to their therapists as authority figures with expertise. This, despite a gut feeling that they must get on with their lives.

My therapeutic experiences with Howard illustrate a partnership with mutual goals, a posture he actively encouraged. I previously stayed in therapy situations with no clear idea where it was supposed to be going, without confidence that the therapist knew, either. No one prior to Howard told me it was my decision, or that I was vital to the success of my process.

Creating motivation to find and stay in true partnership with a therapist is crucial. Neither of us ever lost sight of our goals, even when sessions were intense and frustrating. Equally important is the strength to demand that the process stay on track. Courage in therapy obliges you to see the unseeable and say the unsayable, taking appropriate risks. Creativity in therapy demands that you be innovative and resourceful. The process moves more rapidly if your therapist welcomes your active involvement, ideas, and direction. I discovered I was more likely to accept difficult therapeutic decisions if jointly made.

Writing, no doubt, contributed to a cherished sense of sanity in my life while going through this process. I documented all of my struggles and triumphs as they occurred over 50 months of intense therapy. I sent approximately 300 faxed letters to Howard, all stored in my computer for later review and retrieval. I also transcribed all of the audio tapes from our sessions (and was amazed by the information I'd previously missed by merely "listening"). As such, the documentation herein is not at all reconstructed from memory.

Some original materials presented here are graphic and ugly. Child abuse is not pretty, and any effort to make nice with it is an even greater obscenity. I want these images to create such indelible outrage that no one will hesitate to report incidents of suspected child abuse. I want the limits of a three-year-old's resources and vocabulary recognized, in the hope that the next child automatically earns the benefit of any doubt. I want it on the record that very young children store up memories of all sorts.

Those memories which instill fear and shame color a lifetime, and produce a child who grows into a damaged adult. Unless we, as a society, fully assimilate the ugliness of child abuse, and stop looking the other way, it will continue and be condoned by our silence. I want these pages to be the voice of every child yet unheard and denied.

In my journey, I discovered that this relentless pain, my unbidden companion for 35 years, became bearable with full disclosure and acknowledgment of its source. Then it disappeared. I learned, after countless lessons, that no matter how scary life seems the only really scary part is facing the fear down, and taking another step. I relied upon my instincts whenever I sensed danger, because it invariably was present. I allowed myself to experience absolute trust in another human being for the first time in my life, and I know now it was not a fluke. I confirmed that I was a feisty, creative, and courageous little girl, and that those attributes thrive in my adult self as well. I discovered that life is, in fact, worth living.

Progress in therapy seldom travels in a straight line. Sometimes the value of discovering the truth did not seem enough to offset its impact. Sometimes I longed for oblivion. Howard's message always proclaimed my entitlement to live the life I was supposed to live if nothing traumatic had occurred in my childhood. My past need not negatively influence my life today.

Anyone dealing with these issues is acutely aware of what a tall order that is! Howard's faith remained constant until I successfully merged this precept into my everyday life. It's still an ongoing process, but there is a passage through to the other side. I have been through the door myself.

1

The Myth and Truth of My Childhood

There's a child of joy who pirouettes into daddy's warm embrace.
She's awkward as any other child but she still has her own grace.
Soon she'll leave her father far behind. Soon, he knows he'll be replaced.
He can only hold her to him for the moment when she's still his.
As he lets her smile run through him, he thinks,
"Does all love end like this? Do we have to share?"
But he knows that he won't ask. He will not dare.

There's a lady in her home, alone, forgotten still, and bored.
She's the lady who remembers love and how her hopes once soared.
Now she spends her time in words and rhyme. She tells how her life's scored.
She can't hang onto her happiness the way she can her sorrow.
She knows that somehow her joy cost less.
Once she looked for her tomorrow. Once she thought life would be fair.
She used to ask all the right questions — it's with failure she won't dare.

EXCERPTS FROM "ROADS," SEO, 1975.

I might never have questioned my adult life as portrayed in "Roads" but for the fact that I have distinct memories of being that "child of joy." I've always believed something very bad must have happened when I was young, but could never articulate it. Something transformed me into a child of rage, and an adult who valued pain more than happiness. No one ever asked why I changed.

My parents, Richard and Frances, met in Cincinnati, Ohio, during World War II, and married in 1944. I am the youngest of three daughters: Linda, Charlotte, and Anita, my given name.

My father was 28 when married, a product of city life during the Depression. Throughout my childhood he spent each evening buried in the now-defunct *Los Angeles Herald Examiner*. This was sandwiched between the 6 and 11 p.m. TV news, with a radio earphone plugged in to listen simultaneously to some sports event. In other words, he was totally tuned out to whatever else was happening in our house.

Frances married at 23. She quit work as a registered nurse during her pregnancy with me. She made our lunches and had dinner ready when my father returned from work. She routinely met friends in the neighborhood for Tupperware parties and coffee. She was on the local election commission, attended Bible classes, and taught Vacation Bible School classes.

Her best friend, Cass, moved to Los Angeles in the mid-1940s. She enticed my parents to come West with talk of plentiful jobs and dream housing prices. My parents joined Cass in 1947. By 1951, Cass had met and married her second husband, Ron. He was embraced without question into our lives.

My sisters and I attended church, excelled in school, and didn't run with bad crowds, do drugs, or get pregnant at fifteen. We didn't even have boyfriends. We were never the source of embarrassing neighborhood gossip because we never did anything which remotely qualified. Our mother taught us to be polite and to fear strangers. She insisted that academic excellence was its own reward. She was raised in an era when children were physically punished, and did not hesitate to strike us when provoked. Our lives were full of summer vacations, Girl Scout camp-outs, backyard barbecues, book reports, slumber parties, band auditions, and prom nights. Everyone said we were so lucky to have such wonderful parents.

The myth of my childhood was borne in the notion that our family was so completely normal. By age three, I knew something was terribly wrong. Following the accidental death of our minister's son, I threw my arms around his wife's legs, saying, "I'm sorry you're so sad. I'll be your little girl. I know I'm not a boy, but I'll be good. Please let me be your little girl." This outburst embarrassed my mother, and probably didn't do much good for the minister's wife, either. But I wondered my entire life why was I so desperate to get out of my family at three.

As an adult, I searched for answers and found there weren't any. I spoke with neighbors, cousins, godparents, and even my mother, which took considerable courage. I was consistently given two storylines. My parents were good people with sturdy Midwest values who loved their children, and went out of their way to help someone in need; and I had a reputation that was at odds with itself. I was the family rebel; the spoiled baby brat; spiteful and sarcastic; very good at school; a constant source of aggravation. I was normal, creative, happy, ungrateful. I was Daddy's little Zsa Zsa. I had a chip on my shoulder.

The disparity of these assessments was a shock. I always considered myself a "goody two shoes" who never broke the rules. My godmother labeled me "the rebel," and I really didn't know what she was talking about. The most rebellious thing I remembered was talking back to my mother. I never ditched school when friends begged me to loosen up. I used my milk money to buy milk! It never occurred to me that I had a choice. I often dreamed of running away, but didn't think I was able to leave. I never understood that feeling, either.

I excelled in school because it made my mother briefly happy. I don't have a lot of memories of her celebrating my accomplishments. I do remember terrible fights with her. No matter how good I was, no matter what I did to make her appreciate and love me, it was never enough. Our lives were the picture of normalcy, but I persistently told friends, "You don't really know me. I don't live a normal life." As an adult, I frequently added, "I'm really a bad person." I could never articulate what was so wrong, but I felt certain it was dark and horrible.

The myth of my childhood resided in this facade of normalcy. The truth of my childhood lingered in a series of encapsulated events which were markers for the reality. Someone should have questioned what was happening. No one asked why two little girls were acting out in such strange behaviors. Ron could say with complete confidence, "You see, little girl? Nobody cares."

What is my story? At age three, I was first exposed to Ron's abuses of Charlotte. Over the next three years, I was repeatedly tied down, raped, and tortured. Ron told us often that we were bad, which resulted in our punishment. He promised that if I told anyone, people I loved would die. I told anyway, and no one listened. By age five, I was starring in Ron's child pornography business. He arranged group molestations for money. By then, my mother was Ron's lover, and fully aware of these events. By age six, Ron ventured into the snuff film business, enticing teenaged runaways into their movie of a lifetime. I witnessed several killings orchestrated and filmed for public consumption. I began seeking ways to make Ron kill me or to kill myself.

It ended one afternoon when I wearily asked Cass why Ron hurt me so much. I'd assumed all along that she knew about it. I just wanted to know why. She put a stop to it, at what personal cost I cannot say. But she and Ron continued to visit our house and play cards with my parents until she died when I was ten. Ron disappeared from our lives then. But he was never really gone.

How did these years of abuse and torture affect me? At age three, I retreated into my own little world. Sarah was my secret playmate and confidante. She was beautiful, special, fun, and happy, and everyone loved her best. Paradoxically, no one knew she existed because I went to great lengths to keep her concealed. We talked endlessly during very private tea parties. Sometimes she brought others with her, and our conversations continued inside my head, uninterrupted for hours. Sometimes I pretended I was Sarah.

I stopped telling anyone what I wanted, because I was guaranteed to never have it. I was deliberately noncommittal, and learned very early that I got things by getting them myself. Self-reliance became a survival skill, rather than an attribute connoting strength.

By age four, I'd awaken with aches in my legs so intense I feared I could not walk. I cried in my bed until my mother eventually heard me and brought baby aspirin. She called this "growing pains." They were especially prevalent in summer, when we saw Ron and Cass most frequently. I also began a lifelong habit of picking at my fingernails, in the vain hope that Ron would stop sticking needles under them if they didn't exist.

I memorized the furniture layout in our house so I could walk in complete darkness without tripping or making noise. I took great pride in this skill. As I grew older, I automatically memorized layouts everywhere I stayed. I rationalized it was necessary to retrieve my asthma medicine without waking anyone.

This failed to explain why I also knew where all the exits were located in every building I entered. I told myself it was a game.

I was terrified of doctors. I'd run and hide. I'm also, not surprisingly, terrified of needles, and anything sharp, such as knives and scissors. A few years ago, Charlotte and I realized we share this phobia.

I learned that crying was extremely dangerous. It set off unpredictable reactions in both Ron and my mother. Ron enjoyed it. I felt especially broken when he "won" that way. Crying — or not crying — became a measure of my control. I cried in private, and hated myself for displaying this weakness even to myself.

I became compulsive about many activities. If I didn't stay in the lines in my coloring books, the entire drawing was ruined. Something ruined, by definition, could never be fixed. I also liked the idea of using things up. I'd figure out weeks in advance on what day the vitamin jar would be empty and count the days. It was a way to make sure time passed.

I fought with my mother over naptime. I hated it and refused to cooperate. I knew bad things happened during naps, and became quite adept at faking sleep. This skill was useful with Ron, and saved my life more than once.

By age five, my mother decided Linda was entitled to her own room, which forced me into the back bedroom with Charlotte. I went into hysterics at the idea, but was compelled to comply. No one asked why I was so upset. We slept for years in what once was our parents' double bed. I could not bear for Charlotte to touch me, or to feel her breath on my shoulder if she slept too close. I hugged the outside edge of the bed, in readiness to run. If anyone tried to awaken me by touch I woke up fighting and defensive. No one asked why a child consistently woke up in a combative posture.

I had recurring nightmares of being chased by a shadowy bad man with a knife. I frequently saw him stab me, and sometimes witnessed my dream death. Or it switched to an underground cave where I was tied up for hours. Sometimes QuickDraw McGraw rescued me, sometimes not. Between age five and twelve I had this dream, in all of its variants, hundreds of times. I believed there was a secret passage inside our closet which allowed the bad man to get me. I was terrified to turn the lights out, or to fall asleep. My mother didn't tolerate my fears well.

I believed I was crazy, because the crazy things done to me were ignored by people who could/should have helped me, and were even passed off as normal. No one believed me. No one listened. The only thing scarier than being crazy was being found out. This provided yet another incentive to give in to the abuse, because talking about it made me look crazier than I felt.

By age six, my best friend Stacy decided to not be friends anymore. I never knew why. I can't help but wonder if Stacy was afraid of me, since I was acting strangely by anyone's standards. I had imaginary friends; I saw things no one else saw; I was upset a lot. As I grew older, my need for intensity deepened. Perhaps Stacy was the first casualty of many friends who couldn't take my rapid mood swings.

I lost another good friend that year. Stephen lived just down the street. One morning, our teacher announced he had died, but did not know how. I went screaming up and down the corridors. The school nurse called my mother because I was uncontrollable. (As usual, her primary concern was not over my grief, but that I had created a public scene and inconvenienced her.) What caused this hysteria? Ron threatened to kill someone I loved if I told. Stephen's death seemed quite clear at six. Thirty years later, I learned he'd died of leukemia.

I first considered suicide at six when I decided to drink the bleach next time Ron appeared. But his visits were too unpredictable to complete it. I tried every creative trick possible to escape him. I knew he was not really going to kill us, unless there were some sort of accident. I also knew my mother would never protect us. So I decided to end it by provoking Ron into stabbing me, instead of merely pretending to do so, when I was tied up. I directed all my pent-up rage and frustration at him. My plan failed because he understood what I was doing. I was totally demoralized. The good news (if that can be said without gagging), is that I dumped a lot of appropriate rage directly on him. Charlotte never had this opportunity. I believe that's why I can talk about Ron much more calmly than she can.

Since earliest memory, I said, "I hate Anita," and thought I was referring to my name. I insisted that people call me Nita. No one asked why. I hated every time I was forced to sign Anita for some official reason.

By age seven, the library provided a legitimate escape, but I wasn't one for the children's section. Wandering through the stacks, I discovered survivor accounts from Holocaust victims which included pictures of dead and tortured children. Their accounts were somehow familiar, although by then I wasn't sure why. Terrible things happened to a lot of children, and the books were proof that it wasn't right. I became obsessed with Holocaust literature for the next ten years.

All of these events appeared to happen somewhat randomly. Taken in concert, they depicted a radiant, curious, joyous child consumed by temper tantrums and perpetual fear. This child's nights were permeated by unexplained physical pains and dark dreams. She previously loved life and made friends easily. She became a loner and unremittingly lonely, afraid of new places and people. She became afraid of life.

JANUARY 20, 1992

The following session occurred immediately after I realized why my fingernails are so sensitive.

N: I hadn't told my manicurist why my nails were all gone. She knows the basic story, but wasn't caught up yet. We've had this running joke for six years that I come to her for pain. I'm super-sensitive; everything hurts; I'm always grabbing my hands back, anticipating it. We've always laughed about it. After fifteen minutes, she stopped working, and said, "What happened to you? Your hands are totally relaxed. It's never

been like this before." I said, "What? Really?" (laughs) It was amazing. And it didn't hurt.

H: Wow. It's profound.

N: ***That's what I said, wow. It's like me saying to you, "Show me." This is being shown.***

H: It's a result. This is how it works.

N: ***To have carried around all that pain in my fingertips.***

H: Sure. You'd have to wonder how many other ways it manifests that you just take for granted.

N: ***Well, yeah! I started thinking, "Maybe he did something to my neck." All my physical problems.***

H: What we talk about here must feel like a not very exacting science. But, we're getting more enlightened because the stories of these horrible abuses are coming out. Some have experienced an ordeal others couldn't even think of. We know this now, as a culture and enlightened society. Yet, how many ways are there to deal with it? And success rates — where do you see them? So they talk about it — have the nightmares stopped? Are their relationships good? Does it mean, okay, they know about it, but they're still on drugs or alcohol? The successes are probably a slim few. I want you to be one of them.

N: ***I want it, too. That's why I'm working so hard.***

H: You always did. When you were a kid, you stood out in the family. You did innovative things against the grain. But integrity was the highest goal to maintain, and you're still doing it. When you think about it, there's no difference in this family between now and then. The pattern, the technique, and the way you've gone about doing this has always been more healthy than not.

Myth and truth. Charlotte and I were regularly subjected to horrible pain and humiliation in part because our mother was involved with the man doing it. In part, because our father was oblivious to anything around him. With nowhere else to turn, we created our own coping mechanisms, which followed us to our present-day lives. Charlotte and I forfeited our childhoods and our innocence for the transitory pleasures of a very stupid woman, and for the protection of a man who abdicated his role as parent along the way.

2

Resistance and Sexual Abuse

How did it happen that two sisters were systematically abused, tortured, exploited, and neglected for years with no one taking notice? In part, it was due to the randomness of it all. We never knew when we might be invited to Ron and Cass's house, or if Cass would take all of us shopping or only Linda. We never knew when they (or Ron alone) might appear at our house.

Abused children respond to their plight in two basic ways. A child shuts down completely, preferring to feel nothing rather than risk feeling this overwhelming pain. The child seeks refuge in sleep, reading, obsessive TV habits. Anything to avoid thinking about a horrible reality. The alternative response creates a child who resists and becomes erratic, angry, and combative. This child is screaming her guts out. In reality, it's the same response. The child uses anger and resistance to avoid feeling present terror. Both perspectives inevitably permeate other areas of the child's life where s/he ostensibly is safe.

Both responses played out to dramatic extremes in our house, which makes the fact that no one noticed all the more incomprehensible and dismaying. Charlotte became a nonperson. She slept more than she was awake. She seldom had an opinion about anything.

I became resistant to all forms of authority, especially my mother's. I didn't hesitate to start something with her. I could verbally win any argument because I had a recorder inside me who remembered conversations verbatim. I quoted back what people denied saying. I remained hypervigilant against all danger.

By the time of my involvement with Ron, Charlotte had been dominated by him for years. But I wasn't Charlotte. He frequently threatened to kill us if I told, which I insisted on doing even when no one listened. He tortured Charlotte in retribution. He said our parents sent us there because we were bad, and if I told anyone, they would send us back. It was hard to argue against his logic. I did tell my mother repeatedly, and she kept arranging these "treats" to Uncle Ron and Aunt Cass's house.

The fact that I don't recall Ron ever tying Charlotte up indicates to me that he didn't need to restrain her. She never had a chance to develop basic autonomy. I, however, was a feisty three-year-old with an already acute sense of right and wrong. I was also afraid he would do whatever he was doing to Charlotte, to me. So I told my mother immediately. She claimed, dozens of times, that I really had a bad dream.

Throughout the years, I resisted Ron's brutality in every way imaginable. I bit him, kicked, screamed, and ran away at every opportunity. This resulted in my being tied up for hours, during which time I pleaded with Charlotte to get help while he slept. She was paralyzed by her fear of him. She remembers me telling our mother what happened, very early in my involvement, and being asked, "Charlotte? Is this true?" She denied it, not realizing that her fear kept both of us imprisoned.

My mother's later social life conflicted with my accounts, in any event. She and Ron became lovers, and slept together occasionally after everyone else left for school and work. I was the only witness to her betrayals, which ensured no one would believe me. I began a lifelong quest to protect my father from her.

Linda was not targeted because Ron preferred very young girls. When Ron and Cass married, Linda was an only child and not yet being routinely babysat. By the time I arrived, our parents left all of us at Cass and Ron's house for the weekend. Being with Cass was fun. She loved us as if we were her own children, but it was a crapshoot. Sometimes she left Charlotte and me alone with Ron for hours while she and Linda went shopping. Linda never got left behind, so she was not exposed to his abuse. I grew up hating Linda for this, although I never knew why. Linda, for her part, distanced herself from Charlotte and me, leaving us feeling more isolated and alone.

My mother mentioned once how sad I was at four when Charlotte and Linda's school bus left. The truth was, I had constant low-level anxiety. Bad things happened when I was alone with Mommy. Sometimes Ron showed up, walking in without knocking, like he was welcome. He'd offer to do something special, just the two of us. No matter how I fussed or pretended to be sick, my mother made me go with him. She was tired of her children. I was third in the series, nine years of preschoolers without respite, and an unwanted child at that. I was compelled to go, both before and after she was fully aware of what he was doing to me.

All my life, I retained a memory of screaming, running around our house, trying to get out the back door, finding it locked. Ducking away from my mother, screaming into another room. Diving under the dining room table, thinking I was safe beneath the tablecloth, then dragged out by my feet. I thought this must be a memory of her taking me to the doctor, who terrified me for an unknown reason. But I could not reconcile being ill with how healthy and agile I seemed. My memories always held a "what's wrong with this picture" quality. When the entire memory returned a few years ago, Ron was standing in the dining room, watching this scene, laughing.

He took me out of my house at least four times in addition to episodes staged at his home over weekends. I fought hard not to go. At least once my mother (a nurse) gave me an injection to sedate me. By then all pretense was gone on her part. She knew very well why I fought and became hysterical. When he brought me home, exhausted and unnaturally submissive, she never asked where he took me.

Several months would pass without trauma. I'd slowly relax. I thought if I helped my mother enough she wouldn't get rid of me next time. (It was always an unexpressed certainty that a next time would occur.) If I was just good enough, perfect enough, smart enough, she would say no next time. But she never said no to him.

The minute I was in his possession following these skirmishes I knew there would be later retribution. I have a small scar on my finger that's been there as long as I can remember. It looks like an asterisk. To punish me for one of my many transgressions, Ron stuck the point of his knife into my finger three times to make a star. I was four. My fingers were much smaller then, and his knife seemed so much bigger. I was certain he was going to cut my finger off.

Even so, I resisted in ways he would never discover but were meaningful to me. Ron enjoyed my tears, and tried to provoke them. I learned to suppress them completely. My alter Charyse Noel, who was Inside Sarah's twin, took on all the sadness and managed to suppress the tears while doing so.

In another incident of resistance, I was tied to the bed. My alter Marcie continually chanted that Ron was a bad man, and she was going to tell. Ron said, "If you say one more word, I will kill you." For emphasis, he threw his knife at her. It landed, stuck in the pillow, about two inches from my left cheek. Marcie never spoke again. But other alters stepped in to harass him. And I refused to cry.

FEBRUARY 4, 1992

Dear Howard,

I'm one step away from finding the Rosetta stone for my life, and it's pretty exciting. On Sunday I began "spinning," which happens when I get close to Anita. It began with the memory of using sarcasm as a weapon against Ron, who I thought was very stupid. By six, I knew no one was going to save us. No one believed me. Charlotte denied it was happening to anyone who asked. She called me a liar. I was a very tired six-year-old. I'd lost all hope.

My final resistance was a campaign to provoke Ron into doing something stupid like really stab me, rather than merely threaten. He'd kill or wound me, and either way it would not go unnoticed. (This is what I thought happened when I awoke after my appendectomy.) Either way, it had to end because I had a sense that I was losing my mind, which I then equated with being like Charlotte.

I'd been sarcastic from day one to cover my fear and stop crying. I was relentless. I gave him every bit of spite and hatred in me (I'd had great teachers). Sometimes he broke down, drunk and crying, leaving us alone for hours. I realized a great power in making him cry. Sometime during this period I talked with Cass, and she ended it for us.

As an adult, Nita did this to people who made me feel trapped. I drove my ex-husband to the same kind of breakdowns — or violence — this way. Part of me wondered why I was doing it, but another part enjoyed the results. I couldn't stop myself. I was told I said really out-

rageous things I didn't remember saying. My ex said, "You're like two different people."

My mother and I also had terrible fights. She'd cry, in what I felt was a guilt maneuver, "I don't know what I did to deserve this, but I must have really failed you for you to treat me this way." I remember thinking, "You bet you failed me." I didn't know how, but I knew she deserved everything, and I thought she was as stupid as Ron.

FEBRUARY 17, 1992

N: *It's hard to countermanipulate these people. He was a master. Never leaving clues, always getting there at the right time to make sure everyone got a different story.*

H: *That's not so hard. A person like you would never conceive of doing such a thing. You'd figure you'd have to plan it out meticulously.*

N: *So he was just incredibly lucky for eight years?*

H: *Don't get me wrong, there is some planning. But frankly, the drive is so intense that one thing they tend to overlook is the kid. Like the kid isn't a witness to it.*

N: *I always made sure he knew I was.*

H: *When you made sure of it, how did he conduct himself?*

N: *He hurt me worse.*

H: *The drive is so strong, figuring the kid would never say or do anything about it.*

N: *Charlotte never had.*

H: *Right. Taking the kids for granted. Or, if it should ever come up to Mom and Dad, deniability woven in. The manipulation and strategy comes in not getting caught.*

N: *I'm worried.*

H: *What's your worst fear?*

N: *That I can still be so affected by Charlotte today. I said before I knew all this stuff, "I don't want to be like her." You said, "You won't be like her. You aren't like her."*

H: *(laughs) You do me pretty well.*

N: *That's been the fear since we were kids. Even at six I was afraid of turning into what she was, which was this blob that never fought for anything.*

H: *If you're around her, or talk to her, you're not going to be like her.*

The debate continues regarding whether it is preferable to resist than to acquiesce in any type of abuse situation. One must consider that small children are virtually incapable of making much impact on their world. No matter what path taken as a child, survivors grow up believing they should have done something differently. Perhaps there is no greater form of survivor guilt than "I didn't try to stop it." Or "I should have told." The legacy of a helpless, vulnerable, out-of-control, and humiliated child creates an adult who is generally tentative, insecure, and quite angry. The anger is not often expressed, however, as it is not safe to be angry with violent people. Confrontation and conflict are difficult for many survivors.

All sorts of memories have surfaced which demonstrate that I did, in fact, resist Ron. As an adult, I can confidently say I did everything conceivable to get away, to stop him, to help Charlotte, and to hurt him. The long-term effect is that I don't carry that insidious form of guilt which says maybe I could have done more to escape my situation.

While I believe that no child should be held accountable for whatever s/he did to survive, the issue becomes complex when siblings are at risk. Each of their actions impacts the other. My active resistance, no doubt, caused Charlotte additional stress, if for no other reason than it magnified her fears. There were times she was punished for my defiance. Conversely, Charlotte's lack of resistance and repeated denials most likely prolonged our torment.

In that moment of terror, I believe whatever we did to cope and live was acceptable. I would not change any of my behavior designed to hurt or hinder Ron, or to make someone else take notice. There is a freedom in knowing, regardless of the result, that I did everything possible to not be a victim, and to maintain some small form of control in dangerously unpredictable circumstances.

MARCH 24, 1992

Dear Howard,

It's one thing to say I'd press charges in a minute if I found Ron. It's something else entirely to call men with his name to verify if he's the one. I called three of them! None of them was the right one (I created a great story about long lost money of Cass's), but I'm celebrating the fact that I had the guts to do it. It's a confirmation that I did, in fact, have the guts to do what I did as a child.

3

Self-destruction as an Alternative

To make things better I have to hurt a lot more first. This was a hard lesson at six, and it's kept me in harm's way my entire life.

—NITA, FEBRUARY 4, 1992

NOVEMBER, 1991

N: ***It horrifies me that I could have done this to myself. What else could I have done?***

H: We can talk about that. You stayed married to a crazy person. What were the red flags before you married this guy?

N: ***I knew he was an alcoholic. I was always trying to get him to stop drinking. He collected weird literature about death and dying.***

H: Nita is a very self-destructive individual.

N: ***That's a given.***

H: You're overweight. You don't look to the future in a positive way, or plan for it. These are self-destructive acts. You allow yourself to become overwhelmed by things. Your apartment has gotten out of hand, to say the least. Your apartment being broken into was perhaps the most dramatic and bizarre way to go about self-destructing.[1]

People who were abused learn that no one is there for them, to care for them and make it all better. They decide trust is a myth, and often denounce God for allowing such cruelty to occur. The hurt feels endless and eventually seems more normal than feeling good. They long for the hurt to stop, but with no one to turn to, it becomes an endless loop of pain, constantly recycling itself. Good becomes the absence of bad. These lessons carry forward into adulthood.

APRIL 2, 1992

H: This is very important. I don't want you to sabotage the work we're doing by pushing away the notion that you're more okay than not.

S: ***(quiet and depressed) Is that what I'm doing?***

H: Well, sometimes I wonder.

S: ***Am I more okay than not?***

H: Yeah. But I could say "I love you" and you'd say, "Yeah, but I want to make it hurt." That's the association. I'm saying you're okay; I accept you. But you don't take validation well. You could get very rigid, and say, "Hey! I'll show you something really sick." As if you think I can reach a point where I'd say, "You don't belong living; you're a horrible person."

S: ***It would show far better how sick I am by keeping it hidden, and refusing to talk about it. I may have a hard time talking about it, but I'm here. I don't want to prove to you how sick I am. (softly) I just think I am.***

H: *I think what you are, is hurting a lot. It's far more accurate than calling you sick. I think you're hurting more than we've ever talked about because you can't say enough words about how deep the hurt is.*

Survivors with repressed traumatic memories may repeat old patterns of abuse as adults, completely oblivious to the connection. I grew up to marry a clone of Ron. My ex-husband was an abusive alcoholic who cheated on me. He threatened me with knives on two occasions. I watched him coming at me, feeling helpless and "tied down," even though I was closer to the door with car keys at hand. I tried frantically to make him love me during most of our thirteen-year relationship. A woman with adequate self-esteem would never have taken his abuse. But I felt trapped and unable to leave. This is a legacy of my childhood abuse.

Is it any wonder, then, that children still trapped in horrific predicaments often turn to the only solution they see as within their control? What is "normal" behavior for a child of six? Is there any dispute that a chronically depressed child is not normal? Children who express suicidal thoughts, or who cut or burn themselves, or have constant "accidents," or a fascination with death and dying, are not normal. Children who believe self-mutilation is a viable alternative to their abuse are on the brink of losing everything. Even if removed from the abuse in that moment, these behaviors survive and color the rest of their lives.

Survivors often cut or burn themselves as adults because they can't feel anything any other way. They so deadened themselves as children, that a cut proves they are still alive to feel physical pain. It may delay their having to think about or feel an emotional pain. It may be the only means by which they feel in control.

Suicidal urges are acted upon as adults and, sadly, succeed. Add DID to this mix, and the left hand literally does not know what the right is doing. Not only are some alters suicidal, but others are internally homicidal. They believe they can kill another alter without harming themselves.

FEBRUARY 18, 1992

Dear Howard,

You say it's normal to think of suicide as a fantasy kind of "what will they say at my funeral" thought. I know that aspect is normal. What I don't think is normal is having these "let's jump in front of the bus" thoughts when suicide is the farthest thing from my mind. It happens

when I'm really happy, hopeful, and seeing light at the end of that tunnel. "Normal" would be "my life sucks, nobody cares, they'll be sorry, hey, there's a bus, just do it."

My thoughts as a child obsessed on the idea that it had to look like an accident. Otherwise, everyone would say, "Well, you know she was crazy, it figures." No one would ever know there was a reason for it. If it looked like an accident, they'd say, "Poor Nita." (Hopefully.) For once in my life they would feel sorry for me.

It's when I'm happy and a random suicidal thought jumps in that I worry most. If Anita is the personification of pain, it makes me wonder how many are there inside. The fact that I still get the "spinning" sensation worries me big time. I'm so afraid I'm losing myself. I'm going to wake up and be somebody nobody knows, especially me. It scares me that I could lose all the weight — forestall the obvious suicide — and still be looking at buses with some longing. Things may be connected in ways which we don't even know about yet.

FEBRUARY 26, 1992

*N: **Did you get my last letter? Alternative forms of suicide. I'm sort of not in that mode anymore.***

H: We're walking a tightrope here. While I can say it's normal, I don't discount the seriousness. You may be unaware that it is normal for stable people to have misgivings about their self-esteem or capabilities, or to be depressed. Certainly, to feel that way all the time is a problem. If jumping in front of buses comes up when everything seems okay, it's absolutely significant. But I'm not sure you know what normal is. Just because it's normal, doesn't mean it's good. Frankly, you want to be better than that. Normal's not such a great standard to shoot for.

*N: **It depends on your perspective.***

H: This may sound pushy, but I have high standards for you. You have a right to, soon enough, feel like this is a very good life. You have not been cursed to just get by with minimal or "grin and bear it" pain. That's a lousy standard. It's a reasonable goal for you to like being you.

*N: **I have that, sometimes. (sighs)***

H: I'll fight you, if you think what's happened is so bad that you can only reach some limited place. People who really feel good about themselves have a "sky's the limit" attitude.

APRIL 2, 1992

Dear Howard,

On Friday when I was already shutting down, my doctor said I am self-destructing by eating; I'm running a scam on myself; I don't get it that there's a point of no return. He gives me no credit for what I'm dealing with and still functioning. He said there's always an excuse; in the meantime, I'm irretrievably harming myself. It's not like I'm blissfully unaware, either, but I can't deal with it. I don't know how to change it. He said, "You're killing yourself." I thought, "Finally, he gets it."

You talk of me sabotaging our work, and I deny it, but I'm capable of it. I don't know how to override these destructive urges. If my physical health can cross an irreversible line, it seems like my mental health can too. I'm not trying to convince you how sick I am, any more than I'd convince my doctor that I love being this weight. I'm trying to be realistic. Maybe some things can't be fixed.

October 27, 1992

Dear Howard,

I've been sleeping badly, a sure sign of something working its way to the surface. I'm not losing weight, and feel trapped. Peter and Anita may be out of it, but I must still have a very strong death wish to keep this up.

I started thinking about why I'd want to give my mother the last word, the last triumph, the last breath. Why I would still, knowing what I know, give her that power? All my life I've fought it. For the first time I'm free, and I just roll over and let her go at it one more time. Anita said Erin was going to eat her little face out, and "sooner or later, even Peter dies a natural death." Meaning, the body will give out eventually, if Peter can't arrange anything else. Why dodge all those childhood bullets if this is how it's going to happen now? What was the point?

February 9, 1993

Dear Howard,

My electricity was to be turned off at 5 p.m. today, so I left work to pay the bill. Just the fact that I let the bill go that long — without conscious awareness — is Exhibit A for the disability examiner. Sometimes I "see" (in my head) an accident rushing toward me, and I change course to avoid it. I saw this one coming, but was in a hurry, so I ignored it. I knew there was going to be an accident. About 60 seconds before it happened, I thought, "How do I explain to Jacob how I ended up in Culver City in an accident when I was supposed to be at work?"

I have no idea if I ran the light, or if the other guy did, because "I" wasn't there. Suddenly a car was coming directly at me. I jerked the wheel, and went into a spin in the middle of the intersection, then pulled into a parking lot while the other car took off. I was convinced my car was smashed, but the rubber on the bumper had merely been grazed. I sat a long time, thinking about other near misses; about Peter; about how totaling my car now would really cap everything off.

In a split second I would have hit him head on at 40 miles per hour. But Howard, "I" didn't make it happen. "I" made it not happen, just like with the smoke inhalation. I don't know what's going on here.

FEBRUARY 10, 1993

Dear Howard,

Did I really need to pay $150 to hear some psychiatrist say I should go on unemployment "because there isn't the hassle you get with disability"? He said I'm "on the cusp" of a psychiatric disability, meaning I'm not nuts enough. He thinks I could make a case for asthma, but it's not his area. He reacted defensively at my first sign of frustration (which I admirably withheld till the end), when I said I just came from an M.D. who wouldn't sign for asthma because he thinks it's a psychiatric disability.

I get it now. I blew my big opportunity last August when I was really scraping bottom and no one would have disputed my mental state then. But because I was resourceful, and courageous, and worked goddamned hard, and because I succeeded in making progress, I am now penalized because I am not nuts enough or MPD enough or depressed enough or anything enough to merit disability. This, when I am losing my mind in pieces.

Neither doctor sees the weight, the job, the stress, the MPD, the near-death misses, the lightshows, the anxiety, the depression, the low self-esteem, and the asthma as all being connected, and all part of the same thing. I am so frustrated! Howard, I can't go on like this much longer.

In February 1993, I lost my job due to the recession, and consequently lost my health insurance. I never received disability, and survived financially with unemployment benefits and my father's aid. I hit many low points where suicide seemed attractive.

JULY 1, 1993

Dear Howard,

Sometimes I feel so energized, and sometimes I feel like staring at the wall for hours. I'm floating through time, like waiting for the next train. It'll get here when it gets here, and I have no control over it. Meanwhile, I have so many things I should be doing. So it's hard to see this time as productive. I still have times when I feel extremely fragile, and I don't want to be unnecessarily hard on myself. But I'm not being what I want to be, either, and it's all mixed up!

I want to be a normal person. Actually, I really don't, I really want to be this super-human be-all do-all person, but I haven't even reached the normal part yet. Even though I'm far better than I've ever been, I still have a bunch of overwhelming problems that are. . .overwhelming me.

By August 1993, I'd passed through many crises. I was beginning to feel a sensation of hope for the first time.

AUGUST 12, 1993 *(letter to survivor friend)*

I had one inside named Peter who thought there was no logical reason to keep the body locked in this torment. He tried to kill us many times, but the others were stronger in their will to live, so he failed. He had no hope, because hope could not be empirically measured. He made an agreement with Howard to not make further attempts to harm us while Howard demonstrated (over several months) that hope was real and attainable.

Hope is in every moment of progress, however small it seems. Your inside adults have fooled themselves into believing there is no hope, but you can guide them into a position of trust, strength, and hope. Start by taking care of the little ones. One of your adults may be more inclined to do so than you presently realize. Look for that adult. Find him/her. Protecting your little ones protects you. Dedicate yourself to that task, and you will know that there lies the beginning of hope for all of you inside.

My life was constant chaos, until I began reclaiming myself. DID created massive internal chaos via alters, who then created their own external chaos. This manifested financially, in health issues, work habits, housekeeping. My external chaos was a symbol of what occurred inside. It also demonstrates childhood lessons, such as "I am not good enough" (for love); "I am a bad person" (bounced checks prove it); "I am helpless" (can't change a light bulb). I balked at doing the most elementary things that connoted health and taking good care of myself. This "proved" I was not worth the effort.

Despite the chaos, I've always felt compelled to act "strong," and not let any kind of weakness show. This is tiring, and a mixed blessing. Being strong enabled me to survive my childhood. It provided me with numerous opportunities to explore the limits of my courage. But being strong also made me appear stable and normal. If I'd allowed myself some weakness, perhaps someone would have tried to help, but I could not afford to test it. It also allowed me to overlook or disregard things that needed tending. It's difficult to ask for help, or break down, when everyone expects otherwise. Being the strong one is part of my perfectionist behavior, and not reality-based. It sets up a lot of self-destructive behavior in me as punishment when I fail.

Many survivors agree they are profoundly affected by procrastination, which gives impetus to all sorts of self-destructive acts. It enmeshes me in the chaos it creates, and is intimately linked with my drive for perfection. If I put off doing something important, no one will discover I am really a fraud when they see I didn't do it perfectly. Used to be, I did very little if I could not be certain I'd do it "right." Maybe then someone would love me.

In our first session, Howard asked me to describe my interests outside of work. I stated I am an avid reader, like movies, watch too much TV, love puzzles, and do crafts. He took his first of hundreds of risks, and said I was boring. He claimed these were all solitary, escapist activities which evidenced no passion. I stumbled all over myself trying to justify my activities. I was later amazed that I neglected to mention my exquisite poetry, my enthusiasm for train travel, or my love of Mozart and French Impressionism.

I did not understand for many years that everything I first listed was a recital of what I do to procrastinate. Why did I not just give him the second list? My childhood taught me well that to openly acknowledge the importance of anything was dangerous. So I procrastinated by telling Howard all the things I do to procrastinate. Procrastination served me well in childhood; as an adult, it frustrates my true desires and potential.

The promise in this work of self-discovery is there for those who stay with it. I no longer have suicidal thoughts. In fact, I love my life. Much of my chaos, both internal and external, is vanquished. I still procrastinate, but I don't lose as much time to it as I once did. More importantly, I no longer believe I am a "bad person" if I procrastinate. I may need to face unpleasant consequences, but my behavior does not impute "badness" to me. When I truly internalized my own goodness, my recovery began in earnest.

4

False Memory Syndrome

perhaps once a child
looking at the world with wonder
inquisitive and certain
of sunrises tomorrow
would have seen
this profusion of colors and design
we call life
as the normal course of being
we try to capture the colors
in our memories
maybe nothing could be worse
for a fresh outlook
than the camcorder in our mind
relentlessly recording
every movement
every shade
too many instant replays
to be curious
anymore

SEO, May 23, 1991

This poem was written by my alter, Inside Sarah, before I knew Howard existed. But I knew Sarah existed then. The poem captures the plight of a child who just wants to forget. The child who might have, under better circumstances, relished the colors on life's palette.

Proponents of False Memory Syndrome (FMS) claim that overzealous therapists are implanting memories of heinous abuse into the minds of extremely suggestible and vulnerable people. While I do not dispute that there are unethical and sloppy therapists, I also know many people, myself included, who legitimately repressed their memories. As I combed closets and trunks for older writings, I discovered that much of what I repressed leaked out in various forms. I just couldn't put all the pieces of the puzzle together in any way that made sense until the core memory of being assaulted by Ron surfaced.

MAY 31, 1986 *[written but never sent]*

Dear Daddy,

I used to make myself wake up all by myself at six o'clock to have breakfast with you. I would wish myself awake because the look on your face was worth it. We shared this real special time then. But in the evenings, I was just one of four people trying to break you away from your newspaper. I couldn't compete. But breakfast was just me and you, and Mommy was jealous of our time together. Mommy was jealous of anyone else's happiness and pleasure — even a five-year-old's.

Something happened about then. Life became one big fight. I was so afraid of Mommy, and afraid you'd leave and I'd never see you again. You went off in this faraway place in your mind instead, and Mommy just screamed louder, and threatened us more. You were sick a lot and I knew you were afraid to be alone, too. I began to tell her to leave you alone. You just sat there while she hit us and made life so scary. I never saw her hit you, but I think there were times she really wanted to, and instead she hit me. You deferred every decision to her, never voicing an opinion of your own, never daring to say no, or to protect yourself from her verbal assaults. She couldn't stand it when I protected you. Her rage multiplied, and I got it all, while you buried yourself deeper in your paper.

Have you ever understood the price I paid to protect you? I am a grown woman, and if a friend raises a hand in jest I still cower and cringe, no matter how obvious it is that they will not hit me. I grew up with a rebellious child image. Do you know why? It put the focus on me instead of you. I thought I could take it better than you. I had no one except my dog to talk to because Linda and Charlotte always told her what I said. So I stopped telling them things and pretended everything was fine. Then nobody understood why I got so mad over things that seemed stupid.

And always, I had the feeling that as bad as it was, you were my parents, and this was my family. Somehow, someday, we would be like my friends' families, which were much happier. I knew I was bad so I tried so hard to be good and get straight A's and do all my chores and not fight with Linda. But Mommy couldn't stand it when I got "too good." She had nothing to take out her hostility on then but you. Then I'd see that being good was kind of hollow, so I'd be bad to protect you again. Always that war inside of me — good kid, bad kid. Mommy saying, "Nothing's ever good enough for you." Win, lose, win, lose. When I was ten I knew I could never survive in that house unless I escaped. I was "too good" to literally run away, so I checked out emotionally for the next eight years, which are a blur now.

This letter is as close as Nita ever got to the truth of her childhood. Then she buried it in a stack of half-finished poetry and "to do" lists. But she knew what she knew, even if she forgot most of it. She knew life with Mommy was scary, and Daddy was unavailable to help. She knew the family dynamics well, and that she lost several years as her only viable means of escape. She knew something bad happened at five. These crucial observations demonstrate a reality to my abuse, whether or not I "remembered" it as whole cloth.

The people at the False Memory Syndrome Foundation (FMSF) would have you believe that repressed memories are manufactured primarily by therapists. But I remembered major events of my life all my life, perhaps without detail, but with enough structure and clarity to identify problems. The above letter was written five years before I met Howard. Yet, it describes aspects of splitting: the good girl/bad girl dynamic; the blurring of my teenage years. How does one account for what Nita consciously knew if repressed memories which later filled in details were false?

It is my experience, both personally and in talking with numerous survivors, that nobody who is struggling with memory retrieval consciously remembers a wonderful childhood and healthy family dynamics. It is not as though a functional, rational, "normal" person suddenly becomes emotionally crippled by wildly depicted memories which surface from nowhere. I've never met a survivor with repressed memories who did not previously describe their childhood as hell. They just didn't know why or to what extent it was hell.

I don't remember everything, either. My early childhood abuse happened at a fairly constant rate over three years. Before integration, I recalled a few "entire" incidents of certain types of abuse, and fragments of others. I remembered circumstances where a small child obviously might need to split to cope. I relived abuses that tied my mother to the scene of the crime in very concrete ways. I remembered what I needed to know to proceed with my healing.

FMS proponents claim that such gaps in memory further evidence the recovered memories' falsity. But memory is not linear, even under the best of circumstances. While my memory for other events is excellent, and at times feels photographic, I've probably lost the "camcorder" in my mind, if I ever had one. After all, I wasn't "there" for most of it, and integration was achieved without requiring a play-by-play account.

Even if I could remember every second, I believe total recall would be nearly as traumatic as living it the first time. Our minds are wonderful to us this way, like people in horrible car accidents who wake up and don't remember the impact. They have enough problems without seeing it again. Nobody accuses a car accident survivor of fabricating the accident, or their injuries, merely because they can't remember every detail. Yet, people in psychic car wrecks are told this daily.

People who cast doubt on survivors for lack of linear, completely accessible memories would find something else "wrong" with our accounts even if we could present them so clearly. They'd say "Well, it's your word against his." What are we to do then? Present the tape recording we made as we were raped at age four?

Repressed memories are like trying to hold water in your hands. Eventually they leak out, no matter what you do to contain them. Memories surface when the survivor is emotionally capable of dealing with them (although it often does not feel that way). But parts of these memories inevitably trickle out during the course of a survivor's life, often creating even more doubt and confusion because they cannot be reconciled with whatever else is consciously known.

In a later chapter, I detail a sexual fantasy I held for years which both fascinated and repulsed me, involving a violent gang rape. Everything about my "goody two shoes" image cried against this fantasy. Had I come from that mythical charmed life, this fantasy would create doubt as to my sanity. This is precisely what it did to me, as I had nothing concrete to link it to my childhood previously. It seemed like I was sick to even think of it — Nita, who never broke rules, never slept with anyone but her husband. Nita, who was sexually "normal." But context is crucial. My later memories revealed that I was forced to participate in group molestations at five. My fantasy was a recreation of that experience, from an adult perspective.

As Howard would later say, this was the fantasy that made sense of my life, as did nearly all my newly-surfaced memories. All my life, I harbored certain unassailable memories which I held up as proof of a "normal" childhood. Each appeared innocent and not even worth remembering. The puzzle, my entire life, was why I so intently focused on seemingly harmless incidents.

Memory retrieval is a fascinating thing. My "normal" memories, more often than not, represented the most innocuous aspect of entirely heinous events. One by one, like a photo cut in half and later matched to its missing part, I saw why I had always retained these "normal" memories. It was to remind me, someday, that there was another half of the photo missing. The entire picture, restored, showed something evil and full of pain.

For example, for years I'd held an image of Ron standing in our bedroom doorway. Why would I remember that? It took a year of therapy to get to the heart of it. He was standing in the doorway, flexing his pocket knife open and closed, laughing, because he knew we were desperately pretending our sleep, hoping he would go away. This, with our parents 30 feet away.

AUGUST 6, 1993 *[letter to survivor friend]*

> ***I've been in very intense, aggressive therapy for two years, recovering dozens of memories in a jumbled nonsequential way. I keep saying to Howard, "Couldn't I be making this up?" But there haven't been many inconsistencies. The memories I questioned most as being too bizarre always turned out to be pivotal pieces of the puzzle, if I just waited and was willing to sit with the discomfort of absorbing them.***
>
> ***The most extraordinary event in integration — and what made me know without question that integration occurred — was that I knew with intense clarity that everything really happened. I knew I had not made anything up.***
>
> ***As for the FMSF, if my mother were still alive, she'd be a charter member. I'm very grateful I never had to deal with being believed by her as an adult. I am certain the schism in my family would be insurmountable, and I would always have an active critic discrediting any-***

thing I say, or any progress I make. In that sense, I am lucky, although it is a pain to me that I will never be able to confront her directly about this.

It seems to me that survivors who "recant" must have been gotten to by someone who knows how to push all those delicate scary childhood buttons, and has no scruples doing so. (Who does this describe?) I don't know any survivor who goes through this agony voluntarily. The perpetrators have had a lifetime of practice in denying their involvement and blaming the victim. They're real good at it. They play well on Donahue and Geraldo — but so does Jeffrey Dahmer.

FMS claims are most damaging when they convince very vulnerable people with little self-esteem that they are crazier than even they believed if they come forth with their stories. In the early stages of recovery, it's tempting to go along with everyone else's agenda, and say, "Well, maybe they're right." In the beginning, we don't even realize we have a right to vocalize our hurt. Standing up for ourselves is a new and scary proposition. More than ever, this is the time to stay on course, and be with people who love and support you. Expressing the inexpressible out loud to someone makes it more real, and far less scary, than allowing it to bounce endlessly around inside your head. It's the beginning of your healing.

I still carry my fear that people will not believe my story. But I tell it anyway. I would have loved some "simple" explanation for my life which did not include any abuse. Believing I made the whole thing up certainly would have been an easier road. My memories sickened me for years before reaching resolution. But I've discovered that those who really care about me, really believe me. Those who don't, weren't there, and couldn't possibly imagine what I experienced.

Some people have suggested I am "lucky" to have a sister who can provide corroboration of my abuse. It's rather insulting. It suggests I would not be believed if Charlotte did not exist. Charlotte went through a phase where she "interrogated" relatives as to whether they really believe these things happened; do they believe I have DID; do they believe our mother was involved? These people previously stated their disbelief to our faces. Corroboration does not sway those who don't want to believe. My sister wanted so desperately for them to validate our experiences, she opened herself up to that hurt again. While I hold fond memories of these relatives — their house was a fun, safe place in an otherwise bleak childhood — their belief, or lack of it, does not in any way alter the reality of what happened.

The idea that "your therapist put you up to this" is a fear-based response from people who don't understand the therapist's role. My father, a generally fearful man, still asks if Howard gave me drugs or hypnotized me, neither of which ever occurred. Until recently, he refused to talk to Howard on the phone out of certainty he would be hypnotized against his will. I have relatives who claimed not only that Howard implanted "lies" in my head, but that the money paid to him "wasn't really going to therapy." As if some diabolical plot was happening under my nose. (And I'm too stupid or nuts to see it.)

DECEMBER 19, 1993

I was waking myself up 75-80 times each night, terrified that Ron was in my adult bedroom, waiting for me. Rationally, I knew this was an impossibility, yet I still slept with the lights on, fully dressed, and tried to will myself out of visions of him before I had the courage to open my eyes. I eventually learned, and was able to accept, that I was holding on too tightly to my control of the influx of new memories. I came to see my memories as the only means by which I would be able to get my life back, and as such, was ultimately grateful to have them. By just letting go and not trying to control or suppress them, paradoxically, I gained control.

There may be some people who fabricate memories for attention or revenge. It's safe to also say that perpetrators join FMSF because it provides a convenient shield behind which to cower. Nearly 3,000,000 children are reported abused and/or neglected annually in the United States. Of those, 1,200 die at the hands of their parents, a number on the rise. Many more sustain serious injuries.[1] Who has more to gain by keeping these victims silent?

5

The Early Computer Writings

I sit at my computer, totally exhausted, and this stuff comes out, sort of like throwing up.

—Nita, September 1991

October 16, 1991

N: ***I'm so tired. I'm sleeping with all the lights on, and it's too scary sometimes to sleep with the lights on.***

H: *I thought you keep the lights on because you're scared.*

N: ***It's like the lights aren't enough. So then I put on music, that's not enough.***

H: *You're starting to feel the feelings you had when you were a little girl. The nice thing is, you're not a little girl.*

N: ***(sighs) It doesn't really help to know that, most of the time.***

H: *You don't say, "Okay, this is probably what I was feeling, that drives the fear?" And, "I'm safe." You must add that.*

N: ***I say that, yeah. And I wake myself up dozens of times, 'cause I'm afraid, I think he's there, in the room. I think, before I open my eyes, "He's not here. The lights are on. Nothing has moved." I open my eyes and I'm still scared. I just did this five minutes before, and it's as new and real five minutes later.***

H: *You're feeling it as you felt it. It's not a remembrance anymore; it's an experience.*

As my night terrors increased in the months following Charlotte's revelations regarding my presence during her own childhood abuse, I was chronically fatigued. I tried to maintain a facade at work that everything was okay. Part of me wanted to move rapidly forward in therapy to not waste another moment of my life. I was also terrified of what I might find.

I'd sit at my computer, exhausted, close my eyes, and just type. I transcribed every voice in my head, every random thought. For weeks, all I could express was my exhaustion and fear. One day, however, I was suddenly, in all ways, a very small child. I was there; it was happening. Part of my mind disbelievingly screamed, "What is this?" The more controlled adult moaned, "Oh, this is sick!"

The first writing provided below was a major shock. It made my childhood real to me in ways I really didn't want to see. Suddenly, a three year old was screaming her guts out. It overwhelmed me.

SEPTEMBER 2, 1991

Dear Howard,

After spending a terrified sleepless night, I sat at my computer yesterday and started writing as if I were three years old. I believe Charlotte was involved long before this, but this is the first time I was involved, because I fought so much. I also believe I tried to tell my mother when we got home, and she would not believe me.

Charlotte and I are having lunch tomorrow before her therapy session; I plan to discuss this with her then. She asked that I follow what you said about "being objective," but I have no idea how. This is my memory. She may not remember it even when presented so graphically. It's necessarily totally subjective. This opens whole new vistas of why this "explains everything." I don't think I've remembered everything, by a long shot. So it's pretty scary right now.

. . .

aunt cass went shopping with linda and left us with uncle ron. he made us take naps too much. i pretend i was asleep at naps cause bad things happen. i fooled uncle ron lots. sometime i woke up when charlotte cries. he was mad i didn't want him mad at me. charlotte cries lots i told him to stop i tell aunt cass and she was gonna be mad at him. he chased me it was dark in the living room and light in the kitchen, but the bedroom was dark too. sometime he fell asleep i told charlotte stop crying she was gonna wake him up and aunt cass was gone forever. i tried to make him stop hurting charlotte and he tied me down and i kicked him and i screamed and wished mommy would come and he hurted charlotte again. i couldn't get away sometime he played with his knife and said if i wasn't good something bad would happen he said mommy and daddy sent us there because we were bad and bad little girls had bad things happen. sometime he pretend to put the knife in me then laughs when i get scared i cried i say i'm sorry don't hurt me don't hurt charlotte please please please i won't tell i promise please don't tell mommy i was bad please i won't tell aunt cass. he hurted charlotte cause i was so bad. i say i won't be bad please please he say it was my fault charlotte cry she say don't hurt me she screams she look at me it was my fault i tried hard to be good but sometime i was bad. he say if i tell aunt cass he tell mommy and we never go home cause bad little girls stay here forever. i promise i promise to be good so did charlotte. when aunt cass came home he say finish your naps he untied me we stayed in the bedroom till our naps were over. she say you're my little angel she hugs and kiss me what's the matter, honey? did you have a bad dream? uncle ron looked i say yes and cry she pick me up there's nothing to be afraid of it was just a bad dream. i hold her tight. aunt cass made charlotte wake up for dinner.

. . .

I had no idea from where this account surfaced, but I knew it to be real. I knew I could never retreat into oblivion again. This writing was my first evidence, other than a gut feeling, that I was actually involved in this nightmare with Charlotte. I made an irrevocable promise to myself to face whatever needed to be faced.

SEPTEMBER 15, 1991

Dear Howard,

I write like this when I get totally exhausted. For the last week, I've spent all my time being terrified of falling asleep or afraid to wake up. There's no rest. I know you said it will seem like I'm dying like having a panic attack, but it doesn't feel better to know this stuff after I write. It just makes me afraid of what I'll write next. There doesn't seem to be an endpoint. I don't feel any great relief in making these disclosures. Mostly I feel like I can't breathe and I feel so out of control. The fatigue is affecting my job. I feel like I'm losing my mind, Howard. Rationally, I know it's not happening, but it still feels like I am. Please, can you offer any suggestions?

SEPTEMBER 14, 1991

. . .

he smiles he says you've been very bad. i say i've been asleep i promise. i back up on the bed i can't get out. he's in the way i don't know where i am how did we get here i wish i was home. he says he has something for me. i hold my pillow i close my eyes i wish him gone. it's just you and me honey no one's going to come this time. he laughs he grabs my pillow i'm crying. he says let go and it won't be so bad. i say go away i'm going to tell. he says if you tell he grabs my face real hard i'll make you hurt real bad. he looks happy but he's mean. he pushes my bangs back let go of the pillow honey. i say no i hold tight i say where's my mommy. she's gone little girl no one can hear you he hurts my face i can't get away i can't breathe i can't scream he has his hand on me on my face no one can hear me where did they go why did they leave me please don't hurt me please oh please i'm so scared. let go and i won't hurt you. i say you lie you say charlotte fell down you say bad things you're a bad man you're a very bad man i'm going to tell my mommy on you. he says no you're not because you know she'll never believe you little girl so let go of the goddamned pillow or i'll make sure you're real sorry. i let go and run off the bed but he grabs me holds me down i scream mommy and mommy he laughs all the time put his hand under my pants i scream he puts his hand on my mouth i bite him he hits my face i'm crying he's in the bathroom i run out the front door i run he's coming fast i run i see mommy coming down the path i'm crying i run to mommy i say bad man bad man he hurted me. he comes behind and says she had a terrible dream and was sleep walking again i think she hit her face when she ran out the door. i say mommy crying mommy bad man bad man mommy bad man she picks me up i hug her crying mommy mommy mommy. she holds me she says you'll be okay you just had a bad dream, honey, there's no bad man now don't cry.

My family travelled to the Mojave Desert to look at wildflowers in bloom almost every spring. A month after this writing was made, I perused my father's slide collection, and found several depicting our family, with Ron and Cass, out in the desert, looking at wildflowers. I began hyperventilating. I believe the event in my writing occurred during the same trip. From the look of the pictures, I was about four.

Even after this writing, I still held out, saying this couldn't have happened to me, I was too small, he would have wanted Charlotte because she was bigger. How could a man rape a preschooler? I would dispel this myth in a major way. I still held my breath each time I began writing on my computer.

SEPTEMBER 24, 1991

. . .

i'm afraid to sleep. if i don't take a nap maybe he won't come. but i can't keep my eyes open it's like a dream when he comes. he goes to charlotte i hope he thinks i'm asleep he ties me up if i'm awake. she's crying i turn in my sleep to see. he pulls the covers off she's scared. maybe if i close my eyes and really sleep he'll go away. maybe if i'm real quiet he won't hurt her. he knows when i've been sleeping he knows when i'm awake he knows when i've been bad or good so be good for goodness sake. i hate that song. he sees us when we're sleeping he knows when we're awake. I'm gonna hurt him first and make him go away! he'll be sorry. i'm gonna tell aunt cass he's a bad man he's a very bad man he's gonna get in big trouble. i'm gonna tell i'm gonna tell i'm gonna tell i'm almost asleep the covers come off i pretend to sleep he lifts my gown touches me. wake up run! hurt him! tell aunt cass! i open my eyes his breath smells bad. i hate him! charlotte's like a sleepy kitty she's crying why does she just lie there and be sad when she could go and tell? i say no i want you to go away. he laughs he says you've got spunk, kid, that's for sure. i say leave me alone you bad man. i try to take his hand away but he goes under my panties he's holding me real tight he touches me under there where mommy says wipe good and wash your hands it's a dirty place why is he touching me there he smiles like he likes it why is he doing that i'm trying so hard to get away but it hurts real bad something is moving it's like a bug inside me it's moving down there i'm screaming i hit him he's pulling on his thing i see it now he's hurting me he looks so happy and so mean the thing inside is in my stomach he goes potty on me i'm screaming he's going potty on my face i can't breathe i feel sick i feel so sick oh mommy oh mommy oh mommy he takes the thing out his finger has blood on it he laughs he says next time we'll do it for real i'm screaming trying to get away charlotte is asleep like she can't hear me no one can hear me i try to get the wet stuff off my face with the covers he puts some on his finger puts it in my mouth he says next time you'll get all of it. it's icky and dirty i can't be here someone help me someone will come oh make him go away please i'll be good i promise i'll be good please let me sleep i'll always take my nap i'll be good. he says sleep little girl it was just a bad dream you always have bad dreams he laughs nobody cares little girl. tell them all about it they never believe you. sleep little girl. i'm falling falling falling to sleep i see charlotte sleeping it's dark he's gone it's not a dream not a dream i'm so tired not a dream i'm gonna tell i will i'm gonna tell i'm going to tell

I had not cried once in the six weeks since Charlotte's disclosures, but even this horror failed to bring on tears. I was shocked and revolted. I suppose it must have come as a total relief to Charlotte that at last he'd found another target.

I did not cry until October 3, 1991. As I wrote, a part of me was thinking, "How old am I?" I didn't feel four anymore. The syntax and grammar are that of an older child. I desperately needed to know how and when it ended. Unbeknownst to me then, Charlotte had already concluded it ended when she was eight. We corroborated each other's accounts independently, as this writing indicates it ended when I was six.

OCTOBER 3, 1991

. . .

i say aunt cass why does uncle ron hurt me? she says what do you mean he hurts you? i say, he says i'm bad and he hurts me. she sits up and says how does he hurt you? i say he puts his hand under my panties and goes potty on me. she says he does what? she looks mad i say i'm sorry i'll be good please don't tell him? please? she says what are you saying, honey? you can tell me. i say he'll hurt me if i tell. she says he's not going to hurt you okay? i say he hurts charlotte too, and he ties me up when i'm real bad. she stares like i've been real bad. i start to cry and say don't be mad please don't hurt me. she holds me tight and says i'll never hurt you honey where did you get an idea like that? she rocks a little she says he touches you down there? i say he puts a wiggly bug in my stomach it hurts and he laughs at me then he goes potty on me. she holds me so tight. i say he pretends to stab me when he ties me up. she says oh my god. i say i can't help it i'm bad sometimes. he gets real mad. aunt cass says are you sure honey? i say please believe me. he hurts me he scares me so much. she looks mad she says who else did you tell? i say mommy. i say make him stop hurting me. she looks sad now. i say he hurted me since i was real little and charlotte too. she says how long ago? i say since before kindergarten last year cause i didn't go to school before that. she says how do you know he does this to charlotte? i say she's there she cries lots. it's not fair i try so hard to be good i try, i really try and even when i'm real good he hurts me. she says do me a favor honey don't tell anyone else okay? do you promise me? i say i promise. she says i'll make him stop because you're good girls and he shouldn't do that. she still looks mad but she's crying. i say i'm sorry i made you cry. she says i never want anything to hurt you girls and i'm sorry he did this it'll never happen again, i promise you. i say, he said if i told you he'd hurt me real bad. she holds me tighter and says no honey he's not going to hurt you and if he even tries, if he looks like he's going to try, you tell me okay? i say okay, she says promise me something else promise you'll forget about this okay? i say but aunt cass, she says now please he won't hurt you ever again, so promise you'll just forget about it. she's crying so i say okay but what if, she says no what ifs. i say what about charlotte she says he's never going to hurt charlotte again either but you have to be real grownup about this now or everyone will be real unhappy. can you be my big girl? i say okay but when he comes home, she says i'll take you back home and you won't have to worry about him. i say promise? she says i promise honey.

This writing devastated me. I was certain there was no way this intolerable situation lasted longer than a few months. Someone would have believed me. Someone would have saved us. Nobody did. What hurt most was that the defiant "I'm going to tell" pre-schooler turned into a defeated "Why does he hurt me?" first grader. Initially, I wasn't even asking her to stop it; I was asking her to explain it. I accepted that my life was full of this pain, and just wanted to know why I was such a bad person to deserve it. I didn't seek her intervention until I realized she was actually listening, and that she believed me.

These drastic changes created in me during three years of hell were finally enough to make me break down and cry for eight straight hours, in uncontrollable sobs. I cried because I realized how close I'd come to the brink of giving up, and how very much alone I was as a child. I cried because I knew my mother had grossly betrayed me. I would not cry again for almost a year.

6

The Cast: An Overview of Alters

"I don't know what I am if I'm not me."
—OUTSIDE SARAH TO HOWARD, APRIL 1992

SEPTEMBER 16, 1992

It's shadowy and compartmentalized, like little partitioned cubicles where people stay. Sometimes the cubicles expand to look like the real world when people go out front. They don't see the whole world; they only see the part of it in front of them when they are out. They get a taste of outside freedom that creates conflict because it's good to be outside sometimes, but everyone can't do it simultaneously.

Inside people talk to each other randomly. Sometimes it's accidental that they even know about each other. Lynn knows where everyone is because each is assigned a place. She hears everything inside and out, until she goes out front. Then Lynn discovers how impaired her abilities to look inside are, just like Nita. Nita and Lynn are very much alike, often working in tandem, although Nita refuses to acknowledge this until the end. They are the ones who make this whole thing happen.

Despite tremendous evidence to the contrary, I sustained doubts as to the reality of these inside people.[1] Their presence explained troublesome times in my life. They offered logical solutions to old problems, and created a host of new obstacles. I secretly harbored the idea that I was intelligent (and sick) enough to give my alters a life of their own that had nothing to do with DID.

Through much of that first year, I appealed to Howard to confirm somehow that I was "just really good at making the whole thing up." It was not an attractive choice: either I was experiencing continuous psychotic breaks that I was so good at concealing even Howard failed to see them, or I really had DID. But Howard seldom had trouble seeing anything. There were occasions when I would have been comforted, odd as it sounds, to just say, "That's it! I'm crazy." Better to know it, than to feel it and wonder.

I did not know much about my insiders, however intense some of their interactions were, till after major integration occurred. I never fully understood the impact they had on each other or on the course of my life until then.

I never realized how much I relied on them to take care of me, until it was no longer an option. Because I'd spent most of my life being "one of them," I knew very little about relating to "normal" people.

My pictures from under age three, as Anita, consistently reveal a radiant, joyous, active, and lovable child. If Anita's fate had offered her a loving and nurturing home, she would have blossomed. Anita was not born hateful or self-destructive. She was raised to be like that.

Anita's character was forever altered as a result of the ongoing trauma of her early years. Her reaction was pure rage, acted out as tantrums. She gained a reputation as a difficult child, and anyone who might have saved her tuned her out. Her anger frightened people, but no one wondered why she was so angry. She began to split at age three to cope with her terrors, and facilitated further splits as the intensity and danger of the abuse escalated.

Anita's first split created Lynn, a take-charge, pragmatic alter who organized our resistance. Anita clearly interfered with the rescue effort and had to go somewhere else. Nita was created to prevent Anita from being "out front" unless directly called "Anita." I spent most of my life insisting that people call me Nita until I legally changed my name to Sarah in March 1992.

Nita's primary characteristics were anxiety, depression, and a constant need for reassurances. She saw everything in stark black and white. She feared anything new, and required coaxing to take small risks. Nita, by herself, drew as much unwanted attention as Anita. It was a cruel paradox. I desperately needed someone to pay attention to my plight. Too much attention to the extreme elements of my personality would result in a "crazy" verdict from anyone witnessing it, particularly my mother. I believed her capable of putting me away if I continued to publicly accuse family friends of hurting me. Nita, by herself, did not have it in her to look "not crazy."

Hence, the birth of Sarah. Where Nita was a pessimist, Sarah was radiantly optimistic. Sarah wrote expressive poetry, and was at ease with her own feelings. Sarah created opportunities for fun and healthy risks. She was Nita's secret lifelong best friend, and made Nita seem normal, as most people saw both of them in action more or less simultaneously. Contrary to the popular notion that alters necessarily bring chaos, this singular act of splitting restored a semblance of balance to my life. (However, the chaos continued to relentlessly develop as more splitting occurred.)

Another cruel paradox lay in my belief that Sarah was real. Anita split to avoid looking crazy and protect my good parts from violation. Success required Nita not only to forget her trauma, but that she herself was just an alter. While Sarah was magic and represented safety, she also perpetually reminded me of why we even existed. But the need for her joy became greater than the danger of revealing her source.

Sarah could not risk taint by being present during the abuse. She split into a twin named Charyse Noel, who fulfilled this function at age four. Charyse was the repository of all the sadness Sarah could not feel.

SEPTEMBER 20, 1991

Haven't cried yet. I feel like if I start crying I'll never stop. Having terrible flashbacks. The man was a monster. My mother was a monster. It's a wonder I made it through childhood at all.

When I was little, and didn't know enough to keep quiet about Sarah, I told people that when I grew up I was going to have two little girls named Sarah and Charyse Noel. I've known these names my entire life. Still, Charyse's presence profoundly shocked me. Even Sarah had to split, and in a way that would not be obvious to Nita.

By the time I began dialogues with Charyse on my computer, the implications alternately fascinated and horrified me. Howard had not yet spoken to any of my insiders. Everything I knew about them was surfacing inside my own head, which worried me tremendously. It sounds crazy to say you can talk to people inside. It fascinated me because all I did was type as fast as possible. I could not think fast and far enough ahead to arrive at the undeniably true information Charyse provided at will.

AUGUST 16, 1992 *[written by Lynn]*

Last night I cried for the first time in almost a year. I was listening to the last tape when Nita was so afraid and sad about going inside. I cried because I was sad for Nita. It wasn't like a year ago when Nita couldn't stop crying all night. It was like crying for something, and then letting it go. I thought about calling Howard, but it was after midnight, and it felt normal. It didn't feel unmanageable.

I was intensely observing everything, and felt a swirl of people spinning in my head. I saw Charyse and told her it was good that we were crying, and it was okay to feel sad for Nita. I saw lots of people, but not Nita, and wondered what that meant. The fact that I am able to cry now seems more than ever like this is working. But I didn't become just a crying person. I felt it, absorbed it, and let it go. I am not "just sad." I'm lots of things.

During a session which made me increasingly nervous, Howard asked when he was going to meet some of these people. I thought they appeared only in writing, which was another verification of my insanity. If anyone tried to come out and talk to him, I was convinced I would break out laughing in the midst of it. He believed it would not be difficult to speak with any of them. I became sarcastic and fearful, and asked what kind of magic he thought he had. All he said was, "Lynn?" Lynn responded, "Yeah?" They began talking about my mother.

It was the first time I consciously experienced another alter speaking in my place. To my astonishment, nothing happened when I tried to speak over Lynn. I was, for the first time, aware of being "on the inside." It terrified me. I felt trapped inside. I drove around for hours following this session, trying to explain rationally what had happened.

Howard and Nita created some internal confusion when she legally changed our name to Sarah. Nita knew she was not "becoming Sarah" merely by taking the name. Whenever Howard asked for "Sarah," an internal scramble occurred to insure he was actually talking to Nita. Lynn directed the traffic.

AUGUST 11, 1992

H: I'm affectionately saying this: you're giving me a hard time. Why is that? Is it you?

N: Or you?

H: Or is it anyone else? Who's skeptical? Somebody's giving me a hard time. I've kind of had it with that person.

N: It couldn't just be me, right?

H: What do you think? It's a devil's advocate; an attorney who puts a lot of energy into demonstrating the opposite. Let me talk to Lynn. You know what I'm talking about?

L: Who you are talking about? Well, it gets complicated. It's Nita, but you're calling her Sarah. It's not really Sarah.

H: Have I been a little sloppy about who I address, who walks in the door?

L: Yeah.

H: I don't know if those names get used interchangeably. Does that happen?

L: Well, you haven't talked to the real Sarah.

H: What am I missing? For me, Sarah represents the focal point of integration — the end product, if you will. That may be a bit more in my mind, and too simplistic.

L: Sarah's been there all along. The real Sarah.

H: Do you mean Sarah's like all of you?

L: She's not an end product. She's there. Sarah writes the poems, and Sarah's happy, and kind of free.

H: I should have been seeing Sarah like everyone else?

L: Nita changed her name to Sarah, but she's not really Sarah.

H: Is Nita a name changed from Anita, or is Nita actually another person?

L: Nita's different than Anita.

H: But when Anita changed her name to Nita, I'm guessing that the rest of the world just saw that as a name change.

L: Anita didn't change her name. Nita did.

H: Did Nita have to take over to change the name?

L: Kind of. But she had all of our help to do it. Everyone wanted to not be called Anita anymore, anyway. We knew nobody was going to call us anything else. Kids get nicknames, and nobody cares.

H: So it was the most logical, easiest thing for the rest of them to agree to. Did Nita change Sarah's name, or did Sarah have to take over?

L: Sarah's name wasn't changed. Nita's name was changed.

H: Wait. I am confused, okay?

L: (growing impatient) I said it was complicated.

H: So what did Nita change her name from?

L: (after some thought) Anita was someone who couldn't be out all the time. But sometimes people called her Anita, and she came out anyway. We changed the name to Nita, so people wouldn't call Anita out.

H: That makes sense.

L: So there was somebody else who was Nita. It wasn't Anita who became Nita. Nita was another person.

H: So there wasn't really a name change, from the inside. (she nods) And, like that, Sarah is not a name change. True?

L: No. There's the outside Sarah and the inside Sarah.

H: That's who I had the confusion about.

L: The outside Sarah, it's just Nita being called Sarah. The inside Sarah was always Sarah. She's different from Nita.

Howard subsequently called for the inside or outside Sarah, alleviating most of the confusion. At the conclusion of my integrative processes to date, what remains of me is a new composite entity called Sarah (but different from either inside or outside Sarah). I feel now as though I was born with that name — and in many respects, I was.

My overwhelming need to eat brought me to Howard initially. As my internal chaos grew, we discussed the possibility that I did not always know when I was eating. He asked me to ascertain who was doing it. As a result, I met Erin Elisabeth, a scared and badly hurt six-year-old. The adults in Erin's life horribly brutalized her, and repeatedly failed her. She feared I wanted to make everyone disappear (which, in terms of my therapeutic goals, was more or less true). She thought if she ate enough, I would not physically be able to disappear.

I noticed I lost time more frequently as we identified new alters. Some could take over without my conscious knowledge. Some were co-conscious with me, which means I was "there" inside, as Nita, observing and listening while they were outside. Losing time occurred when I was not co-conscious. During one such event, I carelessly left a pan of grease on the stove, which emitted smoke into my apartment. I learned of the impending danger when Lynn forced Nita back into consciousness. I suffered smoke inhalation severe enough to land in the emergency room.

The following evening, I awakened at 3:00 a.m., staring at a Monet print on my wall, then click! The image distorted, as if I were sitting in my optometrist's chair, and he'd changed the lens for my eye exam. Click! More distortion, and refocusing. I heard voices in my head, children arguing. "It's my turn! I want to look now!" Click! Adults saying, "This is all Peter's fault." I felt the sensation of many people clamoring to look "outside." Click! People mentioned Peter's name so often with irritation until I exploded the thought into my head: "WHO is PETER?" The most coherent responses mentioned the hospital, blaming Peter.

This episode confirmed the existence of alters whom I had never met by name. Howard suggested that these alters were loosely aligned with others already represented outside. Their points of view were gaining expression, thus alleviating their need to compete for outside opportunities. Some of the click! alters probably never wanted, or needed, to speak to anyone outside. They just wanted to take a quick look.

In the last ten years, Lynn and Inside Sarah did more to create the possibility of discovery than anyone, except for the apartment break-in by Anita. Lynn gives Nita constant "wakeup calls" and never lets her forget she is different from everyone else she knows. Nita never gets to feel satisfied. Lynn talks to Nita so much that Nita thinks she's really talking to herself.

Inside Sarah buys expensive suits and beaded silk gowns. Nita has no idea why she bought them. In April 1992, Inside Sarah buys an ivory silk dress finished in iridescent sequins and seed pearls. It is elegant and something someone wears when they want to be noticed. She proclaims it will be her next wedding dress. Inside Sarah writes provocative poetry to make Nita wonder. She tells Nita's friends in high school that someday she will publish, rendering her letters intrinsically valuable. Inside Sarah creates lavish birthday surprises for Nita's friends; one-of-a-kind presents and parties which literally stun them. Sarah's surprises always succeed; Nita's attempts make her look foolish.

Melissa, discovered during a session with Inside Sarah, was an aspect of healthy skepticism, not the destructive element which frustrated Howard. She provided key insights about why Howard could not make headway with Nita. He confided that he did not know how to further reassure Nita that the therapeutic process was moving as intended. Melissa responded that Nita wouldn't know what to do if she did not need reassurances about something, so he was, in effect, catering to her character. This was the first time that both Howard and I fully understood that I (Nita) was really just "another one of them."

As I absorbed the reality of my position, I expressed my exhaustion to Howard. I felt unappreciated by the others, and suggested that Lynn be made the central figure instead of me. Usually, I walked into and out of Howard's office as Nita. Howard proposed that I let Lynn walk out this time. Lynn's confidence and positive attitude would aid the integrative process, plus I believed Nita was becoming a liability. We agreed that Lynn was best suited for the tasks required to complete this switch.

Of course, part of me thought this was like living science fiction. How can you conceive of walking into someone's office as one person, and exiting as someone else? Nita feared she would never again speak to Howard. She thought she was dying. And still, I knew this decision was necessary, and aligned with my stated goals. Howard brought Lynn forward, who was bubbly and excited at the prospect of such freedom.

After Howard worked with Peter for several weeks to extract a commitment to not harm our body, Anita lost her last real ally in chaos. This, and the fact that Lynn took over outside, provoked Anita to the brink of our permanent destruction. Lynn experienced only one week of pleasure and remarkable successes before all hell broke loose.

People who talk to Howard are closer to the front than those who do not. The closer a person is to the front, the better they hear words spoken outside. Otherwise, all the walls are in the way. The only exception is Anita, who hears anything she wants no matter where she is. The others restrain her from going outside, but cannot prevent her from knowing what is happening.

In their first encounter, Anita was bitingly hostile to Howard. She refused to honor his request that she leave the others alone. She tried to implant unspeakable images in Howard's mind toward his own children. Howard, in a surprise bluff, offered Anita the central figure role, in Lynn's place. This served as a catalyst to cause the majority of alters to integrate to prevent Anita's takeover. Anita disappeared for months thereafter.

While we believed integration at that point to be complete, we learned (as many DID patients do), that most integrations are partial. Eventually, Erin and Anita resurfaced, as did Missy, Susan, Steven, Samantha, and Desiree. Steven was Anita's zombie-like henchman. Samantha was a twelve year old tomboy who wanted to shoot hoops with Howard. Desiree was a nineteen year old with a very healthy libido, and no abuse memories to cloud her desires. Missy, four years old, was terrified of "the bad people." Susan's role was to be productively bored. The greatest surprise of all was Original Anita, three years old. Our last, and (we believe) final integration occurred on July 25, 1995.

7

Resistance in the Therapeutic Setting

If it's true, as Howard says, that I'm tremendously insightful as well as totally resistant to this therapeutic process, it's really quite logical. An insightful person does not blindly walk into every get well quick scheme, and draws on past experience to evaluate whether to trust. I don't know how you can be both insightful and not resistant.

—NITA, JULY 2, 1991

JULY 3, 1991

I asked Jacob if he thinks I am resistant. He said yes, he sees it as an early warning system. I'm on the alert with new people, and they have to go through layers to get me to accept I'm safe with them. Then I'm very open. The ultimate goal in life, he says, is to be sensitive without bitterness. Very hard to do. He thinks there may have been a time when I was totally sensitive, resulting in nothing but pain, and I formed this wall so I could be sensitive but not experience it as 100% pain.[1] He agrees that insight must lead to a form of resistance or insight is meaningless.

JULY 15, 1991

N: My mother was a paragon of our neighborhood. People always came up to us with hugs, saying, "You have the most wonderful mother." I'd think, "Don't you see what's going on in this house?" To this day, if somebody even in jest raises their hand to me, I will do this. (raises hands to protect face and cowers) I cringe. Then they look at me like, what's your problem? You don't get that from a great childhood.

H: The resistance I keep bringing up is one of these (repeats her gesture). I'm not here to hurt you. You don't have to protect yourself anymore. You can be completely vulnerable. There's no need for alter ego. You survived.

MAY 4, 1992

[This session dealt with a writing wherein I talked to Charyse Noel on my computer, the first time I ever consciously contacted an alter. It is a prime example of therapeutic resistance.]

H: It was good on a lot of levels. It's probably, to date, the most integrative work you've done. It's real exciting.

N: I don't know what that means. How can it be integration if I was talking to her?

H: I said it was the most integrative thing you've done; I didn't say it's integrated.

N: What's the benefit of doing that if it's not integrated?

H: It gets you where you need to go. If you've never built a house before, then with architectural design, better use of materials, and braving the elements, one who is fairly unintegrated who builds a mud hut has done something more like a house than they've ever done before. It's a matter of degree. You probably don't feel as integrated as I feel.

N: (sarcastic) Probably not.

H: You probably aren't aware there are ways normal people feel unintegrated. "Am I going nuts? Am I falling apart?" I don't know if complete integration is ever accomplished with anybody, but for our purposes you're well on the way. The discussion you had with two selves talking about even other selves, was incredibly integrative. Probably better than mud hut, but not the Taj Mahal. (smiles) Oh, come on. That was clear.

N: (exasperated) No, it's not! In practical terms, what does that mean?

H: You're getting better....You don't trust me, do you? Just say yes or no.

N: (laughs nervously) Not on this. I don't understand it.

H: Fine, but remember I talked about rigidity, and resistance.

N: Do you think she's gone?

H: It's different than gone. I'm going to explain why I figure this is such an important breakthrough. But you're resisting me by not going with the impressions I have. I need you to trust me. I'm telling you it's really good.

N: Yeah, but I don't want to say that.

H: (laughs) Holding out, huh? You want to make this easy, or you want to make this hard?

N: (hesitates) How do I make it easy?

H: By just going with the flow. Come on! I said it was a terrific piece of work. I'll give you the detail. Just be happy that this is good. Why don't you indulge in something in your life that can be nice for the moment?

N: For the moment, hmmm. It's hard.

H: But that's your problem, isn't it? You can use a piece of good news.

N: I get what you're saying.

H: Thank you. Without the detail, you understood what I was saying. Give in, will you? I won't have this. You give in.

N: ***I thought it was neat. I just didn't understand the reasons why you think it's neat.***

H: You know how you think of people as being people? Like, they're not you, but there are people who operate normally?

N: ***People like you.***

H: You think of me as being normal?

N: ***(hesitates) Yeah.***

H: You think of me as a foreign thing to what you are. (she nods) When I use the word "integrative" I mean what you need as a normal person who doesn't have parts of you that struggle for expression and understanding, and other parts hiding out, and who the hell knows how many of them are in there. You figure normal people don't have that. So when I use the word "integrative," we're talking about bringing together in a balance all the alters and characteristics that you are. (picks up Charyse writing) This was very integrative! You're not fighting me anymore, are you?

N: No.

H: Thank you. It was good, and you knew it, too. All I'm saying is, "I like this." Charyse is a very clever girl. Your mind is so clever, it anticipates things I won't get or pay attention to, directly or indirectly. I'll be able to get out of your way, and you'll do what you have to do. But your defenses and resistances are a problem. A big part of what I do — and how you in some ways sought me out — is to make it so they don't get in the way of your natural process of integration, growth, and evolution. It's like, "Howard, you take care of the defenses, I'll do the work, okay? I've got the thing under control. I could do this on my own, please. But these little defenses are getting in the way. You take care of those."

N: ***(laughs) I guess that's sort of been the plan.***

H: You really are on top of it.

N: ***(sighs) I haven't felt that way lately.***

H: This is where I come in. I get rid of your defenses. You're brilliant in your psychotherapy, but something went over your head, or you resisted it. You challenge me a great deal. (she nods) The challenge is not only to take in what I understand, but to express it. I don't do it well, all the time. Don't get frustrated with my inability, because I'll just try again.

Part of my resistance to Howard derived from my certainty that I was crazy, and anything I said could and would be used as evidence of such. We both were confused, however, as to our terminology. In the following dialogue, after several successive sessions where I believed we were not connecting, a lot of the confusion was cleared, and I learned a valuable lesson about why resistance is not beneficial in growth situations.

N: ***We've been talking about a lot of stuff in the last six months. You see me periodically, you think I deal with this stuff pretty quickly. But there's a lot that happens to do that. I don't deal with it if I'm gathering trash or cleaning my house.***

H: Want to go back to psychology? Forget the trash? Forget any of the other problems? Let's just do psychology?

N: ***You're missing the point entirely. I'm going to feel overwhelmed, no matter what. This little kid talks to me in my head, and I can laugh a few days later, and tell people about it. But it's a very heavy process, thinking of all the little things it's telling me. It seems like inconsequential stuff, but I trip out on it.***

H: Or, it brings meaning to your life, that these things aren't just random events, but are connected to something rather significant. Now, I've done this a lot with you. You'll point out some understanding of yours, and I'll say, "Yeah, that makes sense. That's fairly common."

N: ***You say, "Normal people do these things, too." Then I always tell you it's not normal. That's why I was frustrated last week. You've worked very hard to get me to buy into this thing. Now I'm trying to help you out, and give you examples, and you're doing your best to talk me out of it.***

H: Let me tell you how I felt it. I've been amazed, and very impressed by your progress. Like you, I've thought, "God, we've worked all this time," which is really a short time, but still pretty energized and intensive. Then she comes in with something that sort of threatens the whole existence of her progress.

N: ***How could it do that?***

H: That's how I was experiencing it. I was just insecure. It could be anything; it throws you so much, I say, "Wait a second. It doesn't have to offset the whole of what we've done here." You usually come in very unsettled about something. You walk out very unsettled. (laughs) That's just how it goes. I'm not dissuaded by any of it because I also see the progress in a lot of what you say, in your insights, and what you write to me. It's right on target. You tend to come in with something that happened between now and last time, and say, "Well, how does this thing fit in with that? If all of this is right, then how do you explain that?" And I think, "God, is it that fragile?"

N: ***If that one part can't be explained, I'm going to reject everything else?***

H: That's my fear.

N: ***(sighs) No, you got me.***

H: (laughs) It's always good to know. Hook, line, and sinker?

N: ***Pretty much. I was frustrated 'cause you kept saying, "This is what normal people do." I kept thinking, "Why does he want it to be normal all*** *of a sudden? It's not normal." Now I'm even agreeing it's not normal, and you're saying it is normal.*

H: *Do you think I haven't identified the stuff you go through as being pretty far out there?*

N: ***I thought you had.***

H: *There are things you do that are also a slice of what normal people do. You overinterpret that as "this verifies the craziness."*

N: ***I'm not even thinking it's crazy anymore. It's just part of the whole thing.***

H: *So if I say this is normal, what's throwing you about it?*

N: ***If I'm not thinking it's crazy, and you say it's normal, then I think maybe it is crazy.***

H: *If you're not thinking it's crazy, and I say it's normal, that means we think the same thing.*

N: ***No! If I've accepted that all this stuff isn't proof I'm crazy, it's still weird. So if it's not crazy, and then you tell me it's normal, then it's not weird either.***

H: *(light dawning) Oh! It's between weird and normal, not crazy and normal. Okay, so you're sane. I didn't know that. Oooh, this is neat! Of course it's weird! (both laugh) My gosh! It's like, so bizarre! Are you kidding? There's nothing more weird than the stuff you talk about!*

N: ***(giggling) I was beginning to wonder, "Have I lost my touch, or what? I'm becoming so normal? So banal?"***

H: *Forgive me. I didn't understand.*

N: ***(laughs) Now I'm arguing for weird. I can't believe I'm doing this. Like "Oh, please, tell me I'm weird."***

H: *It's very bizarre, but what about it? You want to understand its bizarreness? Where it comes from? Its meaning?*

N: ***I understand the new stuff that comes up better, if I have a real framework. There's a consistency. It's all weird. If I can fit it onto the "weirdness scale" somewhere — that it does fit there — I feel like it's part of everything else. Which makes it...almost normal. (giggling)***

JUNE 16, 1993

Dear Howard,

At the end of the session when I said you didn't understand me, you wondered if it's that you're not getting it, or if I'm just being resistant. I thought we were past this stuff. This really frustrated me because I'd opened myself to embarking on another scary journey with you, with no guarantees. I'm saying, "Let's go for broke," like we did with Anita. Even though I'm terrified. I want to move forward and take risks now. This hardly seems like resistance to me!

Howard and I still have our moments of confusion, nearly always associated with my reluctance to tell the whole story. Only later do I understand the source for moments when I vigorously denied my resistance. It was never a deliberate attempt to cloud our sessions. Just old tapes kicking in, or alters doing their job with methods that served me once and no longer are needed. The more I free myself from resistance to people who will not harm me, the greater my trust, the safer I feel, the less I resist.

8

Hallucinations: A Teddy Bear Named Howard

I held the bear up toward the light, and said, "Howard, make it go away!"

—NITA, DECEMBER 1991

There was a time I never would have believed I was capable of having hallucinations, much less admitting to having them. Insisting that I know what I know is another way to deny what I don't know, especially in terms of my past. Hallucinations would be the first indication of insanity. My life mandated that my sanity be unquestionable. Yet, nearly every night from mid-October 1991, through January 1992, I endured peculiar, and extremely frightening, hallucinations which went well beyond my previous night terrors.

I referred to these strange happenings as "The Twilight Zone Phase." Howard believed that as I worked through scarier memories and got past the fear they created, some alters needed something to feel fearful about. Some alters did not know how to live except in fear. So they worked overtime to keep me terrified.

OCTOBER 12, 1991

> Sometimes when I'm very afraid, I suck in my breath and freeze, like a trapped animal. I've always felt if I were ever in real danger I'd never be able to scream. It would just come out as a hiss as I breathed. Last night I became aware of breathing like that. When I fall asleep I'm afraid to close my eyes and I reflexively gasp. It's the gasping that scares me most so I wake up again. Over and over.

The hallucinations began with shadows moving on my closet doors. I reported this to my physician in January 1991 (six months prior to meeting Howard). I blamed a new hypertension medication. He insisted I should merely close the blinds completely. That didn't help. The shadows looked like dark tree branches leaning toward me. They definitely moved. It was initially an annoyance, but eventually grew scary. After Charlotte's revelations, I slept (when I could sleep) with all the lights on. Imagine my surprise when the shadows moved in a fully illuminated room.

The reflected light created a sheen across the hall door's wooden surface. In that polished glow, nightly I saw faces, hands, trees, eyes. They were all larger than life, moving toward me, talking to me, reaching out as if to take me in. Sometimes I saw bright red blood running down the door, disappearing into the carpet. There was a mark on the door I'd never noticed before in the shape of an "N." Sometimes I swore the door spelled "Nita," as if calling to me.

After weeks of fascination/fright, the hall began emitting a glow in neon pink, yellow, or green. In reality, there was a standard 75-watt bulb in the overhead light, yet the hall was repeatedly suffused with color. When I got bored with (i.e., no longer afraid of) the colors, the hall itself altered shape. Sometimes it turned into an "L." Sometimes it elongated about twenty feet.

The catalyst which drove me out of my bedroom occurred when the open doorway leading into the hall became sealed by a solid wall of glass. Through this glass, I saw the colored lights in the hall. Sitting up in bed, I moved my hand and saw its reflection moving in the glass. I felt as if I were sealed into the room. This happened three successive nights, during which I was too frightened to do anything.

NOVEMBER 11, 1991

H: You wake up and see the glass, which means you see through it?

N: Yeah. Sometimes the hall configuration changes.

H: A true distortion of reality is occurring?

N: Well, I hope so! (both laugh) Don't tell me that the hall is really bending.

H: My questions may sometimes seem silly.

N: I never got up and measured it, let's put it that way! (both laugh) I feel like, if I'm really getting so much better. . .

H: Then why is that going on? 'Cause. You're getting better and that stuff's going on. The reason we're talking about it now, in case you haven't figured it out yet, is to make it stop.

N: How?

H: How do I know? (both laugh)

N: For this, I pay you?! (laughs)

H: A person comes in here, and says she's got this glass thing in front of her. She says, "How am I supposed to deal with this?" I say, "God! I don't know!" You think I've heard it all? (both laugh)

N: I thought maybe you hadn't heard this before, but something like it.

H: Hallucinations, sure. Every psychotherapist who hears this stuff thinks, "Geez, what are we going to do about that?" You've got to know it would drive me nuts.

N: You know what I like about you the best?

H: Oh, the best? What?

N: You're not afraid to tell me your weaknesses. I've never known a therapist who would do that.

H: That, to me, is essential. I'm glad you picked that up. (exaggerated sigh) I don't know. (both laugh) I've got to think about it.

N: Get a ball and throw it through.

H: Yeah, but the scary thing, if it bounces back. . .

N: Then what? Call 911.

H: If it's real, I can't help you! (both laugh) These things are happening very often. It's a reasonable expectation for them to stop happening altogether. You've become so used to them, even though they terrify you, you get revved up for them. It always changes when you get comfortable with it. This is being done to freak you out. "Well, it's doing a good job." (both laugh)

N: It's "being done?"

H: By another entity? No. It's being done by you, with forces you don't quite understand yet. It's true, right? (laughs) You still don't quite understand these forces.

N: That's right.[1]

I decided to throw a shoe through the glass wall that night, but it never reappeared. The possibility of being sealed in my bedroom was too creepy so I decamped to the living room where I hoped the cats would provide a greater sense of reality. This served instead to increase the scope and magnitude of my hallucinations.

The dining room chandelier unaccountably swayed, or cast moving shadows when it wasn't moving. An intricate lace pattern played across the ceiling in neon orange, yellow, green, or pink. The pattern spread from one corner until the entire ceiling was alive with flashes of color. It would suddenly switch to a solid constant green. Sometimes white strobe lights flashed.

I called these episodes "my light shows" to make them feel less threatening. A different light phenomenon occurred which was scarier. I noticed an increasing frequency in power surges, which caused the lights and TV to flare so bright the effect was similar to flood lights. Sometimes I waited for the picture tube to explode. (It never did.) I used an inordinate number of light bulbs (many more than could be attributed to 24-hour usage). My small appliances were dying. But my apartment neighbors noticed no unusual electrical activity in their own units.

Charlotte asked out of the blue if I were using a lot of light bulbs. As I was not confiding my nightly adventures to her, I was astonished. She stated it was "a documented phenomenon" that people with DID have an effect on electrical currents when their alters switch.[2] I have not seen an official study which "documents" this phenomenon. I have had the opportunity (in my work as a survivor group facilitator) to informally discuss strange symptomatology with many people formally diagnosed with DID. All reported hallucinations of wide variety, including their own version of light shows. Several reported power surges similar to what I experienced.

There are still universes within our brains about which scientists can only speculate at best. Whether or not DID plays some role in creating power surges, I do know that since integration not a single power surge has occurred. My light bulbs and appliances now last their normal life span.

Sometimes my hallucinations went beyond light shows and power surges. I frequently feared someone was breaking into my front door. I heard it open (too afraid to look), knowing that the chain and locks were securely fastened. I'd say, "This isn't happening," and still be terrified. Sometimes I heard my mother talking, or more often, yelling in my ear. Sometimes she called my name in a way which sounded so real I was compelled to look around, as if she managed to slip in without my knowledge.[3]

Charlotte has a teddy bear which she takes with her everywhere. She said he gave her courage. I was skeptical, but thought, "Why not?" So I bought one, and named him Howard. I was reluctant to admit this to human Howard, fearing his disapproval at a point where acceptance was critical. I certainly believed it was silly to endow a teddy bear with any kind of power. I feared naming it Howard proved how sick I really was. I withheld this secret from human Howard for weeks while Howard the bear and I became friends. One night when the light show was intense and I felt very threatened, I held the bear up toward the lights, and said, "Howard! Make it go away!" To my amazement, the apparition slowly faded. This incident necessitated telling human Howard the truth in order to explain the outcome. I cringed as I disclosed to him the Other Howard's identity.

Not only was human Howard predictably compassionate, but he offered an explanation as to why the light show faded on command. As in so many things, the lowest common denominator was control. Howard believed this incident demonstrated far greater personal control than I was willing to concede. By imbuing the bear with mystical powers, I could hold tight to the myth that I lacked control to stop these hallucinations of my own volition.

NOVEMBER 24, 1991

N: I've had this voice in my head for years, going, "I hate my life, I hate my life." Since Tuesday, that voice is gone.

H: Good God. You've been holding out on me that you had it.

N: It seemed like a natural element, like breathing. I tuned it out.

H: Wow, that's incredible!

N: So then I started thinking I was almost — but not quite. . .

H: Oh God.

N: Not depressed. (both laugh) How can I not feel depressed? There are so many bad things left.

H: You're experiencing the fruits of your health.

N: ***(sarcastic) Is that what this is?***

H: Yeah! A happy life. No depression. Directed, focused, and communicative with the people in your sphere of humanity you care about.

N: ***But there are so many problems left. It seems false.***

H: Sure, but here's the deal. It used to be you had these same things as well as the voice going "I hate my life, I hate my life." Now you have them without that. It's like you had a bunch of diseases, and one got cured.

N: ***That's what I'm saying, though. I can't get rid of the voice, and then just be instantly happy.***

H: No. But, dare you say, "I'm not depressed anymore?" Now you don't have the voice in your head, and you're not depressed.

N: ***I said almost not depressed. I still have behavioral problems that are depressed-like.***

H: We'll deal with them one at a time. When you go for that last real problem, you'll have a focus you didn't have before. The room is very messy. Maybe we'll pick up all the newspapers. Now the room is messy, but we won't have newspapers. I'm happy about that kind of stuff. Simple pleasures are just fine with me. What other things happen in you that is like background noise, and you just accept it?

N: ***You mean, like the voice?***

H: You know something? I'd rather you not tell me. All those things will drop away as you have no more need, from an emotional and psychological perspective, to have them. There will come a time when you'll have no need to compulsively overeat.

N: ***It worries me that I'll always have that need.***

H: That's the fear of all fears. But if we do this work well enough, you can get used to the idea. The fear won't fall away, but the need to compulsively overeat will.

N: ***Am I really going to get to a place where I feel well?***

H: Yes. Absolutely. And yeah, you're supposed to be normal. Staying normal is easy, not hard.

N: ***Getting normal's the hard part. I'm not normal!(laughs)***

H: I don't know exactly how to respond to that. You're not satisfied with how you are, but you're normal. You can try to convince me how crazy you are, and it's from that position that you'll need to eat. When you know you're normal, you won't need to eat. And you won't go hungry.

N: ***It's really a fear of being unable to control all the things that feel out of control.***

H: You're correct. Like it or not, you're getting more control. With understanding, there's always control.

N: ***Really?***

H: Sure, you understand what's going on. You express the dynamics of your life pretty succinctly. Even if it sounds bizarre, it's truthful. You may not know how to share it because it sounds bizarre, and they can't handle it, but you're more comfortable with it than you used to be. Understanding leads to control. You're not going to lose control; therefore, eating is not a control issue anymore.

N: I guess. (sigh) I moved into the living room the last couple of nights because the bedroom was so scary. Now the living room's getting scary, too.

H: You are freaking you out. You've become used to the feeling that you're supposed to be freaked out. Hard-wired. "I hate my life." All that tells me, which is very obvious, is that if there's a good thing going on, something's wrong. Do you know the rule of soap operas?

N: The nicest, best people always get creamed.

H: Something like that. Nobody is allowed to be happy for more than one episode. "Finally! We love each other, everything's going to be wonderful!" Then there's this car crash. That's what you do. You're not allowed to be happy for more than one episode. An episode could be a minute. (reacting to her cynicism) Oh, come on! That makes sense to you. I hate my life, I hate my life. You're not supposed to have a good life. You are hard-wired that anything positive, good, wonderful, profitable, projects good things, and the outlook is bright — that's not you.

N: Right.

H: (laughs) No resistance on that one. You make sure you don't have goodness in your life by being freaked out. It's how it's supposed to be. Oh, you're losing patience with me, I can tell.

N: (impatiently) No, I'm not losing patience with you, Howard. Being freaked out is how I'm supposed to be.

H: This has real power. The goal — you always do that. (fidgets in illustration) "Okay, I'm actually going to lose those things, too?" Yes. You're going to lose all the symptoms that disturb you. There's one thing you'll be left with when all these symptoms are gone, which is the work of your life.

N: Okay, fine. I do this to myself. I have to be scared of something. Fine.

H: Your life's supposed to be in disarray. That's how you've operated it. Something has to be out of whack. You marry a person who isn't good for you.

N: (sighs) I wrote a poem before we married, saying he would leave my life in disarray. It was seen as a good, romantic thing.

H: One way or another, you invent a way to cause disarray in your life. You call it being out of control, but it's not.

N: I'm like a fish, my mouth just opening and closing. I don't know what to say.

H: Just listen, and absorb it. Every time you come here you must wonder, "What's going to happen this time?" Or are you numb with that one now?

N: (sighs) No.

H: All this other stuff I don't know about you will emerge in its own good time. The issue now is "I don't deserve good things. I hate my life. I'm supposed to have disarray, disorder, and problems." Well, no, you're not supposed to have any of that. You're supposed to have anti-that. And yeah, that's exactly what's going to happen. You'll have to learn how to deal with stability.

N: (whines) But if it's the same person inside who says "I hate my life" and that's gone, then why isn't all this other stuff gone, too?

H: (laughs) Just the way you asked was very snotty and whiny. (going into best snotty and whiny mode) "But it's supposed to be gone!" When you deal with one thing, it illuminates another. You've got a whole bunch of them. More than we've ever even touched. I've always accepted that, right from the gate. Oh, don't get frightened.

N: What does that mean?

H: There's lots of stuff in your life that's really out of line, messed up, not right. You've got to make it better.

N: So how can that be normal?

H: You are normal. Your life isn't. Don't brush that off like I'm being poetic. Your life is completely not normal.

N: That's what I've been saying all along!

H: You're a good person, living a crummy life. Did you think I was implying your life was a good one? Your life is one of the most crummy ones I've known!

N: (laughs) Oh, wow! That's a great distinction! You've known a ton of crummy lives, I'm sure.

H: It's supposed to be a lot better. The way you're living it stinks. Your place is in disarray, your career isn't as on-track as it's supposed to be. You're having hallucinations.

N: I feel so much better now.

H: You should, because it's making more sense. I understand the depth of the pain and disarray in your life. You have all the capabilities to make it different from what it is, and you've done some things that made a difference.

N: (sighs) Somewhat.

H: You're putting a limitation on how far you can go with this. I don't know if you know this, but I've been trying to go for broke. All the things you could ever imagine in your life that should be, and that you want to be for you, that's what I've been imagining for you.

N: ***Hoping it would hit somewhere in the middle?***

H: No, I'm not aiming high, so if it goes a little lower that's okay. I'm aiming high because that's exactly where you're going. I've said I've got plans for you. Career, relationships, your physical and mental health, living arrangements, family, how you relate to them. What did you expect when we first got together?

N: ***Four times or less![4] You said, "You have all the answers inside you." (he laughs) "It's surprising you don't know the answers the first time I see you."***

H: Don't mock me. (laughs)

N: ***It has two sides to it. It's like, you're so screwed up you can't do this in four times or less.***

H: It's about dependency. If I died tomorrow, I wouldn't want you to say, "But I was right in the middle of it, and now it just stops." That says whatever we did had no momentum and promise to it. No one knows when a thing stops, or when I won't be, or need to be, the agent of it anymore. I hope if we never see each other again, it doesn't fall apart, whatever we accomplished. I want you to think about the idea that you're creating havoc in your life because it's become normal. You've defined your life through upset, but you'll start defining it through stability.

N: ***(dejected) I thought I was doing so well.***

H: You're focusing on stuff that's still there, instead of saying, "Wow, got rid of that one! This stuff really works!"

N: ***Yeah! It seemed like it.***

H: "Can't wait for the next one to stop!" It will. Lights out, sleeping the whole night through, without bad dreams. You're giving me very strong resistance. I'm telling you the boat's floating, okay? A little water comes into the boat. I'm saying, "Don't worry; it's supposed to be there. Keep paddling." You say, "Why?" I say, "Look, has the boat sunk? Paddle." "Why? How does the boat stay afloat?" I say, "It does. Put the sail up. Will you do your job, please? You don't have to worry about how the boat stays up."

N: ***So my job is to...?***

H: You have several jobs. Get into a pattern of taking care of yourself, and making nice, healthy meals. Be happy about the voice that's not there. Don't be disturbed if it returns, and don't worry. Listen to this tape, make sense of it, ponder it, feel it. Give yourself credit for how far you've come. Decide you deserve a good life at the highest standards possible. Eat what you want to eat when you want to eat it. The expectation is to be able to sleep through the night, pleasantly, without hallucinations.

N: ***Is that what it is?***

H: You're supposed to have a good life. Not just tolerate-the-crap-and-just-live-with-it stuff. Set your sights high. Get rid of all the crap in your life. Bring as much good stuff in as you can, and maintain it.

JANUARY 3, 1992

Dear Howard,

I feel like I'm blowing away. The hallucinations went wild right after Christmas Eve, but for about four nights there haven't been any. (I know, wow!) I still have trouble sleeping because I expect them. I think they're gone while I contemplate writing off most of the people in my "sphere of humanity." I told Linda about this thing with Charlotte (I fully recognize the self-set-up here). She said, in her own enlightened way, "Why do you have to run to Howard for every little thing?" I'm truly grateful that the hallucinations appear to be gone, but all the good feelings seemed to go with them. One step forward, two steps back.

These hallucinations took a lot out of me, emotionally and physically. They persisted for months without respite, forcing me to question my sanity and doubt my therapy. I tried almost anything to distract myself, and to sleep peacefully. Anything, except drugs. Not that I didn't want them occasionally, but Howard's approach is to use as few artificial means to achieve a goal as possible. He impressed upon me repeatedly the need to sit with and experience all of my feelings, no matter how painful.

Amidst the controversy over whether to medicate survivors, or whether anti-depressants have any appropriate effect upon people with DID, there is one thing I know with certainty, and carry with pride. I can categorically state that my hallucinations — and my retrieved memories — were neither drug-induced nor drug-allayed. I am grateful to have (sometimes grudgingly) avoided the despair created by not knowing.

A survivor needs to understand why one's psychiatrist is prescribing anti-depressants, or any other drug. What is the diagnosis? What is the long-range plan for the drug's use, and eventual discontinuance? How does the drug align with therapeutic goals? Does the survivor want to take drugs, or is s/he being pressured by a therapist who sees his/her client as essentially unmanageable?

As Howard once said, there is a thing of courage where you are frightened, and you do it anyway. I was terrified most of the time for more than three years. To pull this off without drugs, an open and receptive therapist is mandated. Especially for a survivor dealing with DID, the therapist must be consistently available, whether by phone or extra sessions. Howard took on all of my problems from day one, and made no attempt to mitigate them for either his or my short-term benefit.

I eventually became somewhat neutral about these hallucinatory episodes: "Oh, this one's new; love those colors! What might that picture represent?" Their frequency waxed and waned as time passed, to where they only occurred during times of particular stress or upheaval. Within a year, they ceased their torment of me completely.

December 16, 1991

Dear Howard,

Thanks so much for your call last night. It came at a very good time. I know you understand better than anyone what I am going through, but it's still nice to hear that someone is proud of me for what I am accomplishing. Your timing, as always, is exquisite.

P.S. "Poltergeist" seems really phony to me now. I've seen better stuff in my living room.

9

Family Dynamics and Confrontations

The last two calls Linda tried to respond to me, but I know she doesn't get the full scope of the damage. She has no concept of my pain.

—NITA, APRIL 19, 1992

I mentioned to Linda in July 1991, that I'd started therapy with Howard, and was working on why my entire life seemed so chaotic and unhappy. She asked if I could have been molested as a child. I couldn't produce an incident in my memory. She asked if Charlotte might have been molested. I thought it possible. Then she asked, "Could you have been in the same room when she was molested?" Loud sirens went off in my head. I felt dizzy. I told her I'd think about it.

On August 9, 1991, I called Charlotte and learned she had been aware of being molested, and of my involvement, for five years. Not only had she confided this to Linda and my best friend several years previously, but asked them both to not tell me. I was living a new episode of The Twilight Zone. I was furious that these people had all betrayed me. I felt an old familiar sensation of not being able to breathe.

AUGUST 14, 1991

Dear Linda,

It may be awhile yet before I can manage "the tone of voice" you require, so I'm writing. You can decide if you have the courage to read this. Our family didn't excel at much besides keeping hurtful secrets. I'd never have asked Charlotte about this but for the fact that you, Linda, asked me about it. It was so unlike you that I felt I had to ask her. Think about how well you guard confidences in that context.

You protest you "only" knew 1.5 years ago. That's 1.5 years of my life without help. The minute I was implicated Charlotte lost her license to keep the information. So did you, if you cared about me or my welfare.

Charlotte stated she was only telling me because it was good for her recovery — that she had to "make sure in her heart" (what's left of it) that she wasn't telling me for my benefit. If the only thing left in her life that she could control was when baby sis got the news, she was fully prepared to let me go to hell, which I've basically done.

I haven't really believed Charlotte cares if I live or die for a long time, but you made an effort to prolong that illusion the last few years. So I've got my best friend and closest sister watching me struggle in and out of therapy, never feeling complete, always asking, "Why did you turn out so different? Why are your childhood memories so different?" You witnessed my attraction to unavailable men, and listened to my despair over so many things in my life that never made sense. You watched this, month after month, merely because Charlotte said so. She had the gall to say that if I'd continued therapy during the years I thought myself healthy enough not to require it, I might have discovered this on my own. As if it's my fault.

Hank asked, "If you don't remember it, how do you know it really happened?" I said, without hesitation, "Because it explains everything." Here's a partial list.

1. *Lifelong weight problem*
2. *Need for platonic male friends*
3. *Passivity and feeling of helplessness*
4. *Fear of men who are strangers*
5. *Never sexually attracted to anyone I wasn't friends with first*
6. *Never sexually aggressive*
7. *Sexually submissive; can't enjoy it without some form of struggle*
8. *Growing up angry*
9. *Always feeling out of control*
10. *Lifelong feeling I was bad, no matter what I did to be good*
11. *Compulsive need for perfection*
12. *Fear of failure so strong it inhibits me from trying*
13. *Why "Sarah" existed all these years*
14. *Why nothing was ever resolved in therapy before*
15. *Why you grew up different*
16. *Why I feel like I'm a fraud and have said for years that if people really knew me they'd see how horrible I am, never knowing why*
17. *Why all of my happy poems are tentative*
18. *Why when I'm anxious or scared I say "I feel like a three-year-old"*
19. *Why I'm not interested in clothes or makeup, and couldn't act "sexy" if my life depended on it*

I don't need five years to reach a few conclusions. I think Mommy knew. That also explains everything. She was obsessed with having the look of the perfect family, regardless of the cost. Mommy took Charlotte to the doctor for mono when she was sleeping away her teenage years. He told Charlotte she should see someone about depression. I can't imagine that he did not also tell Mommy. But if Charlotte saw someone, the possibility of blowing this wide open was far too risky. Better to let Charlotte sleep some more.

I, however, grew up angry and targeted because Mommy couldn't make me sleep on command. You and Charlotte react to my anger now exactly the way you did when we were children. Did you ever stop to consider why I was so angry? Did anyone ever ask? You get so self-righteous about my tone of voice, but you never say, "Gee, you must feel very hurt now, and I'm sorry you have to go through this. How can I help you?" (Charlotte cleverly asked, "What do you want from me now?" and then refused to give it to me. She gets no points.) You're just like Mommy, more worried about how it sounds and looks than about the content.

I've been trying for sixteen years to rewrite my life, and to get some indication that I'm on the road to mental health. Everyone protects Charlotte's interests, and I'm still struggling. Who are you to make this decision? Who appointed you Charlotte's guardian angel? Where's mine?

Charlotte's still consumed with keeping secrets because that's how she keeps control. Since she's been totally self-obsessed and heartless in her quest to "heal" herself, I'm sure she'll understand when I say that my recovery depends on telling these secrets. I have been victimized twice now. I have done nothing shameful. I'll tell whoever and whenever I want, to the L.A. Times, if I feel like it. The secrets keep all of us sick, and I refuse to participate a second longer. It's sad that Charlotte made this pain so special and precious. It may be the only thing left she can really call her own, but it's sick and sadistic to take me down with her. I had a right to know, and to heal, too. How easy and hypocritical of you to say I didn't have that right.

I understand that forgiveness is an essential and healthy part of living. As much as I am committed to rising above my past, this is going to be very difficult to forgive.

AUGUST 15, 1991

Hank says this betrayal stuff is a smoke screen because I am too afraid to face the scary core issues. He said if it's true this explains everything, I should be joyous and dancing. He thinks I am too passive; I allow everything and everyone to control me. I said perhaps that was learned very young as a survival skill. He said I ask everyone for answers but I have to start figuring things out for myself. I told him all I wanted was a hug. He gave me one, and said, "A hug and a clue."

AUGUST 16, 1991

Dear Linda,

I'm angry at you (not as a substitute for Ron). You've done plenty to deserve it, and your offer to let me "direct my anger toward you" is appropriate, if you followed through. I tried, and you objected to my tone of voice. That's what an angry person's voice sounds like.

The trauma of this revelation is not the fact that I was molested. At least I can work with it. I can see for the first time ever that maybe I'm not crazy or bad. There's a reason why everything in my life seemed skewed. No, the trauma of this revelation was that you and Charlotte conspired to keep me sick longer. You consciously disregarded my life in favor of hers, and justify it as the best thing for me. You call it love.

Call Howard. You have my permission to ask him anything, because I have no secrets. He's a nice, steady, approachable kind of guy. But he's honest, and if you ask for his opinion, he'll give it to you. Got any guts?

SEPTEMBER 19, 1991

Dear Linda,

We've been on different frequencies our whole lives. The current situation illustrates our family dynamic more clearly than usual. You interpret what I say to suit your purpose, and I get to feel a little crazy because there's no way I said what you say I said. You get to be superior, I get to be confused. Well, those days are gone. Not only did I say exactly what I meant, but I put it in writing so there could be no misinterpretation. You persist in creating them.

Stay focused on your pretty little world as long as you can, but I have to deal with horrible realities. I have not turned the lights off in five weeks. I'm too scared to sleep, too scared to wake up. When I'm totally exhausted, I sit at my computer, entranced, and this vile stuff is thrown up on the screen. It just gets progressively worse.

If you can't help me, as you say you want to, I'm not interested. Blaming me for your lack of regard for me is never going to cut it again. Is that clear enough?

P.S. I can't help but wonder where God was when this little girl said her prayers every night.

SEPTEMBER 30, 1991

Dear Linda,

Before you cringe, I'm writing to try to get us to some kind of understanding. On Monday, Howard and I talked about our relationship. He suggested ways which would be conducive to making connections, rather than breaking them. He's just as willing to say I'm wrong as you are. But I don't think I'll remember all the fine points if we talk and I get upset, which seems possible. So I'm sending you the tape, and also to Charlotte, because I'm trying to keep things out in the open. It would be helpful if you did, too.

In my writings, when "I" is "i," I'm feeling like a very small child. Howard says the writings I sent to you were not just memories; it was as if I experienced it as I wrote (and sure felt that way). It seems like someone else wrote them, and really, someone else did. A terrified three-year-old. All my life I've had flashes of her, and never understood why. My whole life I've said, "But you don't understand," then never was able to describe it. If you get nothing else, please know that I've been that three-year-old a lot lately, especially at night. And I (she) keep(s) wondering, if it's really safe to come out now, why do I get hurt when I do? That's what it feels like when I try to be real with you. Maybe Howard has provided the tools to bridge the gap.

OCTOBER 25, 1991

Dear Linda,

Your last letter is the one I wish you'd written long ago. It had compassion, and for the first time cast doubt on Mommy's role. I never expected you to hate her. I've never believed she did anything to cause you to hate her. (Don't you see, that's one of the reasons why I hate her? I knew as a child that she loved you. I never knew that for myself.) But I did want you to admit that she, as a nurse, if not as a mother, should have been sophisticated enough to know something was very wrong with Charlotte and me. Admitting it doesn't make you disloyal to her. It just means you're able to take another look, and that's all I've wanted.

I think Daddy feels a lot of pain over this. He keeps asking, "Where was I when all this was going on?" I tell him it's a good question. He keeps saying, "I can't believe she kept secrets from me." He's seeing the possibility that she did. But sometimes, I just want to shake him and say, "Believe it! Move past that!" Howard asked, "What would he have to face if he moved past that?" I said, "He'd have to face that he didn't know the woman he married very well."

We all have issues to confront. I've been saying I'd never have told Daddy because Mommy had total control. I discovered recently it wasn't about her. I had a wonderful relationship with Daddy until age six. At the same time, Ron was saying I was the baddest little girl in the world. If I told Daddy, he'd find out and stop loving me. My choice was either save myself and lose Daddy, or keep his love and endure everything else. Such an unfair choice! It explains my lifelong feeling that "if they really knew me, they'd know how bad I really am."

DECEMBER 1991

N: My father and I talked about my mother hitting us. She hit everybody, but me more, 'cause I was always yelling at her. Always in her way.

H: What'd your dad say about it?

N: That it was considered okay to hit children then. I told him about the last time she threatened to hit me, when I was fourteen. I decided I didn't care if she killed me. I grew up flinching, and decided to stand up to her. I said, "Go ahead, hit me. It'll do you more good than it does me." I was looking her in the eye, and saying, "I know you get off on this." Real defiant. She never hit me again, but was twice as verbally abusive. My father, amazed, said, "She was hitting you at fourteen?" I said, "Yeah, you were there."

H: *Have you told him yet how astounded you are at the daze you've found him in?*

N: ***That's exactly what we talked about. I spoke to a high school friend who'd been in our house a couple times. Her father gave you a big hug, asked how your life was, very involved in all his kids' lives. She said it was so weird at our house because my father was "totally checked out." She said, "We could have danced nude in front of him, and he'd never have known."***

H: *That's very consistent.*

N: ***Yeah. So he said my mom hit him once when we were little, and he told her never do it again. She didn't. He remembered a few times he told her she was using "excessive force" with us; she stopped that, too. At that moment something gave, and I stopped being nice. I said, "Did it ever once occur to you that if she had the guts to do it in front of you she was doing it lots more when you weren't there?" He said, "Well, I didn't know; I wasn't there." I told him my friend said we could have danced naked in front of him. He smiled, and said, "I would have noticed that!" I went ballistic. "That's great! You would have noticed that, but not that your wife was beating the shit out of me." He kept saying, "I wish I had known." I said, "You were there! You obviously did know." (sighs)***

H: *That's right. There's an inconsistency here. And, of course, what he's saying is completely unacceptable, even now.*

N: ***Yes!***

H: *I give him credit for hanging in there to have the discussion with you. This is completely unacceptable. He had more control in that relationship, and he didn't exercise it, particularly when necessary. Stupidity is always unacceptable. He claims ignorance, but it wasn't. It was stupid.*

MARCH 11, 1992

Dear Howard,

I've kept myself going for years on the hope that someday my family would believe my pain. There would be a day of total redemption. Yet, even when this nightmare is known, nothing really changes. All Linda or Charlotte still see is my anger. My mother would be cheering them on. My father accepts most of what I say without introspection or connection. Sometimes he says he gets it and I know he hasn't. I can't make it any clearer, and I want him to get it without a big song and dance anyway.

Just because I've had to act "stronger than" to survive, doesn't mean I'm really strong. I'm actually quite fragile, and have my break-

ing point. Something very basic fights it down. My survival depended on not having a breaking point. I was close to it in our last session because it's so clear that my family will probably never get it. All my cards are on the table, and it's still not good enough. To have come this far, and still be lectured about "my reality" is, indeed, a bitter pill.

NOVEMBER 9, 1992

I think Daddy has learned a lot about himself, and who he was when we were children, and is responding more appropriately now. It goes a long way for making up for his lapses when we were desperately in need of someone to help us. It's a slow process, and I have days when I'm really angry with him. I don't try to deny or repress it now because I know expressing it is the way to move beyond the anger.

Charlotte and I've always been in sync with how we felt about Mommy. I asked her why, if she has so few memories of direct abuse, she's so clear in her hatred of Mommy? She said it's because Mommy did nothing to protect her. She never taught Charlotte how to say no to a man (probably because she didn't know how, either). She never taught Charlotte how to be pretty, or have style, or to open up with people, all social skills lacking. I'd always felt the same way, but thought that was normal, as it was the backdrop for all the other bizarre things happening.

NOVEMBER 12, 1992

Charlotte's orchestrated this whole Christmas in Seattle thing. Just a year ago I asked her to meet me on Christmas Eve, and she said, "Why?" She now seems open and curious, and wants family around her. It's a major change. For all I know, we're going to become best friends out of all this. But it still seems weird, and I'm waiting for the other shoe to drop.

Our family gathered at Christmas, 1992. Charlotte and I discussed confronting our father regarding his failure to protect us. My memories had surfaced in agonizing detail as to my mother's complicity. I wanted him to know what I knew, but face to face. He and I argued on Christmas Eve when he admitted lying to family friends about why I'd changed my name to Sarah. Then he stated he "knew the whole story" of my abuse, when he did not know half of it. So I told him the other half, and Christmas was "ruined." Charlotte backed away from her own confrontation.

The next day, my sisters agreed to a taped session to "discuss our childhoods." What resulted was a perfect demonstration of our childhood family dynamics. As usual, I became "the problem." Our father was again beneficiary of a child's protection. This time, however, I no longer was confused about my role.

S: Daddy has a personal stake in having others believe Mommy never did this.

LI: He does, and you have to understand that personal stake.

S: He has to understand my personal stake. It's very dangerous for me.

LI: I believe he does, more than you know. He hurts from it. But you have to understand, for him to keep his sanity he may not be able to believe everything that's true about Mommy.

S: ***Why do I have to understand, and he doesn't?***

C: *Can't you understand other people?*

LI: *Can't you come outside of yourself to understand other people's feelings?*

S: ***I've been doing that my entire life.***

LI: *You are acting just like he is. You're very self-absorbed, and everything is in relation to what you think. I'm not saying you haven't gone through a lot, or you don't deserve to have people listen to you. But don't always expect them to do it your way.*

S: ***I guess it's just that after 40 years of no one doing that, I got on a little trip of wanting it. After my entire life of nobody caring what I thought, nobody believing me, nobody putting my point of view first, nobody in my corner. It feels pretty damned good that somebody — at last! — is paying attention to me.***

LI: *I want to continue to give you that kind of attention, but I don't know if Daddy can. He's trying.*

S: ***By telling these lies, he's trying?***

LI: *It's how he's dealing with it.*

S: ***It's my life he's dealing with. It's me he's lying about.***

C: *Everyone copes with their life situations in whatever way they do.*

S: ***Daddy goes off into never-never land. But if he wants to deal with me as an adult, which he said he wants, he can't do that.***

LI: *I know it's not the same situation, but there are some things you have to just let bounce off.*

S: ***And if you were me, Linda, which you are not, you might have found by now that letting things bounce off takes a little piece of you every time.***

LI: *No, it doesn't because I have much more "peace" — the other kind — than you do.*

S: ***(disgusted) Oh, let's not bring religion into this. It does take a piece off of me. I have let things bounce off me for 40 years. I'm through with that. People are not using me as target practice anymore.***

LI: *The one thing I don't think he'd even deal with right now is about Mommy.*

S: ***Then what's the point of this whole conversation? Mommy is a key player here. Mommy made this all happen. We'll just go around that whole subject so he can deal with life.***

LI: *He will not ever accept it.*

S: ***You know that for a fact.***

LI: *He will not change. He had many years of life experience with her, and everything he remembers is contrary to what you're saying.*

C: *Consider the effect of what you say to people when you're telling them. Consider the intensity.*

S: ***I consider it very well, especially with him, because I'm attempting to wake him up.***

C: *How do you know he wants to be woken up?*

S: ***Because he said he wants a relationship with me. I am not going to pretend we have the same one we had before.***

C: *Does he have to be as awake as you to have a relationship?*

S: ***If I'm going to have this relationship with him, here's "A." He understands I changed my name to Sarah because of a bunch of childhood trauma, and Anita is a totally tainted name. Here's "B." He understands that I was molested, what that means, why it affected me the way it did. If he wants to relate to who I really am, and not to the splits he was relating to his whole life, he has to accept that stuff happened back then.***

LI: *I agree.*

S: ***Both of you have to do that, too. Here's "C." He has to understand the depth of it, and how it happened right under his nose. And that he has accountability in it.***

LI: *That's part of his problem in dealing with it. He understands that.*

S: ***But he's not dealing with it. He's still saying, "I think she was forced. I can't believe how all this happened. Where was I?" I'm saying, I've waited years for him to listen to me. And I don't care anymore.***

C: *Great. Don't care. But how will that help you get into relationship with him?*

LI: *If you don't want the relationship, then sever it.*

S: ***(astonished) Sever it.***

C: *Take a separation or something.*

S: ***You two are promoting his fantasy life. If we don't tell him, you're protecting him the way I did my whole life.***

LI: *I still believe he maybe didn't need to know this last part. How does it help him? How does it help you?*

S: ***A father is supposed to provide safety and security. My father failed miserably. What it does for me to tell him is that it's no longer my burden to preserve the good family name. Doing that, as I have my whole life, made me feel very crazy. Made me split. I am not willing to sacrifice my sanity, or my freedom of mental health, or anything to do with my well-being anymore, for his benefit. He blew it big time when I was little. I am not carrying this burden around anymore.***

C: *Why do you want a relationship with him?*

S: ***(exasperated) 'Cause he's my father!***

LI: *So?*

C: *Give us the real answer.*

S: ***(angry) That was the real answer! Who are you to say that?***

LI: *Well, I don't understand, either. If you feel this way, I wouldn't have any relationship with him.*

S: ***I have always wanted a relationship with him as a father.***

LI: *But he's never going to be that father.*

C: *So why are you banging your head against the wall?*

S: ***We all have our walls. He's mine. I have wanted a father my whole life. It's not up to either of you to say "sever it!" when I'm still trying.***

LI: *I get rid of any walls that I'm going to have to bang my head against.*

S: ***Well, good for you. Maybe you haven't had any real big ones.***

LI: *I haven't. I've been very fortunate that way.*

S: ***Confronting him is making a bigger commitment in myself, saying, "I want to try to have a relationship with him." I know I'll never have one if I don't confront him. I can put that off forever. My natural inclination has always been to protect him. But I don't think I should be penalized and put down because I chose to do it on my timing.***

LI: *I didn't put you down. I told you I was angry and upset. There's a difference.*

C: *Is it okay for her to be angry at you?*

S: ***If it's reasonable. A good anger.***

C: *Wait, wait. There's good and bad anger now?*

S: ***Of course there is. Justifiable anger is always good anger. In this situation, I think it's unjustifiable.***

LI: *That's (laughs) your prejudice.*

S: ***That's your prejudice! I am exercising my option to confront, just as she is exercising her option not to confront. Why am I the target of your anger? Why don't you get angry at her for not following through?***

LI: *I didn't know she hadn't. I didn't mean to put you down when I said you were self-absorbed, and I shouldn't have added "like Daddy," because it's different. You have a very difficult time, understandably, of putting yourself in another person's position and mind. Often, that's easy for me to do. It tempers — sometimes changes — what I'd say, or how I'd say it. I understand some of your explanations, and I'm not angry anymore. I still wish you hadn't done it. But I was projecting myself into how Daddy felt. It made me very sad, and then angry.*

S: ***Why did you feel sad?***

LI: *Because I was empathizing with how it must have felt hearing all of this (crying) on Christmas Eve. He did a lot of things wrong, but I'm sure Christmas Eve was a special time for him, with his girls. If I were him, I'd think back to what it was like when we were growing up and Christmas Eve was a happy time. To me, it would be very upsetting. I felt you should have had more control, and been able to see his point of view.*

S: I just wonder, though, if you can empathize so strongly with him, how come you can't with me?

LI: I empathize with you, too. That's why I'm not angry with you anymore. I didn't have your side of the story.

S: I guess my problem is, I saw people getting murdered, and all he wants to talk about is why I should eat the vegetable quiche.

LI: It's hard for him to deal with the fact that you saw people getting murdered.

S: (incredulous) It's hard for me, too! I'm still looking for the father who'll say, "I'm sorry that happened to you."

LI: You won't find it.

S: Well, that's part of what this whole thing is about. I want him to be that father.

LI: (laughs) It's too late.

S: He's not dead. I don't believe that. Anybody can change if they want to. Part of the reason he doesn't want to is because people continue to coddle to the belief that he can't. I say he can change anytime he chooses, because he has free will, whether he uses it or not.

LI: He doesn't want to use it.

S: Right. So if he says he wants a relationship with me, and then doesn't give it to me, he has to account for that.

DECEMBER 27, 1992

Dear Howard,

I forgot to mention that this outpouring of compassion toward me took place immediately after I played for them the tape of Erin's account of "the bad place." It had little effect on them, apparently. They are accusing me of being what my family has always accused me of: making unnecessary problems; being selfish; being spiteful. The difference now is I'm not buying it.

Sometimes, Howard, I feel like I'm back in the Twilight Zone. Linda cannot possibly acknowledge that these "special" Christmases Past were based on tremendous lies and treachery. She can look back fondly on them because she was not being terrorized round the clock. She can easily give value to my father's pain, but readily admits she does not really understand what I went through. Which means she cannot

easily give value to my pain, even after listening to Erin.

DECEMBER 29, 1992

I cannot accept that it is okay for Daddy to not believe Mommy did these things. If Mommy didn't do anything wrong, then Daddy didn't, either, since we're saying his fault lies in not protecting us from her. We are then left with "two model parents taken in by some criminal." The next leap is: Mommy would never have allowed these things to happen if she were, in fact, this model parent, so maybe none of it really happened. "You know how she tells stories." I refuse to participate in this sick game to let Daddy shirk his responsibilities. It's also fascinating that Linda can choose between his sanity or mine.

MAY 15, 1993

Dear Howard,

My father and I had another long talk. My more integrated self isn't big on nonsense these days. He couldn't explain why, when I genuinely ask for help, he thinks I'm attacking him. He said I'm punishing him because I think he's "culpable of something." I (amazingly calmly) told him why he is culpable of being an ineffectual father then, who didn't protect me because he was too busy playing passive-aggressive mind games with my mother. That he systematically tuned everyone out, because he didn't want to know what was happening, which, in effect, means he did know. He denies everything. By the way, his idea of what we talked about with Linda was that I must be suicidal. Are the changes in me really so subtle he couldn't figure out that I'm farther away from suicide than ever before in my life?

As of late 1995, Linda and I have made peace, and are friends. Charlotte and I still struggle to communicate without kicking up each other's fears. My father thinks "the bad part" of my life is over so it doesn't need much air time anymore. Even so, he's done more to be a father than I expected from him in the sense of listening to my story and my pain, and in helping to defray therapy costs. I still find myself feeling angry at him as I read these passages, but the hurt is slowly fading.

10

Charlotte's Role Then and Now

I've always longed to be close to Charlotte. Always tried to figure out why it doesn't happen. Knowing now why it doesn't happen doesn't make me feel better.

—NITA, FEBRUARY 17, 1992

My relationship with my sister, Charlotte, has long been a source of grief, profound longing, and aggravation for me. Although she is two years my senior, I grew up with a secret belief that we were twins, and that it was "us against them." I could never articulate who "them" was, but I knew Charlotte and I were united in our struggle. Charlotte, however, distanced herself from me increasingly as we grew older. She became rather eccentric and isolated. She certainly didn't seem happy. I feared all my life that I would become Charlotte. I saw myself heading in that direction after my divorce, but didn't know what to do about it.

Charlotte has feared me and my anger since childhood, to my continual astonishment. I believed myself to be a great debater with an excellent memory. Sometimes I'd get angry, but everyone does. So her claims that my anger frightened her seemed disproportionate to anything I actually did. She described me as violent. That was not my perception of myself, until I realized that Anita could be downright nasty.

Charlotte deliberately withheld her knowledge of my involvement with Ron for five years. She might never have told me had I not asked. Even then, she flatly stated she was telling me only to benefit her own therapy, and that I should be grateful she told me at all. My response was full of the kind of anger she fears so much.

Charlotte's nondisclosure created all sorts of echoes back to things she'd done "for her benefit" as a child. As an adult looking back, I empathize with virtually anything a child might do to survive. I understand it. But I cannot condone perpetuating the same behavior into adulthood. I reached the point, as an adult, where I didn't want to be in the same room with her because she frightened me.

DECEMBER 31, 1991

Dear Howard,

You're saying "to get my foot in the door" I should tell her I'm the

Problem. But I've been designated "the Problem" for 37 years. It's real familiar for Charlotte to do whatever she wants and I get the rap. I'm able to admit when I really am the Problem. I'm so good at it I often apologize for things I had nothing to do with. I didn't sign up for abuse on Christmas Eve, or engineer it so I could once again be the Problem — anymore than I did at three. My worst fault is being incredibly naive.

I've allowed a lot of bad things to be done and said to me over the years because I was called "sensitive" and "touchy." It's a great way for rotten people to justify their behavior. It's never that they are hurtful, irresponsible, or obnoxious. I'm the Problem, and if I value their friendship, love, or presence, I sell a piece of myself to make nice and make up. I know that's not what you meant by "squaring it," but it's what happens in reality. On Christmas Eve I finally reached a point where no one is worth feeling that way. I thought you'd want to celebrate.

You say that as a child I used Newtonian physics because it worked then. Now we have to look at quantum physics, and all the rules change. Charlotte is still stuck in Newton, and I don't have the time or energy to drag her into this brave new world with me, especially when she isn't real eager to explore it.

JANUARY 14, 1992

Dear Howard,

This writing gets more disturbing and scary each time I read it. I realize she was a kid and every bit as much a victim as I was, but she sold me out to save herself. As a three-year-old, I jumped on him to make him stop hurting her; this is what she did for me. Not only was I getting it from Ron and my mother, but from her as well. There was no escape.

. . .

charlotte speaks for ron now. she's going to hurt me real bad. howard doesn't know how mean she is. she hurts me no one believes me she's quiet she's real quiet when ron hurts me she never makes him stop even if i try to help her she hates me she hates me she hates me! she says it's my fault she didn't know i talked to aunt cass she didn't hear me nobody hears me but she hates me for waiting she hates me! she looks at me she smiles when he hurts me sometimes he doesn't hurt her then. when i hide i make myself real little she tells him where i am she watches while he hurts me she tells lies to make him mad at me instead of her he says she likes to watch she's my little helper i don't know why she hates me i tried to tell i tried so hard nobody believes me she hates me she hates me!

JANUARY 15, 1992

At Ron's house there was a closet big enough for me but not big enough for Charlotte, even by herself. I hid there, behind a mirror or a big box, for a long time. He looked, but never saw me. If he threatened Charlotte, she'd tell him where I was. By age seven, he was losing interest in her, but he used her however he could. So she blew my closet cover, and other hiding places, rather than endure whatever he said he'd do to her. He'd praise her for turning me in, then be very cruel to me. Sometimes he put needles under my fingernails, or stuck pins in me after he tied me up. I began picking off my nails down to the quick, hoping he'd stop if I had none.

At five I still had the new bedroom to myself. I had nightmares and my legs hurt, but it was as far away as I could get from Charlotte. Being with her was a scary thing, and bad things happened. When Mommy forced me into the back bedroom with Charlotte I screamed that whole day — when Mommy wasn't hitting me because she thought I was backtalking her — because being with Charlotte terrified me. I thought she'd bring Ron into our bedroom to get me. I felt trapped and desperate.

I've had lifelong issues of betrayal with Charlotte. She's always been in this for herself, and I believe she'd sell me out for anything she wanted bad enough. My adult can see this is how she survived as a child, and we've both carried things with us from childhood that we'd do better without. But my child cringes and doesn't want to be in the same room with her. I know what she's capable of doing. I spent this weekend feeling terrified of this meeting, even knowing Howard would be there. So terrified that I picked off all my fingernails. Just in case.

JANUARY 15, 1992

H: The strides made by Nita are rather phenomenal. It's unfortunate that these difficulties in communication have the appearance of a setback, but they're actually wonderful opportunities. You're better off having a crisis than not because it promotes a possibility of catapulting to a better place.

C: That's true, but do we need to be in crisis all the time?

H: Sometimes. You're talking to a very practical person, who doesn't want a lot of drama. So I agree with you. But when I do see crises all the time, I ask myself, "What the hell happened here?" Particularly when I know the person's of sound character. I hope you'll continue to have faith in your relationship, but you've got to walk right in the middle of that storm because there's stuff to find out.

N: I know you were a kid. But the little five-year-old is really afraid to be with you. Afraid to be in the same room with you.

C: 'Cause what will I do next to you?

N: Yeah.

H: It's a pattern that got hard-wired. Wherever you don't offset it, it's just seen as another violation. Nita's expressing an extreme form of isolation. No one to go to; no one to turn to; having to deal with it all on her own strength. Being told she's not good, not strong. Not being able to explain it well enough. What does a person do? All kinds of dramatic things that could be interpreted as unstable, nuts, crazy. But they're not. Credibility is lost. Nita is a difficult child, people will say. A temperamental child. Even today, in some ways, it plays out. "Nita doesn't take responsibility for her feelings; she doesn't say what's on her mind; you do your best, and look what happens." That may be a correct report, but it's out of context with a bigger picture which you can't possibly know you're stepping into. You must have faith that something's happening, even though it may look ugly on the outside, crisis-producing, a little nuts, disturbed. It really isn't. She hasn't done a disturbed thing yet. She's never said anything that made me think, "Oh, God. This person's one step away from the loony bin."

N: ***I wanted you to think that.***

H: *I know, but it just isn't true because there's context. It all makes sense. Even so, Nita has to take responsibility for herself and make her way in the world, coming from strength, not weakness. She has to get continually more skillful with herself and other people. But, it's like a toddler. The way they first start to walk doesn't look so pretty. Most right-thinking people have an appreciation for the stumbling. I don't want anyone to make excuses for her. I'm the last person to do that. But she needs to be taken at face value and given a lot of credibility. That doesn't mean, her credibility against yours. Everybody's got equal credibility here. But it can't be questioned. Make sense?*

C: *In a vague way.*

H: *It gets clearer and clearer. You'll talk more. The interpretation I make is that Nita wants to love you. She wants to have the relationship with you that she idyllizes of any close sibling relationship. Attempts have been made, but for lack of skill, understanding, or insensitivities, it just doesn't happen. What's hard-wired in her is that you hate her. Why does she think that? I saw, as she spoke here earlier, the immediate compassion you had, totally non-defensive, it made a lot of sense to you. There was no reason to refute it. When you put that in the recipe, all it means is, you hate her. You get this opportunity now, because you know where she got it, to identify with it, and to attempt your reassurances. It's not hate. It's sort of like, without assuming guilt, 'cause you're not, you ask for forgiveness for the things that didn't happen the way she wanted. When you allow her to process that, there will be a time she can recognize she didn't do so well by you, sometimes. Thank goodness you're adults, because you can have adult compassion that couldn't, in a sophisticated way, play out when you were kids. More so, because there were survival issues of the highest order. She can't bear you any malice for her feelings that you weren't there for her in those moments. That's her adult. But where that gets hard-wired it's difficult, but not impossible, to override. It shouldn't be overridden until it's acknowledged. You can't discount it. "Well, whatever happened when we were kids, that was then." That's an attempt to not feel the feeling, and to override it without even knowing what you're overriding. The pains should be felt very acutely. Don't worry if that happens. Go ahead and feel the pain. Why is it that the two of you don't get along now? Charlotte's an adult; she's mature. She's always been, in here, very responsive to what you say. She can't know why these responsive things have never been acknowledged, understood, or appreciated. So she'd say, "What is it? I'm crazy? You're crazy?" Now there's context. It's not a mystery to her how she can do a good thing today, and you'd wonder if it's good or not.*

FEBRUARY 12, 1992

Things to discuss with Howard:

1. I decided it was better to die than end up like Charlotte. My entire life, I have said in various ways I don't want to be like her.
2. A front of anger, sarcasm, and resistance represented saving my sanity.
3. Have I mixed the signals all these years to do self-destructive things because I think it will make things better? How does this get reversed?
4. Because I resisted and fought back, I endured a physical pain entirely different from what Charlotte had to endure. Not more or worse, but different.
5. Charlotte may not trust me because she perceived my resistance as a danger to her.

FEBRUARY 13, 1992

Everyday, something new comes to me. Some new remembrance. It's real consistent. I was fighting, resisting, and doing everything I could to get away and out of it — and to get Charlotte out, too. But she wasn't this sleepy, passive, quiet, helpless person, as she claims, who did nothing. She directed her energy towards turning him on me, instead of her. It wasn't isolated, it was a pattern.

I understand clearly that she was a scared little girl, and if she'd not told him where I was hiding, the consequences would have been serious for her. But not any worse than what happened to me after he found me! Although Charlotte was both older and bigger, I had to be stronger emotionally, just to survive. But there are physical and emotional consequences to that kind of resistance. As a result, I continued to split. Charlotte had her way of coping; I had mine.

Charlotte has said she felt a lot of terror and helplessness. I understand that, because I had it, too. But I never saw her as truly helpless. What would Ron have done with two mad as hell little girls? What would it have been like if two of us had said, "He's hurting us?" Would my mother have claimed, "You know how she tells stories?"

I believe there must be some resolution on old issues before we discuss what our relationship is today. Resolution for me would be Charlotte not saying things like "you ought to be grateful I even told you." I don't need to hear she is so in it for herself. I cannot have a relationship with someone who withholds information key to my survival, and says it's for her benefit to do so.

I am still viewed as the troublemaker, the angry one. A relationship now would require a lot more empathy with my feelings, not just hers.

When we were at Howard's, I was hyperventilating. I told him, "I'm scared of her." We got through this very intense session, me divulging some horrible things that happened to me due to her actions. I poured out all this fear of her, and when we walked out the door, she said, "Can we hug?" I didn't want to be in the same room with her. Oh, sure! I want to hug the person who made me hyperventilate for three hours. There was no connection with what I was feeling, at all.

Charlotte later said she could see I was saying "back away from me, I'm afraid of you." At the same time, she felt my pain, so she offered the hug. I didn't think there was any evil intent. But I didn't want to get in the elevator with her. That's the reality there. She's saying she got it, but she did it anyway. So I don't think she really got it.

There's a part of me that really wants to believe everything can be worked out, that we can be close. That part keeps getting smashed. It gets harder for that part to get up and do it again each time. Pretty soon there isn't going to be anything left to try. It's just going to be gone.

I would like to not have a million conditions put on me for whatever I'm supposed to do around her. I know she does it because she feels unsafe. But the more conditions she demands, the more unsafe I feel. I feel trapped. She sets conditions because it's like a little wall she can build up, and then say, "If nothing else is true, I know this will happen." To me, all these little conditions fence me in and make me want to break out. I can't breathe. She said she does that when she's scared of me. She comes to peek over the wall. All I see is the wall.

April 2, 1992

Dear Howard,

Charlotte decreed a nine-month separation; she won't accept my calls or letters. After December 29, she wants a relationship based on "present issues" — no childhood stuff — since it's "all about blaming" her. She'll call in November to "negotiate" who will go where for the holidays. Of course, nothing is being negotiated now. I'll go where I please for the holidays.

I'm grateful to her, because now I don't have to fret over her well-being, or pretend she really cares. I don't have to compromise myself to try to make her happy. As with all this stuff, it's far better to know than to keep guessing.

March 8, 1993

Dear Howard,

Last night, for the first time, I got Charlotte to see that being passionate about something does not automatically mean I am angry, which has always been her assumption. That's a major leap for both of us, and is a product of integration — because now I know when I'm angry. This was a revelation to her.

MAY 9, 1993

Dear Howard,

Charlotte's crossed a very real line now. She's literally placed me in the same category between my mother and Ron, as to how she is/was affected. This is morally outrageous and unacceptable. Since day one, every time her actions have angered me, you've said I should be more generous. I've been very generous, because I've naively hoped for that "twin" thing to happen. She's consistently and deliberately pulled the rug out from under me. When I react, she does her "I'm so scared of your anger you're just like Mommy I'm so overwhelmed" routine, and never acknowledges her role in any of it. It stops here, precisely because I am more integrated and healthy.

Charlotte and I talk sporadically. She seems genuinely pleased that I've found a new, happier life with Dan. She said she's proud of the work I've done to change my life. But she still refuses to open herself up to me. She still keeps that wall up. Since this book was originally conceived as a way to tell her my story at her own pace without pressure, I'm hoping she will read it. We are two little girls who could have been best friends for a lifetime under different circumstances.

11

Thirty Years On: The Fear of Being Crazy

I spent most of my life believing I was crazy because all the crazy things I experienced in childhood were treated as nonexistent or normal. This belief colored every decision made, from something so basic as what to wear today, to the more esoteric boundaries of whether I should kill myself. I understood very well that killing myself under the wrong circumstances would establish my insanity forever. So I analyzed every word, every gesture, before committing myself. (Which probably accounts for why I am alive today.)

This strategy more immediately resulted in considerable lag time in conversations, which in itself appeared strange. I learned to remain silent and noncommittal, constantly updating my position to match that of a "normal" person. It became an elaborate game to correctly anticipate a conversational break so I could "naturally" participate.

Even greater than my fear that I was crazy, was my lifelong dread that someone would find out. As a child, that someone was my mother, who I felt certain would put me away permanently if my behavior grew too extreme. I continually tested her resolve in that area, but for the most part, faded into the background to not draw undue attention.

This created an ongoing conflict intellectually, as I was naturally curious and inclined toward study. Excellence and achievement focused a spotlight on me whenever grades were due. I learned early that being noticed for anything was dangerous. Good grades also briefly appeased my mother. My dilemma was how to receive justly due accolades without simultaneous detection of some form of defect. (A defect was anything not readily explainable, with which my life seemed replete.) I was forever searching for a balance between satisfying myself intellectually and not letting anyone else know I could.

The fear of discovery created a "push-pull" between perfectionism and its partner, procrastination. Perfectionism might guarantee no one would notice I was crazy, especially if I was supervigilant to every detail. The chain of prediction and probability could be calculated endlessly. (And often was.) Focusing so tightly on perfection could, temporarily, block out feelings of craziness. But "too perfect" would tip someone off, so I constantly procrastinated doing anything that might create the essence of perfection.

This kind of thinking creates entire conversations in advance, yet does not allow term papers to be written until the morning they are due. It anticipates and remembers everyone's birthday to engender goodwill, yet fails to timely pay bills. It allows one to dream, but never quite succeed.

I carried my fears into adulthood, marking time between obvious insecurities and a desperate bravado. Strange, unexplained things continued to occur, but it seemed best to pretend nothing happened at all. So I endured ridicule and confusion, created anger and tension, and lost credibility with the people from whom I most needed it. This, in the hope that my fundamental flaw — that I was truly crazy — remained unnoticed.

I never opened up completely in therapy prior to working with Howard. I felt intellectually superior to therapists, and played games. If a therapist was blind to my obvious insanity, s/he would never uncover my secrets, either. It never occurred to me that if Howard could recognize "crazy," he might also know what "not crazy" looked like. I quickly realized he was three steps ahead of me. There was no time to play games. He constantly challenged me to expand the limits of my thinking.

Howard vigorously campaigned to convince me I was not crazy, and that DID was, if anything, evidence to support his conclusion. His model suggested that DID, by its very nature, indicated a desire not just to survive, but to triumph. He repeatedly used the metaphor that I had cast a lifeline into the future for a later, safe reunion. I wanted to believe him, but needed proof of an unequivocal nature.

September 13, 1991

Dear Howard,

I've been doing my usual family thing — trying to make them see, come, call, do — and while I've been successful, focusing on them stops me from focusing on me. (So much for resistance, hmm?) I feel like I'm drifting, waiting for the next wave to wash over me. While all this stuff explains the craziness of my childhood, it also feels crazy to have these memories pop up. It's like reading a bad horror novel and realizing it's about you. Sometimes it really frightens me.

The new memories and hallucinations I was experiencing terrified me. I felt isolated, but certain I could handle anything. I reassured my boss that nothing happening personally would affect my work, since work created my major escape from the terror in my mind. Even with that certainty, the next six weeks took a tremendous toll on me.

October 30, 1991

I feel myself disintegrating right before my eyes and no one sees me disappearing. The disease of the week bores my friends and they want something happy now. Performances at eight and twice Saturday. Nothing is real now. Everything is pressure. I can't stand it. I will explode from this pressure and nothing will be left of me. Nobody calls, nobody cares. I

smile, I laugh, I sigh, I commiserate; no one sees this shell making the moves of a person. No one sees; they can see right through me because I'm not here. Every day I am less here than yesterday and no one sees, no one cares.

What happened to take me from full-of-bravado to becoming invisible? I constantly awakened in panic with night terrors and drug-free hallucinations. I heard voices from within my head. I feared something inside beyond my control would make me kill myself. I longed for a day when some heinous memory did not descend upon me. And still, I worked and "acted normal," pretending everything was perfectly okay. To do otherwise would invalidate everything I'd fought for/against my entire life. After six weeks of this pressure, becoming invisible was beginning to look attractive.

Since childhood, my much-needed outlet for pent-up emotions has derived from writing poetry. I keep it honest. I take each poem seriously, and nearly always know exactly what it means. But my poem "Thirty Years On" (see below) was a great mystery. The first verse seemed likely to be about me, while the rest seemed odd. It was written three months before I met Howard. I could not unravel whatever the title meant, which bothered me for months. I tried repeatedly to change it, but found I was "unable."

Sometimes poems with very complex rhyming patterns poured out of me faster than I could write, and I'd wonder, "Where did that come from?" The notion that my poems might originate in some uncontrollable internal interloper was distressing. For years, I'd claimed that Inside Sarah wrote my poems, but never took the implication far. This notion fueled the fire in my "crazy" debate with Howard. Then I looked at "Thirty Years On" one more time, and knew exactly what it was about. It was a conversation between Nita and Sarah. All I did was add "who" was speaking when.

Thirty Years On

Nita: *Nothing feels so lost and lonely*
As the sound of one heart beating
Late at night when din of traffic
And apartment neighbors ceases
Might have been a time I welcomed
Solitude booked through September
Might have longed for my own space
Without regard for old subleases

Sarah: *I've been touring once upon a time*
A place in which you won't be found
And still I keep the searchlights on
In hope of late-night revelations
I wish you chose to speculate
In happily ever after dreams
The kind that other people have

Without default for fabrications

Nita: *Have you lately read a sonnet*
Pledging love to last forever
Time can fool our best intentions
Or, at least, it's sure fooled me

Sarah: *Do you wonder where I am tonight*
Or does my silence comfort you?
The guardian of my secret thoughts
Custodian of the only key

April 17, 1991; revised October 30, 1991, SEO

This poem presented a compelling picture of what my life looked like after pretending and not being real for 30 years. The "Nita" verses captured the aloneness and fear of being Nita. The "Sarah" verses portrayed someone who hoped for her future and enjoyed the present. The reference to "old subleases" recognized that other people were in residence, and that they had some formal right to be there.

I felt invaded, out of control, and more alone than ever. I demanded of Howard, bordering on belligerence, "When is this going to be over? When am I going to have a week when something major doesn't hit me?" It felt unbearable.

October 31, 1991

N: ***This is like being in a really bad movie.***

H: I want to know if you're aware of something. All people have something that bothers them, which they feel unsettled about, and provokes anxiety. That's normal.

N: ***I think your typical anxiety doesn't really match this kind of thing. Sarah has been like a little joke. A little secret. It really upsets me. My poetry is something I thought I could call my own. Now I don't even know if I'm writing it. I've always said, "My best poems kind of write themselves." Maybe I wasn't even doing it.***

H: Are you worried that you're splitting off? Fragmenting?

N: ***Yes.***

H: When we talked before about it, didn't you get a feel for the direction of how this whole thing was put together? You actually fragmented to stay stable and operating.

N: ***Yes. And you said to lead my (sarcastic) "best, fulfilled, happy, productive life" I needed to integrate. But I could go on without doing so.***

H: You threw yourself a lifeline, and now you're putting it together on the other side. You did a good thing.

N: ***(agitated) It feels like it's coming apart! It doesn't feel like anything's coming together! It feels like . . . like I'm not going to be there. Maybe that's real irrational. (laughs nervously) What's rational, when you're***

talking about someone else writing your poems? All of this has a very unreal quality to me. That we're even having this conversation.

H: Okay.

*N: **It doesn't seem real. It seems like we're both going to start laughing any minute now. Like this is really funny.***

H: It's not that funny.

*N: **It's not enough that I have to deal with everything Ron did, and what my mother did, but I have to deal with this, too?***

H: I need a name. The "this" is what? Fragmentation? (she nods) That's the result of the Ron deal. It's not an addition. While it feels like you can't connect and rejoin and integrate, you will. I've seen this. I know how it operates.

*N: **I feel like I have no control. I don't even know what I'd be trying to control.***

H: Sometimes when there is a need to reintegrate, it has to break down first. You're holding on and controlling probably too strongly. Look, you're in a safe place. If you're nuts, you're nuts. If it doesn't make sense to you now, frankly, you're far more animated and personable in this state than I see you many times. It's true.

*N: **(very sarcastic) Oh, and you're pleased. You're happy.***

H: Well, no, I don't like that you feel pain, so I don't get any pleasure out of that. But the nature of what I do is being present in other people's pain. And it's a privilege. I'm willing to sit with you in this. I'm also here to reassure you that there's another side. You've got to break it all apart before it comes back together. It must sound lame to always hear, "Oh, you're doing so great."

*N: **And I'm here bouncing off the walls. I have to do everything I can to act "normal" at work. Whatever normal is. I see a correlation here. After we had that talk about Linda, it dragged on for another month. We were writing hate letters, and not handling it well. So I sent her the tape because every time I talked with her, I got upset really easily.***

H: What happened?

*N: **She turned into the person I wanted her to be. And I see that my focus now is not on her or Ron. The distractions are over, so now I'm falling apart.***

H: You don't make a very good case for yourself when talking to people who are significant to you. You can't get out the essence of what you want to say, and have it understood. You came up with a creative thing to share the tape. She says, "I understand where you're at, what you're dealing with." That's triumph, okay? You don't know how to deal with triumph. You go crazy.

*N: **(arguing) I'm happy!***

H: *(exasperated) I know you are, but you're not. You've never been validated.*

N: ***But I can't focus on that now, 'cause it's over. So now it's like all this is happening.***

H: *That's absolutely correct. Now you've got to deal with this other shit.*

N: ***Well, yeah. All the other shit I didn't know existed. I have no control over anything. It's just one thing after another — major things I have to cope with.***

H: *It's not likely you'll get broadsided more than you already have been. This is the voice of logic now. I've been with you through this whole thing. You are a person — and I rarely say a thing like this — who has trouble coping with the success of your own understanding. Things making sense to you. Finally making a connection with people whom you felt could never understand, which made you feel more isolated. It's all new. You're being completely validated.*

N: ***No. The understanding with Linda is new. I don't know that it's in cement yet.***

H: *You might be a person who is out to test it by staying in a state of turmoil.*

N: ***So I'm making all this up?***

H: *No. You go into turmoil to see "How much can I decompensate and they'll still take me in and accept me for who I am?"*

N: ***(agitated) That's what this is about? My poem was written six months ago. Until yesterday, I had no idea what it was about.***

H: *You're freaked out. I can understand it. Do you understand splitting off, and the whole phenomenon of multiple personalities? (she nods) Are you worried about that? Badly?*

N: ***(sighs) Yes.***

H: *Do you think there are other lives in you?*

N: ***(hesitates) Possibly.***

H: *We've never talked like this before. It seems to terrify you, which you get angry about, because that's how you deal with terror. (sighs) This isn't fair.*

N: ***No. It's not fair.***

H: *But I will have the courage to sit with you through whatever feelings you have to share. I will be present with it. And however painful this is, you are, for all that I've known you've gone through, 500% better off than you were before we got together.*

N: ***Just for knowing?***

H: *The way you put things together, you do more than know. You have great insight and survival instincts. You're very creative and extremely talented. It's hard to hear, unless all that stuff is integrated. You don't like hearing it, because some of it that you can't relate to you're wondering if there's an alter within who can relate to it. Have courage, though. You'll be okay. It's a very traumatic thing you're going through. It cannot be determined, based on what we've talked about thus far, that you are hard-core MPD. I guess I'm asking you not to worry.*

N: ***(loudly exasperated) I'm floating off into the universe, and I'm not supposed to worry!***

H: That's right. You don't have to hold on. You've never been more free.

N: ***(agitated) Free to be nothing.***

H: Free to be — come on — nothing?

N: ***I don't know what I am, if I'm not me!***

H: Well said. (she laughs) I don't know how to define what you are, because it doesn't need to be defined.

N: ***But I thought I was creative, and now I don't even know if I believe that.***

H: Integration always means that it's you writing your poems. You're just more in touch with it than before. When you say it got written by itself, there are two ways to look at it. The scary way, which is that you're out of touch with some entity within that's writing the poem. Or, if you allow yourself to get out of your way with whatever emotional blockages you have, poetry comes out. I'm in the latter camp.

N: ***(sighs) Right.***

H: I was asked not long ago, how do I do therapy? I said it's a process of always getting out of my way, so therapy happens by itself. When I am ego-involved, it turns into shit. Same process you go through. You and I are more alike than you know; you are more like normal people than you know. Are you aware of how insecure a person I am? Or how anxious I am?

N: ***Sometimes.***

H: You pick that up. I have a recurring dream, one not to be cured, but which causes me great distress when I dream it. My goal is not to eliminate it which, interestingly, makes it not happen that much. The dream is: an old man, sitting in a rocking chair. I realize this old man is me. I see this person; it's not me; then I realize it is. There's nothing more to this person's life. I wake up screaming.

N: ***Are you screaming as you, or as the old man?***

H: I'm this old man; I don't want to be this old man. And I feel that's exactly what I am. I feel I am a person without purpose or direction.

N: ***(incredulous) Are you serious? It's not what you put out.***

H: Because I'm not out to correct it. It's my "thing." You've got your thing. It'll always be your thing. That one will always be mine. My dreams speak very directly to me, but knowing what they're about doesn't make me any less insecure. It doesn't make me any less anxious, or concerned about my competency as a person. I carry that; I'll die with it. My integration process is to be able to say it flatly like that. And it's totally neutral. The thing that would happen to you at the completion of whatever needs to occur, is that this becomes neutral to you. It has meaning, but it's not bad or good. You could have nightmares for the rest of your life — that's not a curse — but you'd wake up in a fright. However it manifests. "Geez, that one again." That's all. "Oooh, I haven't had that one for a while." It's both accepting and resolving at the same moment.

N: ***I don't understand.***

H: The implication is, there's nothing wrong. Oh, you feel bad. I don't feel great when I wake up in my anxious state. But symptom relief, as odd as it sounds, is not always the goal. Acceptance and acknowledgment is where you're at. You're getting a lot of validation. Qualitatively different from anything you've ever gotten. And it's like, "God, can I handle this? I don't know how people who accept themselves as okay handle that kind of stuff." So you have to invent it. How does a person handle this kind of validation? With class and grace.

N: ***They don't have a nervous breakdown.***

H: If you have a nervous breakdown, I'll do anything I can to help you pick the pieces up. I'm not that impressed with them, anyway. I know they happen, but I don't get thrown by them. It just doesn't have to come to it. People avert nervous breakdowns by doing one of two things. They either deny a lot of feelings, which really doesn't avert it. It'll come eventually, and probably be more severe. Or, they understand some important thing about themselves that they accept and resolve in the same understanding. The nervous breakdown is averted because there's no need for one. Handling the situation with grace and class might be to say, "Linda, this is very meaningful to me. Thank you for acknowledging where I was coming from."

N: ***I did! I wrote her a letter.***

H: That's good! It's not beside the point, it is the point. You come here in a fairly decompensated way, you tell me all this stuff, plus you tell me who is speaking in your poem. There's more texture to your revelation. You're at a point where you can't help but understand more. You're on a roll.

N: ***It's a roller coaster.***

H: Stay on it. It's moving in the right direction.

N: ***(agitated) Ups and downs, very fast!***

H: It happens when you put yourself in a risky situation — and not one where you take stupid risks. I'm talking about growth-producing risks.

Talking plainly and directly about this stuff has always been risky. Life is supposed to have ups and downs. Everything you're feeling now is exactly what is supposed to happen. "Oh, great. This is how a normal person feels?" Yes. Maybe you don't want normal anymore. Maybe you want to revert to before.

N: ***(agitated) The other stuff, I know it's going to happen! Life, yes. You have ups and downs. But you know what your situation is. You don't think you're losing your mind when it happens.***

H: Yeah, you do. Go through a graduate program, sometimes you think you're losing your mind. (she sighs) You think I didn't understand you. Try me again. You're losing your mind.

N: ***That's what it feels like. And filling out some application for law school isn't going to make it all better. You're saying this is real life. I don't think it is.***

H: What you're describing is more normal than not. At any given point of the day, a person could wonder if they're okay; if they're who they are; why are they sitting here? That's really normal. It shouldn't be very frequent. You're going through more of it, probably, than a person who we consider normal. That you go through it, doesn't mean it won't find a time and frequency that is more regular and appropriate. And in the event there is more profound splitting off going on, you and I will talk about it.

N: ***As I said, Sarah has been this unique little thing in my life, who nobody really took seriously until you.***

H: I think you're both appreciative of me and pissed off at the same time.

N: ***(sighs) I'm appreciative, but not pissed off.***

H: I know this has been really hard. The courage I'd want you to have is to entertain all possibilities. Even the MPD problem. I think it's more common than most people know.

N: ***I think it's crazy.***

H: That's what most people think, too.

N: ***(anxious) I don't know what to do. It's like okay, fine, all this is fine.***

H: It is fine. It hurts. I'm not out for relief on it. It's like putting relief on insight.

N: ***Do you think twenty years from now you're still going to wake up screaming? (he nods) And that's okay?***

H: It's fine. There are a lot of other things that function well enough that this is not my life's focus. When I'm thinking about it, it's always on the surface. But there's no attempt to resolve it, because it's like trying to resolve brown eyes. It is fine.

N: ***(very agitated) It's not fine!***

H: I'm proposing the idea that it is. Every time we meet, there's more illumination. In three to six months, if we should talk, you'll be saying, "You know, I do have those pains, but it's not any big deal."

N: Three to six months?

H: Have the courage to feel the feelings. I don't wish them on you. But I don't believe there is anything to do with them other than acknowledge them. Be shaken by them in the moment. "God, that again." Give it a name. And none of it should dissuade you from doing any of the other stuff you do in your life. Do that, and you can avert a breakdown. Repress the idea that it's okay to feel, debate with me that point, and resist it, and it sets you up for a breakdown. Either way, you'll come out okay. Whether you do it with a breakdown, or avert one.

N: (incredulous) No matter what happens, I'll come out okay?

H: Oh, yeah, you can't lose.

N: How can you be so sure?

H: This is how this works. Knowing the truth, and understanding and defining what's going on — as you've shown every time we get together — always works a benefit. I'm not happy for your pain, but your progression is fabulous. And you've done it very rapidly. You've demonstrated better understanding with a great deal of courage and strength. But you haven't yet developed a creativity and confidence in your purpose. You're very much in the childhood of your understanding. It's a very successful, integrated childhood, from where we started talking about it. But it isn't mature yet. And if you never saw me again, it would get that way, because there's no stopping you.

I realized that the only way to move on would be to openly discuss DID with Howard. I sent him a letter confessing every bizarre event I could remember. I hoped that if he really did know "not crazy," he would have a logical explanation for these events which precluded the possibility of either DID or insanity.

NOVEMBER 12, 1991

N: I've thought about having MPD for a long time, not just when you brought it up. And now I feel really weird. I don't know what you're going to do with that information. Or what it means.

H: Are you frightened?

N: (hesitates) A little.

H: I'm not going to do anything with it. Just process it. You presented it as though you've done something bad.

N: That's how it feels. I think it's crazy.

H: That's your fear, that you are crazy.

N: (agitated) Yes! I'm afraid I'm crazy. And you're going to lock me up.

H: Can I reassure you?

N: I don't know! Can you?

H: There isn't any good, just cause for locking you up. You're not a danger to yourself or others; you're stable and healthy. Even with all the stuff we've talked about. The last thing on my mind is thinking about how to get you locked up.

N: I'm sure it is.

H: Hmm. (laughs) Sort of a tone there. We're talking about a disturbing subject. It's best to grapple with it that way, not with what its consequences are. It's far more productive to deal with the meaning of it on that level.

N: (accusatory) Why do you keep smiling? You think I'm silly.

H: No, To the contrary — I don't think you're silly.

N: Then why are you smiling? Quit smiling.

H: (laughs) You want me to quit smiling?

N: (miserable) No. Do whatever you want.

H: I only smile when you smile. It's a reflection, see?

N: My smile is full of anxiety, so you probably don't want to reflect that, do you?

H: No, I try to create as much comfort as I can so we can talk about a disturbing issue. What you are saying is an increased enhancement of perspective. And it's a flood. Every week there will be something that fits in the puzzle, probably for the rest of your life.

N: I should be able to remember this stuff quicker.

H: It hasn't been that long. These are the pieces of integration, and when it's all coming out, it looks kind of messy.

N: One piece is that I've felt like I'm being played with.

H: Played with in what way? By whom? With what?

N: By something inside of me. This thing about having to look at the clock, or waking up, at a certain time.

H: Is this a thing of good motive or bad?

N: Enough that it scared me.

H: That's the point. Is it trying to victimize and mess you up further? Or is it trying to have you take a look, and you're better off for seeing it?

N: It was never "bad." It went on for six weeks, every morning at 10:34, no matter what. I would say to myself, "Just don't look at the clock." But I had to look, and it was 10:34. Every single morning. It got so I avoided my office, then I'd look and see it other places.

H: What you're talking about is a superintuitive, sensitive thing. Certainly, an obsession.

*N: **How is it my obsession, when I didn't want to look? I feel like I wasn't in control.***

H: The obsession is not to look, and doing it anyway. That's what an obsession is — feeling like you're not in control. Feeling anxious and concerned about it. Using a lot of energy to combat it.

*N: **There was no alarm going off, literally, which made me know it was 10:34.***

H: I understand that. So what's your account for six weeks going by, and every day you look up and it's 10:34?

*N: **I have no idea. It was just something that made me consider there was a split personality in me.***

H: How would it operate?

*N: **(anguish) I don't know! I just thought I was being played with.***

H: By something outside of you?

*N: **Inside of me.***

H: Did you think it was you?

*N: **No.***

H: Just something in you, other than you?

*N: **(sighs) Yes. It's crazy.***

H: Well, it's disturbing to think about it and feel it. So we'll talk more. Now we're on another level, about something in you that is not of you.

*N: **That's different?***

H: There's a different slant on it, sure. (reacting to her upset) We're just looking at every angle, okay? Try to have courage to talk about it. MPD is just different aspects of you. They're all you. The quality you're talking about now is not of you, but something of someone else.

*N: **(quietly and tense) If I were, even for a few minutes, kind of spaced out, and lost time, the time I lost could have been . . . (tortured) God! I can't believe I'm saying this!***

H: Can I share something with you? Keeping your thoughts inside makes them more disturbing than sharing them with someone you trust. Sharing may make it seem more real. If you don't, it stays unreal, and fantasy. But it's a release when you talk about it, and trust is an important part. I'm not going over to the telephone, and say, "Guys? You got the white coats on? I got one for you."

*N: **Not yet, anyway.***

H: I'll warn you, okay? Short of you telling me that you've got a gun, and you're going to shoot a particular person with that gun, I'm not telling anybody. I have no duty to warn here.

*N: **What? Oh, God. (very frightened) If I spaced out, and it was 10:32, and*** *someone else takes that time (voice cracks) besides me, inside of me, the someone else could trigger me to come back and suggest, in a very strong way, that I look at the clock.*

H: (long silence) Okay. We're still here.

N: (agitated) What? Are we?

H: Well, yes, we are. Both of us. That's how it operated.

N: (trembling) That's how I thought it operated. Until it stopped. One day, suddenly, I didn't care if it was 10:34 anymore.

H: Did you wonder why it was happening when it was happening?

N: Oh, sure. Why it was happening, why it ended. It's the same thing.

H: So one day, it went away. And left you with not knowing.

N: (softly) It always leaves me with not knowing. This happens regularly. With waking up, or sometimes (in utter anguish) it's like there's this rubber band in my brain going boing! I cannot describe how it feels to talk about this stuff.

H: You never did, right?

N: No.

H: You know that's like testing the waters, just telling another person.

N: Testing the waters for what?

H: For sanity. To see how it plays.

N: It plays crazy is how it plays!

H: I dare say this is just the tip of the iceberg for the kinds of things you could share that have been your experiences.

NOVEMBER 13, 1991

Dear Howard,

Whatever makes me look at a clock is no different to me than whatever makes me aware of Sarah. For all I know, it's Sarah who makes me look at the clock.

This stuff doesn't seem to have much to do with my childhood, or have I missed the point entirely? Does everything that feels crazy have to do with my childhood, or are there things that would feel crazy anyway? You said this is probably the tip of the iceberg. What does that mean? That I may not be lock-uppable, but it plays crazy to you, too?

Things aren't coming together, Howard, and it's not fine. If total control is at one end, and total confusion at the other, I've just exchanged extremes. You say I am more like normal people than I know. I say I'm more unlike normal people than you know.

NOVEMBER 14, 1991

Last night I tried to let go of my control, to stop resisting the feelings like Howard said. After 37 years of doing everything I can to not let anyone know, it's very hard to just stop and go crazy if that's what it's going to be.

What was all the suffering for? Why don't I get to savor the triumph of my survival? Why, after all this time, do I now go crazy? It's like now I let down my vigilance, and there's nothing left but feeling crazy. Thirty years of absolute training is screaming out that I will lose my mind if I feel these feelings, even if I'm not really crazy. Which, of course, makes me crazy anyway.

12

Dissociative Identity Disorder (MPD) and Denial

I've been depressed all day. I feel like such a fraud. People say how special and wonderful I am. I think, "Can't they tell?"

—NITA, SEPTEMBER 18, 1984

All my life, I've hoped things could be different. Either that it gets better, or wishing it wasn't so bad. Always trying to minimize the damage. Always expecting things to get better via something external to me. Always knowing things are bad because of something internal. It's always my fault. I always fucked up in some way. Things get better because someone else does it. Someone else, someone better, does the talking for me.

—NITA, JULY 10, 1985

JUNE 4, 1987

When I told Bill that my Wednesday "friends" are a therapy group, there was a quarter-second flash in his eyes which I decided was probably surprise, but also perhaps anger at me for lying to him. In fact, he's never asked questions I could not answer truthfully, but it was a spiritual lie, if not an actual one. It has nothing to do with him. It's my fear of being hurt, and my lack of trust in myself. I have other spiritual lies out there, but it's becoming safer to let them out. Every time I give him a poem I cringe. The fear is that he'll fit all the pieces together and get the "real" picture. It's also the hope, because it's wonderful to be able to be real.

Being in a state of denial is a universally human response to situations which threaten to overwhelm. People who were abused as children sometimes carry their denial like precious cargo without a port of destination. It enabled us to survive our childhood experiences, and often we still live in survival mode decades beyond the actual abuse. We protect ourselves to excess because we learned abruptly and painfully that no one else would.

We say, "It wasn't that bad. It was my fault. I'm making all this stuff up." All my life, I spoke bitterly of my mother's treatment of me as a child. Friends asked, "What did she do to you?" I couldn't really describe it, and in frustration would say, "Well, she didn't lock us up in closets." In fact, my mother behaved much worse than that, but by focusing on the empty closet, I avoided looking at what waited beyond it.

The reality is, no matter what you were told, whatever happened to you as a child was not legally or morally your fault. Abused children are instilled with guilt regarding their "participation." It's an especially complex issue if the abuser is a family member. The child is told/believes that by his word his family will disintegrate, or harm may descend upon other loved ones. He fears he will lose more by telling than not. His denial of the truth perpetuates his guilt and self-loathing.

The reality is, if you were fabricating your memories now, life would have been very different from the way it turned out. My first husband, not surprisingly, was an abusive alcoholic who acted in similar ways to my childhood menace. But since I had no conscious memory of childhood trauma, I figured my first husband was the best I could get, considering how bad I really was. I believed I deserved a lot of what he gave me, although I never knew why.

I used to look friends in the eye, and say, "You don't really know me. I'm really a very bad person." I've never acted like a bad person, so they were astonished. I felt more than a little crazy when compelled to explain myself. But my abuse systematically taught me that I was nothing; I was worthless; I was damaged; I was bad. My life exemplified these thoughts until therapy taught me new, appropriate lessons.

If our early childhood lessons were really about love, and about being good enough and precious, we would not need to fabricate stories now, much less ones that demonstrate the opposite. If my parents' example had been one of stability and security, I should have attracted a mate who would not automatically and predictably abuse me. If I somehow managed to do that anyway, I would never have confused the abuse with love.

Do you believe that the memories, once aired, will create nothing but relentless and unendurable pain? That makes sense, but actually the reverse is true. While memories create an initial pain of recognition, it dissipates with acknowledgment of their truth and reality. Denial is what keeps the pain lingering.

Do you tell yourself you were better off not knowing? This is the single biggest lie you can create about your life. It is always better to know than to not know. Denial merely traps us in a suspended crazy state, because deep inside we each know our truth. No matter how scary the memories get, that's all they are. They have no further power, but it takes a lot of courage to discover this.

NOVEMBER 7, 1991

Dear Howard,

It isn't true that I first considered MPD after you suggested it. It was just too much to admit. I've considered it many times. When my ex-husband said, "She's like two people" I took him very seriously. When I've lost time, it's surprised me, and yet, it really doesn't. You said to have courage. Here are other times I've considered it:

I cannot explain why I had no clue who the Beatles were until sixth grade (1966-67), even though Linda was crazy about them before then.

I often know the time without looking at a clock. I go through phases where something compels me to look at my watch or wake up at a certain time, day after day.

I've had a lifelong fascination with identical twins. I thought it was neat to look like yourself and be someone else, to be able to fool people.

When I read Sybil years ago, I tried to imagine different people in me, not because I was intellectually curious, but because it seemed likely. I tried to recall blocks of lost time, and couldn't. I've always trusted my excellent memory, so I believed myself.

At the office Christmas party three years ago, I made a conscious decision that I was Sarah, which freed me to have fun. I was so high on being her. Co-workers said they'd never seen me like that in four years. (This, without alcohol.)

I've always considered myself to not be very logical. Yet every lawyer I've worked with has praised me specifically for my logic. It always throws me.

In my first performance review, Jacob said I spend a lot of time staring into space. I could not figure out what he was talking about.

When you first said Sarah and I need to integrate, you said, "I'm not trying to kill Sarah." The depth of my reaction — that you might try to kill Sarah — alarmed me.

It isn't thrilling me to put this on paper. It feels like surrender. It scares me and makes me sad at the same time. I'm sending it to you now because I can't be trusted to bring this with me Monday. You are a great solace when I listen to the last tape, and I am trying extremely hard to see how this really is "fine." I'm not there yet.

SEPTEMBER 14, 1984

I experienced pure magic in finding my apartment, and felt I'd been led to it by God. I was happy for two weeks while I made it my little haven, where I could be and do whatever I wanted. Then someone broke in and did sick things in it, and I was filled with fear and revulsion of the very things that made it seem special. I'm resigned to live my old tape that I don't deserve good things, nothing special lasts, God has deceived me (again). It's been a tremendous struggle for months. My apartment is tainted. I'm sad for having lost that rush of excitement over what it symbolized. I'd like to create a new kind of magic here, but I don't know how, or if I'm willing to risk it again.

Howard and I were five months into our process, during which time I'd had terrible flashbacks, night terrors, wild hallucinations. I thought MPD would prove my insanity, and Howard hadn't caught on yet. As one example of many weird things in my life, I told him about my apartment break-in. Nothing was taken. Just weird, sick things were done with my possessions. Mind game stuff. As time passed, I couldn't tell if this person had gotten in again. I felt very crazy. I slept with the lights on, and felt certain it didn't matter if the door was locked. Every night, I sat in the hall with the phone, watching the living room and bedroom windows, waiting for the glass to break.

After warning that he was about to pose a provocative question, Howard asked, "Did you ever think it might have been you who did it, as a different identity?" That was the closest I ever came to walking out. My agitation grew as he calmly blew all my little alibis out of the water. I felt dizzy, like something was shifting inside my head.

NOVEMBER 1991

N: ***What?! You are making this twelve times weirder than it was. It was already so weird, it didn't need to be weirder.***

H: But what do you want to do with it? Do you want a better understanding?

N: ***I wanted you to have a better understanding about why I have a hard time keeping my apartment clean.***

H: Well, I don't.

N: ***Oh, God. (extremely agitated) Isn't that a totally bizarre thing you just said?***

H: I thought I made that real clear. I even warned you.

N: ***I had no idea!***

H: Now you know (both laugh), when I warn you, I mean it. Next time you'll say, "No way. I've got to pace myself." Now look. Since you are experiencing a lot of strange things, it gives us license to talk about any of it. I want you to have some resilience in discussing this.

N: ***You think that really happened?***

H: Don't look at me like I know what happened. Do things happen like that?

N: ***(sighs) Yes, I'm sure they do.***

H: People with MPD sometimes do things like that, and don't remember it. It's one of the unsettling parts of it.

N: ***Well, it's even more unsettling because the things that were pulled out of the boxes.... (sighs)***

H: Ah, tell me what was pulled out?

N: ***(slowly) Things that only somebody who knew me really well would know were meaningful. Which is why everyone said it had to be my ex-husband. But I never believed it was him. Geez. And I'd never told anyone about my dream of walking into this place with the pink light, and***

there I was, running toward the pink light in my bedroom. (sighs)

H: *Let's say it's what I just said. That somehow you dissociated so completely. . .*

N: ***I am doing everything I can to stop myself from totally freaking out right here in front of you.***

H: *Okay. But it starts to be the cleanest explanation of what happened, because you could never make sense of someone coming into your house, and going through those things. Why don't you take a deep breath?*

N: ***As I told you the story, is that what you thought? From the beginning?***

H: *How two and two got put together, was that the story sounded so incredibly strange. I felt just like you felt. But I knew you weren't crazy. And, if what I'm saying is a possibility? It means you're not crazy.*

N: ***Why?***

H: *If nothing else, I want you to understand this: if MPD is operating here, it's to make you healthy, not crazy. A person finds himself in a position so untenable, and so unresolvable, that he splits off. Only a healthy person would utilize multiple features. All this really means is you didn't get a little abuse. Splitting off occurs in extreme situations where it couldn't get any worse. It's a verification of how bad it was.*

N: ***Why would I do this to myself?***

H: *It's complicated. I'm trying out hypotheses which seem to add up. Maybe your reflecting on it brings a greater certainty, either rejecting what I'm saying or confirming it. Why would you mess up your apartment? Your wanting to make it a safe place may have, in some way, been a cover-up for something that another part of you didn't want covered up. Something that couldn't be denied because it was going to get you one way or another, and in a bad way. Your own processes created a crisis by which you would have to analyze it, and here we are talking about it. What you're doing now is almost like "I don't want to see it."*

N: ***I don't.***

H: *There was something you were supposed to know about you. You have intellectual integrity — you want to know why. That's your strong point, but it causes all this grief.*

N: ***Do you think, on a scale of one to ten, that this is possible?***

H: *Anything is possible, but I haven't thrown "anything" on the table. I've thrown out specific things that have a connected possibility. You don't feel good about this. MPD is a more healthy phenomenon than not. If multiple features are occurring, do you know that by talking about them like this they go away, and more integration occurs?*

N: ***Talking about it integrates it?***

H: *Yes. What we're doing makes it more likely not to happen. I think I understand the disturbing features of this discussion. But you also should feel a certain amount of freedom. And relief.*

*N: **(fearful) Relief that it's all out in the open now?***

H: It's just you and me. You are talking to a person who is completely on your side, always has been. We're putting everything on the table to see what fits. Putting the pieces of this puzzle together, which I'm sure would be much more fascinating if it wasn't you.

*N: **(laughs nervously) Oh, yes. Let's go read*** **Sybil.**

H: Don't put yourself down that way, okay? Don't use the word "Sybil" like "one of those." Thank goodness for those mechanisms, or you wouldn't be doing as well as you are.

*N: **(frightened) This stuff doesn't go away.***

H: It goes away when you allow the full depth of possibility to be entertained. What gives you more comfort — not having an explanation for these weird things going on in your life? Or knowing multiple features are operating, and that's why these things happen?

*N: **I'd rather just know there were these weird things, sorry.***

H: Oh, okay. Let me invite you to the other one.

*N: **You're so logical about everything. All of this really defies logic. But there's a part of me that says. . .could be.***

H: It's a healthy part that can entertain this.

*N: **I don't really feel healthy. It's not good.***

H: The other way of feeling was good?

*N: **(in anguish) Nothing has ever been good! I look back on my life, and think, "Well, last year was a really bad year. But the year before was like really, really bad." I can't come up with a year where I thought things were working well.***

H: This year's been pretty interesting. (she laughs) And, has given you more promise in your future than you've ever had. However painful this is. So maybe next year you start to say, "It's better now. I understand myself more. I have more direction than ever before, and more reason for hope." I feel like I'm fighting to keep you on the side of confident stability when you talk like this. You're stable, but you just want to go back to feeling crazy. It's easier that way. "I just want things to be weird. I'm sick and tired of the explanations!"

*N: **I'm getting there. It's a bit much.***

H: It's a hell of a lot. I'm astounded by it. But none of it is hopeless.

*N: **It seems hopeless. If I could do that to myself, it's really freaky.***

H: I am, frankly, less shocked by this, than that you stayed married to your husband, which was a lot more self-destructive.

*N: **Maybe I didn't feel as crazy, in his craziness.***

H: That's even more disturbing. It's like, if I can be around a real crazy per-

son, then it makes me think I'm stable.

N: ***That's what it was, part of the time. People have relationships. This was the one I had.***

H: *Yeah, but it was a bad and crazy one, and it demanded you to be less than good. It told you to do yourself in. Great relationship! I'm more disturbed by that, than you had a loss of consciousness and did things that aren't all that crazy in the context of your life. Does a person have to be nuts to get to a place where they say, "I don't want anymore already, enough!" Does this define insanity?*

N: ***No, but it's like a window on it. If the person does that all the time, he could be insane.***

H: *If you do it all the time, you may not be insane, but you are dysfunctional. Maybe that's the most we can say. We cannot say you're crazy. It's why I liked your last letter. I do know health when I see it. You're in that category.*

N: ***The letter saying you would know crazy when you saw it.***

H: *I'm not disturbed by what happened to you, even though you are. The language we use is that you went into another identity. We could be just as accurate to say you shut off for awhile. So this would be a good reason not to progress in your life. Nita is not supposed to have a good life. This is hard-wired. You created a crisis that gave you a reason to make it filthy and horrible to be there. And you're still there. You know what? You're not married to this man anymore, but you would never have left him. Say that on tape, so we can hear it later.*

N: ***I thought the tape was finished. Oh, God! This is all on tape? (miserable) I would never have left my husband.***

H: *The same is true with your apartment. "Now I've made a new icky situation; now I won't leave this one." The purpose of your life is to be in a bad situation.*

N: ***It's what I keep finding myself in.***

H: *It's also what you create. This should be hopeful to you. Instead of saying, "God! Am I going nuts?"*

N: ***Hopeful?***

H: *It demonstrates just how much control you have over your own life. We're not talking about bad things that aren't of your doing or control. That's bad enough, without you adding to it. That's a life destined, or programmed, for misery. (long pause) I really don't want you to go into a depression over this.*

N: ***(loudly, very agitated) Oh, yeah, let's just make this today's exercise! "Maybe seven years ago you zoomed into another identity and created all this chaos, and it's been a mystery ever since. Don't get depressed."***

H: *I was going to say "don't get sarcastic with me," but you put it into con-*

text. The deal is to do what you're supposed to about what you know about yourself today. If you think you're better off if you never considered these things — but they occurred anyway — then you're nothing but a big lie. You don't want that . . . . I guess you'll think twice about walking in here again. (both laugh)

NOVEMBER 25, 1991

Dear Howard,

I asked Linda if she remembered the weird things that happened in my apartment, and that you, in discussing MPD, proposed that I did these things as another part of me. She said very forcefully, "I don't believe it!" (Maybe she thought that's what I wanted to hear.) I said, "But I do." Long, long silence.

You're probably wondering how I made that leap so quickly. It just seems likely. It's no more weird, really, than everything else. You say I'm a person with vision, that I see things, and on tape I unequivocally say yes. No one ever asked before, but I see little point in denying it. I am curious as to how you knew.

For example, at a wedding reception, I said, very casually, "Watch them drop the top of the cake." There was no prior indication of this occurring, but about a minute later the waiters dropped the top of the cake. I felt terrible, like I was responsible.

It becomes not only a matter of telling the future, but of somehow altering it. I've always had visions of dying in a car accident. Sometimes when driving I see it rushing toward me, and always turn out of the direction in which I'm going. Sometimes I refuse to go on the freeway, because I see me dying on one. I've never had an accident.

If this is what you meant when you said I am "talented," why not add MPD? It might explain my handwriting, which at twelve changed from school-taught cursive, to an unpredictable mix of printing, cursive, and calligraphy. Its size shrank three times smaller.

None of this feels any different than whatever makes me look at a clock at 10:34 for weeks. Why not believe that another part of me broke into my house to keep me feeling icky and oppressed? What bothers me is that it wasn't the "me" who's writing this letter who did it, and it certainly wasn't Sarah. I'm turning into a committee, and the new kid doesn't have anything going for her besides fear and self-destruction. Why should I try to integrate that?

JANUARY 1992 *[Excerpt from session after Howard talked to an alter the first time.]*

H: I'm with Nita, right? This feels firm and solid? We've gone a step beyond where we've been before.

N: No! (laughs nervously) We've gone 2,000 steps beyond.

H: It frankly just shows how dramatic a thing it is. It's not just conceptual. It's real.

N: It makes it impossible for me to go back. Before, I kept saying to myself,

"Maybe this will all just end someday."

H: It can end. But I guess you more deeply appreciate the profoundness of this condition.

N: When it's all in my head, I can say I made it up. But I left your office really in a daze, sort of shocked.

H: I want to reassure you. You have complete control of this. It's like riding a bike.

N: (sighs) I just didn't know which magic button to push to make her go away?

H: It's too sarcastic when you say "magic button." You didn't know how to work the levers. Stay with me. It's just a skill factor. We've been talking about this for awhile. This was the first time we actually brought it out in a real way with another person, out loud. That would have to be a real dramatic and profound experience.

N: And scared me out of my mind.

H: Right. You've been scared before. Things have moved very fast. You've had courage, and stuck with it. Not only did you experience — I don't know what to call it — the coming out of this person, and you're trapped, and banging on the walls to get out. There was also a newer understanding of what happened in your childhood with Ron and your mom. That's a whole load of stuff. Maybe in some ways it's more than can be managed in one shot. Do you understand, the whole phenomenon is to develop new alters because others couldn't do certain things? Integration is like this: you are one person, and someone says, "Act sad. Act strong. Act weak." The one of "you" acts all those ways. You can't do that yet. These alters are somewhat caricatures because they're all one-dimensional. I want one person to have all the feelings and all the thoughts. That's what complete integration is.

N: Maybe this is all a little too overwhelming. Why did you say that the worst is over?

H: It was the first manifestation you've had with an alter, in such a direct way. It was like jumping into a cold pond, with all the shock value that has.

N: It won't be so shocking next time?

H: It shouldn't be. Even if it's scary, you've got explanation going for you. I'd bet it was a lot more scary not knowing why these things happened. It's a hell of a trade-off. If you know what it is, you've got to face the dynamics of what's actually happened. But I contend to you, you're better off. The worst is over when a great deal of the unknown has revealed itself. I'm wondering something. Did you think you weren't multiple? Did you think we were just talking in an academic place?

N: No, I thought I was, but it wasn't real. I keep having it shown to me that

it's real, and I say, "Oh, that's nice." But, it's not real enough. This seemed pretty real though.

H: *I might have underestimated your acceptance of how real it was. I haven't been bringing this up just 'cause it's an interesting model.*

N: ***I accept all this stuff about Ron, too, but it would be a shock to actually find him. It would be real seeing him again. Knowing it on one level, and then experiencing it...***

H: *That makes sense. Do you think you can get used to it? Not like it should happen continuously. You could integrate, and that's the end of it. But, get used to the idea that it is real. And that it actually played out in a significant way.*

N: ***That's why I said I felt like a freak. I didn't before. Now I feel like Sybil.***

H: *You're in good company, you know.*

N: ***What does that mean? All the wackos in the world.***

H: *(laughs) No, no. That it could play out, and even as much as you feel like a freak, you're with somebody who understands, and doesn't see you as a freak.*

N: ***Oh, you mean you.***

H: *If it's going to happen, it's best that it happens with me, 'cause I understand it.*

N: ***So you don't think I'm losing my mind.***

H: *How many times do I have to say it to you? (laughs) No, you're not losing your mind.*

JULY 17, 1992

Dear Howard,

There are so many things going on and I can't deal with it. I feel like I've struggled my entire life, and what's happening now is just the current struggle. There's no end to it. It's a struggle at work, with people, with living. Now it's a struggle even inside my own mind. Even being real doesn't feel real anymore.

APRIL 11, 1993

Dear Howard,

I've been thinking about how I said I still wonder if everything that's happened is real. Whenever I've not challenged something that happened as an alter, I've thought I just wasn't trying hard enough to override it. I say things I think are proof that I'm fabricating the whole thing, and wait for you to say, "Oh, come on!" (Still waiting.) When I do challenge it, I get freaked out that I can't "do" anything when another alter is out. I still freak myself out to avoid knowing I'm really making it all up.

But there have been physical things that made me think I'm not making it up. I don't mean like Erin not being able to stand up when

my leg cramped. I thought she really could have if I concentrated hard enough, but the pain was increasing. However, last August when we were downstairs before Marianne popped in, I was dizzy and as I sat down, I looked at my hand which was turning into a fist, and thought, "I'm not doing that." When you hugged me/Erin, I had a very clear thought, in a sarcastic, critical way, "Most people who hug you think it's nice if you hug them back." I was looking over your shoulder (it was all very slow motion), and my left hand came up to hug you. I watched in amazement because it wasn't "me" making my arm do that.

So I have hundreds of hours of talk with you that alternately fascinate and horrify me. And give me doubts (even though I know I deserve an academy award for sustaining it so long)(sigh). But here's the topper: I accept that I'm not crazy, even if I am making it up. This part has to be programmed because it's otherwise not logical. And if I'm programmed...then I can't be making it up.

December 19, 1991

Dear Howard,

My favorite Stephen King book is a fantasy called The Talisman, *co-written with Peter Straub. The premise is that there's another reality to our world which exists in another dimension. On the other side, we have "twinners" who usually correspond to our weaker parts. If you're a loving, kind person, your twinner will be the dark, weaker part of you. If you're evil, your twinner will be a good person, but probably strongly influenced by your shadow (and never know why). There's a seamless force field between the two worlds which is sometimes torn. People get pushed from one world into the other, ultimately with good and evil fighting for control as they seek the talisman which may forever unite both worlds.*

I read this six years ago and was enchanted. It offered the first explanation that made sense of my crazy feelings. I never went so far as to adopt it as the explanation — but I thought long and hard about it as a possibility. So imagine how delighted I've been (beyond the fear and resistance) to find there really is another world to discover where the rules are all different, and everything is seen in a totally different light. I'm sure this book enabled me, in part, to entertain some of the very bizarre things we've discussed.

The rest is because of you. Life is pretty strange. You never know who you're going to meet, or what they're going to teach you. It's like you've opened a door on this other world. It gives me so much hope for my future. I have never looked forward to a new year quite like I am this one.

13

Trust in the Therapeutic Setting

Howard's Poem

I have wandered without purpose
Across precarious borders
Not located on any fold-out map
But substantially fortified
With elaborate defenses
Refined by repeated assaults
And sanctified by time
Like a petrified forest
It looks a lot like a tree
But it is really a rock
And eventually one forgets
It was once a living thing

We met in one such forest
Where I'd staked my claim
You opened a modest box
Brimming with various seeds
Harvested on your travels
You mastered in agronomy
An inexact science but
Laden with possibilities
You study crop enhancement
By planting exceptional seeds
In ground previously deemed
To yield no more than sighs

While I wait for the new moon
With heavy heart for my harvest
I cannot help but mention
That trees made of solid rock
Seldom bear edible fruit

And that this rough terrain
Cannot bear one more false start
You continue, unperturbed
So assured of these outcomes
You leave nothing unattended and say
The goal may not be to bear fruit
But to discover a new life

SEO, NOVEMBER 26, 1991

NOVEMBER 18, 1991

Dear Howard,

About trust. Despite tremendous fear, my last letter provided what I thought was evidence of my craziness, fully knowing that if anyone had the ability to know crazy when you see it, it's you. (It never occurred to me that you'd also know not-crazy.) The fact that I ask too many why's, in light of my fear that someone was going to find me out, cannot offset what I consider to be an act of total trust. I will make an effort to be more conscious of it, but I don't think it's a real measure of my trust in you.

DECEMBER 5, 1991

Dear Howard,

It's so much harder to leave a session which ends positively than one where I feel overwhelmed and afraid. Last night I went home thinking, wow, maybe this stuff really works, maybe I can be normal. Maybe Howard is right. Then I had a migraine which responded only to codeine.

I tried to describe to a friend why seeing you gave me a major headache. "It's like we know how to make each other laugh now." As if that's a problem. I can make almost anyone laugh, but someone has to know me well before I'll laugh. So how did we get to that point? Am I that easily read? Or is it just you?

It seems, paradoxically, that the more comfortable I am with you, the more afraid I am that this is a very elaborate practical joke. Like you're going to say, "Sorry, I'm really an accountant, I do this for fun, but we're getting into tax season." Every time I've really trusted someone it's come back at me in some horrible way.

It's hard to see therapy as nonadversarial. I tend to play games to see if the therapist is really there, and I've always considered myself intellectually leaps ahead of any therapist. But with you, I haven't had time to play games. I feel challenged whenever we talk; there's nothing adversarial about you. Do you see how this could be stressful?

DECEMBER 6, 1991

Dear Howard,

I think it's all about control and that you're a man. You say things that make me directly compare you to men in my life. Is that intentional or just unavoidable? Like how you deal with kids. I see a totally involved father, who adores them, and respects them as individuals. When I was a kid, my father couldn't even keep our names straight. You tell me things you do with your kids, and I think, "Is that how it was supposed to be, or are these kids just incredibly lucky?"

When you said it was disturbing that I stayed with a crazy man for thirteen years, I thought, "What's the fuss?" My ex-husband's bad boy image appealed to someone trapped in goody two shoes. It didn't seem like a reason to not see him. You get worked up about how self-destructive my marriage was, and say, "Great relationship!" like I had lots of alternatives, or know the difference between a good and bad relationship. My experience with men is very limited. I look at you and think, "Is this what normal is? Is Cro-Magnon out?"

I've spent my entire life seeing men as either cruel or weak, and never what they say they are. You consistently present someone who doesn't fit anything I know. It's kind of fascinating, but also scary. You say you've got plans for me, and no one has ever, ever cared enough to imagine what you say you are imagining for me. So you've got a scared little three-year-old who desperately wants to believe you're really not an accountant. If I buy into that, it's like willingly opening a wound that might never close again. It goes beyond resistance, and into survival. Migraines begin to make a lot of sense.

DECEMBER 11, 1991

If I've always seen men as cruel or weak and never what they say they are, in a sense, they're predictable. If Howard isn't these things I can't predict what he'll do, and I can't even create the illusion of safety by thinking I'm in control. So here's this unpredictable man saying not only that he's got plans for me, but he knows how to make them happen. What a big relief, but he's also got the control. The three-year-old says who cares? Let him do whatever he wants! At last, someone who can help me! The cynical adult says he's really an accountant and I'm going to be taken again. I don't think I can stand that.

DECEMBER 11, 1991

H: By the way, tax season's coming, and I'll need to administer to my other clients.

N: That's not funny!

H: No? Does that add to the anxiety?

N: Yes!

H: It makes me wonder. Do you want this to be a good session or a bad session?

N: *I have a choice?*

H: *If it's a good session, you're apt to find out all kinds of things you don't want to find out, and it'll add to your anxiety. If it's a bad session, you'll just waste your time.*

N: ***Well, gee, let's make it a good session. So you're going to accounting school at night, right? (both laugh)***

H: *What you're talking about is the level of trust, and what can be expected in a process like this. I make myself as available as I possibly can. But I don't like to create dependency, as you well know. So I operate like I'm never going to see anyone again. The truth is, I'm not an accountant, but I could get hit by a car tomorrow and die.*

N: ***That's out of your control. It's not like you skipped town for six months to go to New York. I understand that in theory.***

H: *But? What's the but?*

N: ***(agitated) Why talk about how you have all these plans for me if I might never see you again? What's the point?***

H: *If I'm here to talk to you, you'll get all that stuff.*

N: ***(agitated) The assumption is that you will be, isn't it?***

H: *A fairly good bet. It's what I do.*

N: ***I think I overdid the vulnerability stuff in this last letter, and that's why I'm having an anxiety attack.***

H: *With the vulnerability comes the possibility that you'll be betrayed. Now that you've laid yourself wide open, I am the agent of this betrayal? It's not my style.*

N: ***I've thought it wasn't other people's style, too.***

H: *Sometimes a betrayal can be so subtle that it clouds the whole thing.*

N: ***It would have to be a real betrayal. Not like canceling an appointment. It would be like you'd end the relationship in the middle.***

H: *Why would I call it off?*

N: ***I don't know!***

H: *Well, we're done! (laughs)*

N: ***"It's tax season!"***

H: *Yes, you are vulnerable, but there's still a guardedness about you. A resistance. Certainly far less than when we first met. That's what "playing games" and being adversarial is about. It's a form of defense and resistance, using your humor or intelligence. You say that with me you've been able to be nonadversarial. However, that you know there's an adversarial thing means you're exercising great restraint, which is one of your defenses.*

N: ***But I'm not exercising great restraint. You asked if I thought we were having a debate. I had no sense of that, but you did. I thought, "It's adversarial, even when I don't want it to be."***

H: That's important. Maybe things just don't strike you that way. The potential for bullshit is very great, on both of our parts. The potential for me to interpret something you say that's very genuine and twist it into some psychological bullshit is very great, too. That's why it's on tape. Keeps us both honest. The second letter was more meaningful to you, you said. As a matter of fact, I am more normal. The way I am, is the way it should be.

N: ***But you would say that! Later, I thought, is he going to say, "No, I'm abnormal?" "No, I'm an anomaly?"***

H: If I'm not normal, this is what normal should look like. Statistically, there's just a bunch of shlubs out there. You make reference to my kids. Yes, this is how it's supposed to be, plus they're lucky. Kids should feel like "Wow, this is neat." That's a good, safe feeling. You'd like them to feel appreciative, but you don't do a head trip on them if they're somehow not. What are we going to do about this anxiety? You can predict what I'll do within limits.

N: ***Not if you're not who you say you are.***

H: It's like living in a two-dimensional world, and finding out it's really three-dimensional. There's a whole new dimension you never knew anything about.

N: ***(sighs) I don't know anything about anything.***

H: That's what it feels like when you discover a three-dimensional world. Come on! You've been operating in two-dimensions for a long time, and I say, "Well, lift your head." Am I making sense, or just making you mad?

N: ***You're making sense. In a strange sort of way.***

H: (laughs) Well, that's how I make sense.

N: ***I'm having a very hard time.***

H: You need reassurance. What's reasonable to predict about me?

N: ***Sometimes you say things with an inflection that's exactly like how this guy said to me. Like, "You think you don't deserve good things." He sort of went off and became an accountant. He was there in the beginning, when I was an interesting subject, but left when he got tired of it.***

H: Well, in spirit? He had to do his life.

N: ***He literally left. He called and said, "I want nothing to do with you. You're nuts." But he also was very there and helpful to me in the beginning.***

H: That's called conflict.

N: When I met him I was incredibly needy. I feel really needy now. (laughs nervously) If I get better, are you going to walk out?

H: In your mind it could be the same thing. "That's what happens. You get vulnerable, you get into the same situation where you can rely on somebody" — and by relying I mean the way that normal people would. So here it is. At what point will I dump you?

N: Yes! God. But it's more than that. If I go forward with this, and put everything into it, because it seems like my last shot, and then you dump me.

H: This is a good risk. It's not my style. This is a professional relationship. There are those kinds of safeguards. Does that reassure you, or not? You're supposed to feel resolved.

N: You know when I had the stomach pains? At the end of that you asked how I felt? I said I felt relieved, and you seemed surprised? I figured you thought it was because in the first hour you convinced me, more or less, that I wasn't crazy. But I was relieved because you said, "I have plans for you!" It was like, (looking to ceiling) "Oh, thank you!"

H: I do have plans for you. No one ever said that to you. "Let's plan this. Let's figure out how this will happen."

N: No.

H: Well, that's what you're supposed to have.

N: I was just relieved that at last someone could help me.

H: That someone could express that level of caring.

N: (near tears) Yeah.

H: It's probably easy for me to discount it because it seems so easy and natural to me. A person comes in with a problem. Let's say what the problem is and figure out its elements; let's make a plan so the problem's not there anymore. That's the kind of world you ought to be living in. With people who are in your life who plan forward and positively about their lives, and if you're in it, they would be planning for your life, as well.

N: I don't know anybody like that.

H: That's really sad. I don't think I'm an anomaly. I have people who care like that in my life. So I know at least in my own sphere of humanity that's what people do. If somehow, in this universe, I occupy the speck of all specks, and it's totally not there anywhere else, I'm oblivious. But, I say to you, be oblivious, and only be with people who are of that type. Positive people gravitate toward each other.

DECEMBER 24, 1991

Dear Howard,

I guess I haven't gotten it yet. Part of why I told you about naming the bear Howard was because it was a test, or a very self-destructive

urge, since I was certain you'd say it was bad. You went the other way, offering this "lifetime" arrangement. (Like I said, you're unpredictable.) I hope you understood I was totally overwhelmed. Is the point in this process supposed to be that you're there, no matter what silly things I do to sabotage it? Or that I'm not even trying to sabotage it — I'm just totally needy? And that's okay, for now?

This is so hard, Howard. I can't discount the fact that whatever we're doing, it's working. You say you aren't telling me anything I wouldn't have figured out by myself, but that's a stretch. Everything we discuss goes further than anything I've ever thought about. I understand that you don't like to create unhealthy dependence; I also don't get how I can not be dependent on you right now. Is there a healthy dependency? I often feel like I'm three years old with you. Is that part of what we're doing? Do I get to grow up with you?

APRIL 6, 1992

The more heinous my memories become, the more depressed I am, the more hopeless I feel. Howard's sure everything's okay; that I'm okay. He predicts that I'm near an "emotional breakthrough," which I'm sure involves an emotional breakdown. He says I control Sarah too much. He says she's been busy holding this together, but it's getting to the point where she can relax.

I don't feel okay! I don't feel integrated. I don't feel there's hope for me because the damage is so great, I can never possibly be normal. Some broken things can't be fixed.

MAY 6, 1992

Dear Howard,

I'm sorry I give you such a hard time. I know I understood what you were saying long before you got into your "mud hut" analogy. I don't know why the idea of integration scares me so much. I think it's that I'm afraid I'm not going to be me when this is over. If that's not enough to scare me senseless, then I guess I wonder just as much what if I'm not any different? What if the integrated me feels just as confused and alone?

Most of what I've done the last eight months has felt very unreal. What if the only difference is, before I did unreal things and wasn't aware of it, and now I know I'm doing it? If "weirdness" is an attribute that can't be blamed on Ron or DID, does that mean I'll still be doing weird stuff (like everything I do now that we both agree is weird) even when I'm integrated? Or is the weird stuff a product of my intellect? Would Mozart understand my dilemma? Such anxiety.

JUNE 3, 1992

Dear Howard,

I have so many questions! I really don't understand how these relationships are supposed to work. My confusion about integration is that I still feel like Nita. Sarah is when I feel good. Nita has a wider range of emotional responses. Nita performs for approval and is crushed when it doesn't happen. Nita is shy and self-effacing, doesn't take compliments well, and feels like a fraud. Nita's convinced that life is one big cosmic joke. I display all of that sometimes. Am I Nita, or am I Sarah acting like Nita?

You've always pointed out my sarcasm. You wished you could "snap your fingers and make it go away." (I'm sure Lynn was amused.) Nita is also sarcastic. But how can she be if Lynn is the sarcastic one? You've said I walked in as Sarah; you've only known Sarah. Has Sarah always been sarcastic, too? You said I know when I slip into another alter; I'm sure I don't know. Can it be that Lynn pops in to say sarcastic things that I consciously wanted to say and I never had the sense of being shut out by her (as in your office) because she was saying what I wanted to say and I thought I was saying it, so nothing seemed odd?

Regarding my being in control when Lynn is speaking, if it's like riding a bicycle, you're making a big assumption that I've already ridden one. If I've never controlled Lynn before, how would I know how to do it now? Could you please tell me what it is so I don't totally freak out if this happens sometime when you're not around?

P.S. The majority of my sarcasm is self-directed, and the only one I am trying to hurt is me. I have nothing but the highest respect and affection for you. I appreciate your presence in my life more than I can begin to tell you. Please forgive me if I have ever lost sight of that.

July 21, 1993

Dear Howard,

As I meet people in exponentially faster numbers, and get so much affirmation and appreciation for just being me, everyday seems to get a little better. But there are still times when I just want to come running back to you, because I'm still like a child at all this stuff, and being an instant grownup is sometimes unbearable. (crying now) Sometimes the sensory overload is oppressive, and I shut down. Sometimes I just want to be Erin again. I try to put on a brave face because I know I'm doing great, but sometimes it's so hard! I have this huge ball of pain welling up inside of me, and I don't know why.

I miss the feeling that, as a six-year-old, everything's okay because you're here. I know as an adult that everything is okay, and you are here. But Erin threw herself 100% into your care and custody for awhile, and you were wonderful with her. That's what I miss. Most people get to do it gradually, like they get to be six and seven and eight. The developmental stages in a relationship with you as "parent" would change accordingly. My six-year-old still hasn't learned a lot about separation, other than wanting it from people who hurt her, but you're the last person she wants to let go. I recently went from six directly to 39, as you say, at warp speed. I feel it acutely and it's hard to make that adjustment sometimes.

DECEMBER 10, 1992

Dear Howard,

For the first time ever I'm looking back on a year filled with turbulence and pain, and feeling it was worth it. It all makes sense, and no one can tell me otherwise. There is great freedom in realizing and recognizing the truth. You said ages ago, "This is how this works!" I've come a long way, with your guidance at each step. The journey continues, with hope for the future and tremendous admiration for you and your particular brand of magic. Thank you for caring so much about and for me.

14

Confusion Stimulus and Sexual Dysfunctions

I told Charlotte I slept with my ex-husband. She said, "How could you do that when he's such a jerk?" I told her about when he went crazy drunk, searching for the knives. I had no idea if he'd go for me or himself. All I could think was, "I love you so much. Why are you doing this?" In that moment, loving him so much made me helpless. I stood there, like I was tied down, waiting to see what happened. Obviously, it takes an incredible amount of shit for me to stop loving someone.

—NITA, JUNE 12, 1985

MARCH 26, 1992

Dear Howard,

I've had a recurring dream for years where I meet a sensitive, generous, charismatic stranger, a different man in each dream. I do something totally "out of character" and go with him. We don't even know each other's last names. We have this totally free sexual experience which seems so real that even in the dream I'm asking myself if this is really a dream. We kiss goodbye, without regrets. I never see him again.

This dream happened a dozen times in the last fifteen years. I always wake up in the middle of the night, with that surreal feeling. I wonder what day it is, feeling quite disoriented. (It was always the day I thought it should be — but what about the date? One of my biggest unresolved complaints at my last job was that someone was using my office at night. My things would be different from how I left them. What if "I" was gone for a week and didn't know it? What if my office was left the way my other self left it the day before?) I'm always amazed at how real the dream seems, and then move on fast, because how can it be real? "I" would never have sex with a total stranger.

If I left home in this dream state, who was I? These liaisons were self-affirming and pleasurable. Anita is too angry to have great sex. How I know what "great sex" is remains a mystery to me, and is about as scary as having these bizarre "#9" thoughts. They both are beyond my personal experience, as I know me. Sarah wouldn't endanger me. It wasn't Nita, or I'd remember it. So who was I? Was this real? How will I ever know?

MARCH 31, 1992

N: I brought you a letter. I hate this. (He reads it; she endures the silence in agony.)

Dear Howard,

This is excruciatingly embarrassing. I can only tell you now because I see it as necessary, but will save lots of time if you read this and don't have to drag it out of me. I want so badly to leave parts out, because this is so humiliating, but what's the point? I am relying heavily on your statement that we can talk about anything.

The #9 fantasy:

I am in a warehouse. I don't know how I got there. Lots of men are looking at me. One says, "It's your choice. Either we kill you now, or you do whatever we want, and maybe we won't kill you." I say, "Please don't kill me. I'll do anything, please." He tells me to undress. I am strapped face down, spread eagle, on a contraption. Several men begin touching me, hands all over me. I am repeatedly assaulted, simultaneously, in different parts of my body. It seems endless.

Someone says, "Have you ever done it with so many men before?" They all laugh. He says I'm really being prepared for Rob. I ask who is he? More laughter. One says, "Rob is hung like a horse." Someone says, "He's really a jackass." More laughter. Someone says, "You know what a jackass is, don't you?" Someone says, "Yeah, Rob is a real animal." Someone applies oil to my genitals. The men cheer as Rob approaches. I try to see but can't. The men are reaching for me. Something huge pushes between my legs. The men are calling bets. One of them makes a noise like a donkey. More cheers.

The man nearest to my face says Rob will not come until I do, so I should relax and enjoy it. I beg him to help me. He says, "If you don't do this real nice, honey, I will personally kill you." He thrusts his penis into my mouth as the donkey makes his first thrust into my vagina, which is immediately seared with intense pain. The donkey thrusts again, men cheering wildly, touching my breasts, masturbating in my hands, the man in my mouth making me gag, tears rolling down my face. The donkey begins a rhythm, the man comes in my mouth and forces me to swallow. He tells me to open my eyes and I see that this is being filmed. I close my eyes and try to stop breathing, but I can't. Everything seems like slow motion, the sound is fading, when suddenly I realize this is beginning to feel good, and I'm horrified, but maybe that will make them happy, maybe they won't kill me if I come. The donkey is thrusting harder and faster, and I give up and give in to it, and feel the wave of contractions wash over me. The men are going wild. The donkey comes in massive amounts, semen running down my legs.

My analysis:

Maybe I judge things I think about harshly because somewhere inside I know these are really things I've done. If thinking and doing are two dif-

ferent things, then the only thing worse than the #9 fantasy is the #10 actually living it.

You asked, "Did Ron ever engage in this #9 weirdness with you?" It made me laugh (briefly) because I got a picture of him with a donkey's body. I said, "Well, he had sex with a child — that's pretty weird." I played that part of the tape over and over. What suddenly hit me was that the reality of the donkey was never confirmed, and from the perspective of size, and physical pain, there's no difference between a donkey with a grown woman, and a man with a four-year-old girl. A child might well believe noises she heard sounded like an animal.

If I found any of this pleasurable as a child, I'm sure I also laughed sometimes when he tickled me. It's far more disturbing that I get pleasure out of it now.

My recollections about this incident: I was given a drug to take the fight out of me, and driven to this place by Ron. The other men were only allowed to penetrate me with their fingers. I don't know how I know this. Only Ron was allowed to have vaginal sex with me. Still pictures and home movies were taken. It was after these events that I would wake up with pains in my legs that my mother called "growing pains."

H: *(breaking the strained silence) This isn't that uncommon of a fantasy. I think you just feel so terribly humiliated. (she nods) On the one hand, that's good because it means you're trying to deal with healthier things, and a more normal way of seeing things. But just because you've had images like this doesn't make you unhealthy.*

N: ***It really happened.***

H: *That's what I'm thinking, too. The images are becoming strong for you. Throughout your life, they've pervaded as a fantasy. A fantasy usually is something pleasurable.*

N: ***That's why I think it's very strange.***

H: *It is strange. But we're going to make sense of it, okay? When you first talk about it, it's anything but pleasurable. With child sexual abuse, there's a crossover confusion. It goes something like this. "I want to be loved, and cared about, and the thing happening to me isn't really pleasurable, yet it seems to give pleasure to other people. So if I can see it as pleasurable, then pleasure will be equated with doing these things because I want to be loved."*

N: ***I think it was a purely physical response.***

H: *This is why the word "confusion" is important. Vaginal stimulation is pleasurable. So here's this horrible thing going on, mixed with a pleasurable thing.*

N: ***But if that happened as a child, and I got pleasure out of it, I see nothing wrong with it. I couldn't help what was happening. It's just what I've done with it since then that bothers me.***

H: *That's where the confusion continued. Do you know how associations are built? If you pair two things, the tendency is to see that the two go together. When you got older, you buried a lot of this stuff in out-and-out blocking, and in other identity formations. But the stimulus response was still connected. As a mature individual operating in a particular identity format, you get these fantasies, and wonder why a thing like that would be pleasurable. It would be, because a normally pleasurable thing was paired with a toxic thing. So it isn't completely felt either like a toxic thing, or a pleasurable thing.*

N: ***Isn't that kind of sick?***

H: *Do you want to make an argument for sick? Yeah, you're not in good shape with it. If that's what you need — validation of your sickness, sure.*

N: ***Well, it's not normal.***

H: *It's not normal. People don't grow up this way. Most people don't have experiences like this. You were violently and viciously abused. The sickness was in the minds of the persons doing it. It's normal to have a fantasy like this under those circumstances. If you had it when you grew up with love, devotion, support, and encouragement, it would get me wondering. Would you rather have this fantasy without anything leading up to it? You just purely like these kinds of images?*

N: ***That's what it seemed like.***

H: *Until we talked about the other parts of your life. This is the fantasy that makes sense. You were totally denied by everybody. No one trusted you; no one believed you; people labeled you as difficult; you had no support or affection, or encouragement. The sick thing about all this is that this was the only kind of attention shown to you that you could crossover, as a kid, and call affection.*

N: ***I don't think so!***

H: *There are kids who will do anything to get a laugh, even if it's humiliating. They don't feel validated any other way. You were so completely invalidated by various elements of your life, even a humiliating thing that gave someone else pleasure was a way for you to be validated.*

N: ***I'll have to work on that one a bit.***

H: *Here's how you work on it for your life. You were validated, but you couldn't stand it. So you compartmentalized into an alter who allowed you — it's a very neat trick — to feel the validation, and in another alter, to abhor this. That resolves the conflict. At least till you and I talked, but it got you here. This is a normal fantasy that would be expected from all your experiences, and it would haunt you. It might even seem pleasurable as an adult because of the crossover confusion. See, you haven't gone for the best, which is someone in your life who respects you, who laughs with you, and not at your expense; who gives to you, supports you. That's the best. You went for the laugh.*

N: ***What do you mean, I went for the laugh, in my life?***

H: *These men validated you. As an adult, that this is still a fantasy for you means you go for the pleasurable experience connected to their getting off. Their laughing. "I'm bringing pleasure into another person's life even though I'm the target of their abuse." Sarah, these are the dynamics. You're having a hard time buying this.*

N: ***I'm sure it's very textbook.***

H: *It is textbook. It's also true.*

N: ***Whether I was getting gratified from it, I don't know. The fantasies that stuck with me the longest are always about being out of control, and thinking I'm having sex with someone I know and trust, and suddenly, it turns out there are other people, and I'm not sure what's going on. It's usually scary.***

H: *That's hard-wired. Imagine growing up in a situation where you're slapped across the face five times a day, and they're saying they love you. That's a mixed message.*

N: ***It's not that hard to imagine.***

H: *I figured. Then, you get into a real relationship as an adult, and the person says, "I love you," and you can feel the sensation of your face getting smacked. That's what's going on. You might even sabotage the situation to make it so you actually do get hit. A confusion sets in that says "I guess that's what love is." Intellectually, you'd know different. This is a classic case of confusion stimulus. And it doesn't go away until you talk about it. I'm shocked that these things happened to you. But no right-thinking person could hold you accountable for the crossover confusion and pleasure you might derive by thinking about it.*

APRIL 2, 1992

Dear Howard,

After last time, I was sure you were upset with me. On tape, you clearly weren't, but I felt I'd let you down. It has occurred to me that if I'm in therapy for sexual abuse issues, sooner or later I'd probably have to talk about sexual abuse. I thought it would be a relief, but I feel like you've lost respect for me. (How could you not.) You made it very clear you haven't, but I still feel so ashamed.

SEPTEMBER 25, 1992

Dear Howard,

I have an increasing concern about what we discussed before about sexual fantasies, and that whole thing about "confusion stimulus." I can't even figure out what to say if I were pretending that I'm not really sending this to you. I'm very uncomfortable. Oh well, here goes. The fantasies we discussed previously aren't exciting anymore, but neither is anything else. It's a good news/bad news thing. I may not be in a good, intimate, loving, and committed relationship now, but I'm not

dead, either. It just feels that way. I wish I could talk to Lynn, because I never asked her about my sexual history, or if the dreams I had about meeting nice guys in the supermarket really happened.

Suddenly I feel so sad, I guess because it's hitting me how little I know about what is normal. Sometimes knowing what you know only lets you catch on to how much you don't know. Mostly, I'm feeling unprotected, and not sure why.

SEPTEMBER 28, 1992

H: *I'm looking for a way that you can be thrown by something with quick recovery, without it undermining, or threatening, your well-being. This discovery should not do that.*

S: *Why not?*

H: *'Cause you're here today. You're okay.*

S: *I'm not okay.*

H: *You hate the way it feels. You hate what this is. You hate the endless memories. This was evil. If you're embarrassed that you have these fantasies, you don't have to be. You didn't conjure them up; they were put there. You got nothing but mixed messages. There's supposed to be some kind of consistency in values, and there wasn't any. Good was bad, bad was good. Love was hate, and hate was love. You were systematically brainwashed. It all got mixed up.*

DECEMBER 17, 1992

Dear Howard,

Erin is offering new insights into my behavior with men in general. I'm not real happy with some of these insights. I asked what she wanted for Christmas, and one thing she wants is a hug from you.

I'm sure you give great hugs, but Erin doesn't understand. It would be like asking you for sex. She wants to hug you for exactly what you said, to reach trust with father. But Nita never did anything that could be wrongly interpreted by a man, so it's a sticky issue. I've always had platonic friendships, but the men must initiate even hugs or they don't happen. After a couple of years of being friends, rejection seems like a long shot (even to me), so I take tiny risks to initiate hugs and kisses. After realizing that's okay, I start to sexualize it. Of course they have no idea what's happening. Everything gets mixed up and no matter what happens, I always feel bad.

So I can't do that. I don't even want to talk about it, but she'll probably talk about it! She's more open with you, in many ways, than I am. And if you can't tell, but I'm certain you can, this really bugs me.

JANUARY 6, 1993

Dear Howard,

I don't know why I feel so insecure. But I do. Erin is pushing for things I have difficulty dealing with. I pulled the tape from last April when I first told you about that really horrible "fantasy no. 9" and I see why I've done a lot of things based on that false information. But my knee-jerk reaction takes me right into the same behavior, and I hate it! I hate feeling so confused. I hate acting in old patterns even when I know it's an old pattern and I don't want to do it. It makes me feel out of control, but it's the need for control that makes me do it. I don't know why I feel so out of control when I'm supposedly in control.

JUNE 7, 1993

Dear Howard,

When I first told you how Charlotte asked if I ever had sexual feelings for you, and I said, "All I want Howard to do is adopt me," you said, "Well, isn't that just as profound? Isn't that kind of neat?" I thought, "Would he think it's so neat if I did feel sexually attracted to him?" It all seemed equally unthinkable. I kept saying, "No, it's weird." Which you couldn't believe I really meant, but I didn't understand, even at that late hour, that therapy can enlighten or even heal certain relationships. I thought I wasn't supposed to want you to adopt me!

I don't have anyone left (like Inside Sarah) to pawn this off on, so now I have to be very brave. I read something about when a woman was never mirrored sexually by her parents, the therapist can do it without sexual contact. I was mirrored sexually by Ron. Confusion stimulus all over the place. I have negative attitudes about sex, but have never been specific, other than about sexual fantasies that were not especially healthy. So I'm going to tell you more, and want to know if there's a way to work on this.

1. *I have a fascination with pornography. For many years I considered writing the absurd "stories" that accompany photos in hard-core magazines.*
2. *I cannot seem to finish my romance novel. I have a legitimate plot, but once the characters have sex there's literally nothing left to say. I cannot write dialogue for people who are happy after sex.*
3. *I have a general fear and mistrust of men, which hasn't lessened just for knowing you. I don't think you're like most men, even though you claim you are.*
4. *I was interested in dating as a teenager, but it seemed scary. I had no conscious knowledge of what sex was, and never masturbated until my future husband taught me how at nineteen. Even then, I had a feeling it was bad to touch myself. I don't feel that way now, but think some of my thoughts while touching myself are bad.*
5. *My ex-husband enjoyed questionable sexual practices, for which I faked unusual interest and orgasm to please him. I felt such contempt for him, that he couldn't tell the difference.*
6. *His biggest complaint was that I "didn't move enough" during sex. This always surprised me (no matter how many times I heard it), because either I thought I was moving, or I didn't realize I was supposed to move. It was like a new concept every time. This may be a*

DID problem, but echoes back to the fact that I certainly didn't think I was supposed to move as a child.

7. *The last time he and I had sex was about a year after our divorce, and it was our best sex ever. We pretended he was pinning me on the floor. I struggled and said, "No!" This was a standard ritual which I found (find) extremely arousing. I guess I'd finally learned to move enough for him, because he was impressed, and asked who I'd been with. (The answer: no one. I think he encountered Desiree.) "Good" sex has always involved some conscious element of struggle.*
8. *(gulp) I've noticed a marked difference in how I look at you. (Is this profound!? Is this really neat?!) You must realize, it's like watching a play. I'd never walk on stage, or even want to. While you fit my old pattern of being totally unavailable, which seems very regressive, I also trust you, which is new. Are you safe because you're unavailable, or because you're you? Hmmm.*
9. *When you hugged me (Erin), it felt wonderful. Sometimes I feel so untouchable. It takes a long time to feel okay about initiating touch with someone, which I realize may signal I don't want to be touched, but that's not true. I just want to feel safe when touched. Your hug was fascinating in that I was resisting it, while Erin was bringing my arm up to hug you back. I guess I didn't realize that touch was, or could be, an important part of therapy for someone who is very afraid of it.*

I want to deal with all of this. Down the road, it won't matter how much I weigh if my attitudes about myself and sex result in poor choices in men and inappropriate behavior.

JUNE 16, 1993

Dear Howard,

I flinch in terror virtually every time someone might touch me. This certainly will affect any future sexual relationship, but is much more damaging in an everyday context because I can never relax. I said your hug was wonderful, but I also said I was resisting it.

The dynamic is clear: I might feel something good if I'm touched, which is bad. If they're close enough to touch, they're close enough to hurt. I know for sure that feeling bad when people touch me is bad, so I steel myself against feeling anything because it's bad either way. I hated when my mother touched me; it goes more to her than to Ron. I knew where he was coming from, but my mother was unpredictable. Sometimes she acted like she cared, which I couldn't afford to believe. Feeling good when she touched me was not a good thing.

It's for this aspect alone that I bravely inquired about the therapeutic use of nonsexual touch. If anything can convey the level of trust I have in you, sort of saying, "Okay, touch me" is it. I disguise my fear so well that often I don't even know I'm doing it. Nothing makes me feel more damaged. I wondered if it's something to which I could be desensitized. ("Test it with someone you admire.")

I want to break free from the last remnants of my abuse so I can have that life you keep saying I was meant to have, including the guy who goes with Inside Sarah's wedding dress! It's more than physical transformation that gets me the guy or into that dress. I must stop flinching at life. I also don't want to end therapy feeling like life is great except for this one little problem.

July 16, 1993

Dear Howard,

You gave me the greatest gift today. You said you've always known I am extremely sensual, erotic, and sexual. You've never said anything like that before, but I've never talked so freely about my sexuality, either. All things in good time. Don't I seem different to you?! I feel so free! Sarah is emerging as my "self" — all her strengths, joy, and sexiness. I know it's "just a report," but I can't tell you what it means to me that you, as a man, see beyond my body. That I am not my body.

October 31, 1994

Dear Howard,

Things with Dan are wonderful. He's genuine. He cares deeply, not just about me, but Erin as well. I find myself going through different phases of emotions in getting such royal treatment. I feel quite special and cherished. Sometimes I feel an overwhelming sadness that I had to wait this long to feel so good in my life. Sometimes I feel unworthy of his devotion. Most of the time, I feel happy.

You know how you said Dan would follow my lead sexually? The only little problem is that it's not just me and Erin here. Desiree made a star appearance the last few nights. She's much more sexually aggressive than I am, so he was wondering what was going on.

So, speaking of Desiree (clearing throat)....I'd never experienced successfully doing oral sex on a man (in conscious memory), and wanted to know what it was like. My ex-husband said I didn't do it right. Gave me quite a complex. So we tried it, and although it was pleasurable, he did not climax. But last night, Desiree took over (and he knew it was her). She has, shall we say, better technique than me.

I went through a very quick set of emotions. I felt powerful and sexy. (Me, Sarah, beyond anything Desiree felt). I stepped into my "new" integrated sexuality. I also had to do everything in my power to not throw up (which, of course, was very obvious to Dan), because I had nanosecond flashbacks from childhood. I had this adult rational person who knew there was nothing horrible about this, and that it was actually quite sweet. And I had my memories haunting me. (Categorically, Erin was not part of this.)

Afterward, Desiree commented to Dan that it was she who made it happen, and Sarah who got sick. She said this to protect me, so he would not assume I'd be ready for this again soon. He took great offense, thinking she was attempting to denigrate me in his eyes, and elevate herself. He called her a not-nice name, to which she rightly took exception, pointing out she'd just given him the treat of his lifetime, and it was extremely bad form to call her names. So they talked.

She has no childhood memories, so is completely unaffected by them sexually. She first appeared at fourteen when Nita couldn't handle her interest in boys. She arrested at nineteen when Nita began dating my ex-husband, as "there was no point" in getting older. She is not sexually submissive (she says I am), but likes to experiment and role play. She explained differences between her and my technique (for our edification). She believes something subconscious stops me from doing it in a way to ensure a man's orgasm, precisely due to childhood issues, while she does not have this problem.

Dan was dismayed to find Desiree not integrated, but also intrigued. He told Desiree he wants to have sex with me, not her. He asked if she doesn't integrate, in the next few years when my body gets to a normal weight, is she going to go out looking for sex elsewhere. She said Sarah is highly monogamous and she will respect that. She agreed to not come out again unless invited.

Even now, I have diametrically opposed reactions to what happened. I still gag when I think about it. But I also am extremely pleased! I don't especially want to try it again soon, but I do. It's strictly childhood memories that make this unpleasant. Certainly not Dan.

I'm telling you all this not at all because I feel I am in some sort of crisis. I'm not. I'm just a little amazed. A little confused. I'm sure you knew sexual contact would stir things up. Although you focused on Erin, the rest of me was bound to have some echoes, too. I don't think it's a bad thing. I'm emotionally ready for it, and I've picked the right man to venture forth with.

Is Dan wonderful, or what? (Say yes!) I cannot comprehend having anything like this conversation with my ex-husband. He would not have cared what was important to me, nor would he have been willing to openly examine his own assumptions and insecurities. I feel like I'm graduating, Howard.

15

Losing Time

We don't have a sense of who we are without knowing what we were before. You survived your childhood with sheer creativity, will, and intellectual prowess. You would have been greatly more disturbed without your intellectual tools. DID is the most profoundly creative coping skill a human can manufacture, under circumstances that would literally destroy anyone else. I see multiples as heroes.

—Howard, July 30, 1993

In kindergarten, we had nap time after snacks. I seldom slept, as I was consumed by fear that bad things happened when I napped. Afterward, we listened to our teacher tell a story, which I loved. She told of adventures, happy children, and places faraway which seemed like good places to go to get away. I wasn't sure why I wanted to get away; I just knew it was a good idea.

One day, I opened my eyes, and (like magic) I was listening to a story. I had no idea how I'd gotten to school. The last thing I knew, I was at home with my mother, which felt like a distant event. All the other kids seemed their normal selves, but I felt panicked, and did not know why. The teacher spoke as if nothing unusual had occurred. But I knew I'd not done my usual routine. I knew I had not taken the bus that morning. I knew something was terribly wrong, and it scared me.

I was compelled, for some unknown reason, to look beneath the collar of my dress, and was horrified to discover I still had my pajamas on. For the remainder of the day, nothing was more important than ensuring no one saw my pajamas. Looking back on this, I rationalized that it must have been because I feared embarrassment from the other kids. But I could never account for the terror I felt. Or my extreme confusion at "waking up" in a place I knew I should not have been.

Embarrassment was always the best rationale for these bizarre incidents of psychic teletransport, until my memories began surfacing. I realized, thirty very odd years later, that I had, in fact, not taken the bus that morning. I'd spent a nightmare weekend with Ron, who hurriedly dressed me, and dropped me off in front of school. (It would have looked even more odd had I carried my pajamas with me into class). An alter attended school until it was deemed safe enough for Nita to "wake up." This is the essence of losing time. It's why I felt crazy my entire life.

OCTOBER 31, 1991

H: In the event that there is more profound splitting off, we will talk about it.

N: How will I even know?

H: What clues have there been? Are you suspecting more than Sarah?

N: (hesitates) Yeah.

H: Are there major gaps in your life, as an adult?

N: Where I lost time? Not blocks like months, but whole evenings.

H: How often?

N: I don't know. I just suddenly realize it's 2:00 a.m., and I don't know what I did.

H: How much time lapsed?

N: (agitated) I feel like this is a joke! I don't know! It's 9:00 p.m., and then I just suddenly realize it's 2:00 a.m.. I wasn't reading, or doing anything to absorb my time.

H: You're not talking about time where you're so wrapped up, it goes quickly. You're talking about an actual gap.

N: (sighs) That's what it feels like. But I just think, "Oh, geez, I spaced out. I don't even know what time it is."

H: When did that kind of stuff start?

N: (sighs) Long time ago.

H: Can you give me a fix on frequency?

N: Maybe once every couple of weeks. This isn't making me feel better.

H: Have courage, okay? The worst case is, you've got that going on, and talking about it makes the integration process occur. The best case is, we talk about it, and we can't make a case at all. It's just a moment of shutdown.

MARCH 18, 1992

Dear Howard,

When I was sixteen, my mother told Charlotte not to lend me $10 because I couldn't be trusted to pay her back. I was stunned. I seldom borrowed money, and always paid people back. I thought it was more maliciousness on her part. But, I've had a lifetime of financial chaos with Anita signing checks and credit cards. I wonder if Anita was "out" and doing things with money I was unaware of. The next leap is: what other things could I have thought my mother was being cruel — and I never understood what I'd done to deserve it — but she really was reacting to Anita. I never thought I'd give her the benefit of any doubt, but the $10 incident seems clear now. (Things that make you go "hmmm.")

May 7, 1992

Dear Howard,

Is it possible I could still be losing time? In the last two weeks, I've twice had a distinct sensation of it. The first time I shook it off; after this morning, I'm pretty sure. But it seems so odd. I noticed it when watching a TV show. I thought, as usual, that I must have fallen asleep, but also was very sure I hadn't. I had a creepy feeling, but thought I was exaggerating it, and let it go.

A similar thing happened this morning when watching the news, and resulted in my being 45 minutes late to work. This morning, I woke up at 6:30 a.m. I'm wide awake, it's 8:00 a.m., I'm looking directly at the TV, and literally, the next thing I see is not the news anymore. I called time, and it was 9:14 a.m.

Why is this happening now? Or has it been happening all along, and I'm only now able to discern it? Is it a form of integration to be aware that I'm losing time, or am I going backwards? I don't think I went anywhere or did anything unusual during these lost periods. It didn't feel the same way it feels when I merely zone out. Is there something I should do to try to make this happen more? Or less?

May 11, 1992

S: *Is it possible that I'm still losing time?*

H: *Well, I could lose time. It's possible. But, I'm not aware of it.*

S: *Yes, but how?*

H: *Through processes I'd be unaware of.*

S: *It's happened three times. But only the last time was really clear to me. The others, I just blew it off.*

H: *Try to make yourself aware of anything that triggers you. Something that has emotional content for you. It puts you in a dilemma, where it would challenge you in some way. Some kind of stress.*

S: *It was nothing unusual.*

H: *That's what you want to pay attention to. Otherwise, what you're saying is that these are just spontaneous lapses or loss of consciousness as Sarah. You'd think, "Was I someone else?" I'm sure you'd like to believe these things happen for a certain reason. Once you know the reason, the likelihood of it happening again diminishes. As opposed to, it just happened, and there is no good reason.*

S: *Which makes it random.*

H: *Random and hard to control, which would be fearful. You wouldn't like to think you could be that much out of control. I want Sarah to ask who was there. "Who came in?"*

S: *I also had another really weird experience. I was writing you a letter, which I never mailed, which also made it seem weird, because I didn't want to mail it to you.*

H: Yeah, you didn't send me anything this time.

S: I was trying to explain...(laughs) Oh! My mind just went blank! Oh, geez! (ponders) I said I was sorry I was giving you such a hard time.

H: I like that. (both laugh)

S: I was trying to explain to you. . .what I meant. . .oh, why is this so hard? My mind is fading in and out. (struggling)

H: Did you throw it away?

S: No. But I felt...you said I was too patient with you about not reading the Charyse writing, and it was my "nice way" of saying we weren't connecting. I tried to explain why I said it was a reality check, and you didn't get it. I said, "When I start feeling too important." And it was like (struggling to speak)...I started to write that there's this narcissistic part of me. When I wrote "narcissistic," that buzz started, like that weird feeling? It was the cynical person talking about other ones. The narcissistic part says that if I'm so fascinating, then you wouldn't be able to resist reading anything I write. (laughs) "Oh! What a thought!" That I have that kind of control over you.

H: You're really pleased by having this sense of control. And the interest another person could have about this.

S: But that's why it's a reality check. Obviously, it's not true. (laughs) You resisted. For two weeks, you didn't read it. That's why I said it was a reality check. There's this narcissistic part that says, "How could he not read this?"

H: Yes! Exactly.

S: I wrote this, and was spinning around, and all of a sudden I thought, "This isn't real." That's why I didn't mail it, 'cause I thought I was really making this up.

H: I want you to encourage the emergence of parts of your personality. I want these people to come out. I want you to be in touch with them.

S: You said before that when it happens integration is so fast. So then I started thinking, "Well, it's 'cause they're integrated, and that's why I don't think it's real."

H: A person can be very sure of himself, very clear-headed, and still have times when he's fuzzy, and not certain of anything. You have a spectrum of moods and personality shifts that happen with all people. In any moment, the integration is complete. But in another moment, it feels split off. "I'm just not me." You're frightened by stuff like lapses of time, the emergence of a person who has a name, or who shares a name. When you get frightened, you suppress anything else that might come out. I'm telling you to do the opposite. Go home and say, "All right, listen! Does anyone know about this person who was around earlier? Who was watching TV?"

S: And I will get an answer?

H: You are very expressive in written form. You might want to do it that way. You will get all the information. "Okay, it was us. We had a picnic."

MAY 10, 1992

Dear Howard,

I'm sorry I've been giving you such a hard time lately. I hate saying I don't trust you, because it's basically not true. There's so much crap to rise above, starting with, if I believe you, then it's not going to happen ("I know what you want and you can't have it.") It must be odd to have someone resist you who wants what you say to be true. (Or maybe it isn't odd.)

[Howard: The following was intended as a neutral explanation, and turned into something else. My head started "spinning" when I typed "narcissistic".]

When you forgot to read the Charyse writing, I said it was a reality check for when I start to feel too important. There's a narcissistic part of me that knows my writing is brilliant, and is secretly quite pleased when you say, "You're fascinating," because it's true. And you'll be unable to restrain yourself from reading anything I write. She craves attention she makes sure she gets it, but she's held back by the one who refuses to do anything obvious like read her own poems. She downgrades her achievements because someone might notice her. They're always pulling at each other. They're always fighting. And there's the one who's so patient, so nice, so eternally nice, because it's polite and we try so hard to be polite because people like us and nobody knows about us when we're polite. She's also forever nice out of fear of reprisals. And there's the little one who wants to please you so much and do everything right because you hold so many keys you are magic. You see her even when she is invisible even when she is magic too she's afraid of what will happen if she doesn't do it right every time she's afraid that her magic is gone she's afraid

My head is spinning again. That same weird feeling.

MAY 14, 1992

On two separate occasions I am certain I lost time, and I wasn't asleep or zoned out. I wonder if this has been happening nonstop this last year, or if it's a last hurrah for the masses. I've also had sporadic light shows in the last few weeks.

JUNE 12, 1992

It happened again. This time I lost an hour and screwed up Jamie's schedule. It seems that now I know about the others the more aware I'm becoming of when I've lost time. It makes me feel so out of control. Like maybe they'll be able to do it any time they feel like it.

June 18, 1992

I tried so hard last night to connect with Lynn and Erin, and I couldn't do it, and I couldn't stop myself from overeating, and I lost at least another hour this morning. It's such a struggle to be at work, to get out of bed, to do anything meaningful. I'm being pulled in a million different directions.

October 27, 1992

I always thought the Cuban Missile Crisis was made public years after it happened. While watching Maria Shriver's special I realized it lasted a few weeks and everyone knew while it was happening. My father was addicted to TV news. (He could then say, "Where was I?" thirty years later when our private missiles started flying.) But missiles aimed at the U.S.? That would get his attention. The news would have been on constantly. There would have been drop drills in school, which I remember vaguely, but not in connection with this. I remember very little about being eight.

I was stunned when Howard once estimated I had lost perhaps one-half of my life this way. "Reality" becomes an extremely relative concept then.

16

Nita (The Outside Sarah)

I say things on paper I'd never have the nerve to say in person. Some of my poems I wouldn't even read out loud because they're so unlike the typical me that I'd be embarrassed to say them. People don't know what goes on in my mind most of the time. I take my frustrations out in my writing; swearing, screaming words that take some of the fight out of me.

—Nita, May 1972

I often use confusion to stay stuck, and demanding things from people is an element of my confusion. I see it as a big cover-up, which surprises me (and yes, also confuses me). I need to identify legitimate, as opposed to my scared little kid, confusion. The second kind, deep inside, I always know the real answer, but I don't want to take responsibility for knowing it.

—Nita, February 10, 1986

He says we all have a darker side
With a little grin that makes it safe
To reveal pieces of that shadowy phantom
Bit by bit into daylight and noncompromise
He thinks he knows mine well
But it's like he's got a Michelin guide
Pointing out the best attractions
And nasty detours to avoid
He's never actually been there
Or tried to traverse its minefields
We don't take the scenic route
I fear he'd no longer see the light
In my eyes trying so hard to be free
He says we all tell little white lies sometimes
Sometimes little white lies are all we tell
Till everything's so white it's dark

And who knows how we got
From there to here
On our good intentions and
Sincerest forms of superficiality

SEO, July 24, 1990

I wish I could just go poof and make everything different. New name, new focus, new career path, new opportunities. I wish.

—Nita, August 2, 1991

May 22, 1985

It's like there were two of me at group — one who was angry and hurt, and one who was observing, objectively. The angry one is so caught up in my bullshit she doesn't see anything else. I sort of spaced out (they were talking about me like I wasn't there anyway). The observer thought, "Why do I insist that these people care for me the way I want them to?" Although I'd told them three times what I really wanted, I experimented. I told them, (observing, but also humiliated), that I need them to love and care for me even when I'm not "Sarah." (The humiliation was in the way I said it — no pride, no hope, no defiance.)

Presto chango! "Of course it's okay!" (When nothing I said before was okay.) I had to totally humiliate myself to get a loving response. So their response — even though it was what I wanted — made me feel sad. Why must I go through these contortions to get what I need?

My ex-husband and I played this scene a lot. He'd say something designed to wound, and rather than show how hurt I was, I'd become angry, and chip away at him. He either exploded in anger, becoming dangerous, or he felt so terrible, he'd cry. Either way, I'd humiliate myself, say I was sorry, it was all my fault, I'm such a bad person blah blah blah. Then he'd agree. And say he loved me "anyway." In exchange for this crumb of pseudo-intimacy, I'd promise anything.

If I must humiliate myself to get love, it's far too high a price. It's really easy for them if I'm "Sarah" all the time, but Sarah isn't just fun, pretty, and together. Sarah experiences pain to grow. I was being real with them on one level, but on another, I knew Nita (which is what they got) was not real. It seemed like I could only get what I wanted by not being real, and then when I got it, it didn't feel good because of that.

Nita brought me to Howard in 1991, and acted with courage during the worst times in therapy. She was ever fearful and negative. As my history unfolded, and more alters became evident, she realized why so much of her life seemed a great mystery. Why her confusion seemed endless. Why her strongest defense all her life was to ask "why." Her life both fascinated and terrified her.

AUGUST 5, 1992

H: *I'm real impressed. I see continual signs of our integrative process happening in you. It accelerates all the time.*

N: ***But now there's more people.***

H: *That's Nita talking. (both laugh) That's just a call for me to reassure. Those other people are real helpful. Thank goodness for them!*

N: ***God, now you're going to be reading me constantly.***

H: *With me, you're under a microscope, no question. Are you feeling comfortable with me, getting into this highly intimate thing?*

N: ***Yes. I just feel insecure, generally.***

H: *That's Nita! (laughs) But it's less complicated than it was.*

N: ***(sighs) It's very complicated. It's weird to think of myself as being just another one of them.***

H: *It will make a big difference because you're all equal. That comment you made was very integrative. It's not you and them. It's every one of "us."*

N: ***Which is also a pretty scary thought.***

H: *It is, because you're not comfortable yet with the idea that an integrated person has a lot of different feelings and approaches to life. It's amazing that we've been able to stay on track, because words have not been invented to aptly describe the process, the treatment, and its dynamics. It's why I use analogies so much. But it's not about you as central person, bringing the flock in. You're really just another one of them. Even I might be an alter that doesn't exist at all in you. You don't have a rallying person in you. Someone who says, "Come on, get the little ones."*

N: ***Lynn tries.***

H: *I'm aligned with Lynn. But what I did was, I got into your "you" — your whole structure of "you."*

N: ***Oh. (laughs) You mean like right now, or what?***

H: *The whole of my existence with you. Geez! Sarah would understand this.(laughs) I can use a figurative term, and she's there. Nita, she just says, "Who me? Where are you?"*

N: ***(irritated) Oh, please.***

H: *(laughs) You really give me a hard time.*

N: ***I don't, really.***

H: *Sometimes I wonder if you just do it to make me jump through hoops. That you do understand what I'm saying.*

N: ***I don't know what you're talking about enough to make you jump through hoops.***

H: Oh, God! (laughs) That! Sometimes I feel like I'm doing "Who's On First" with you.

N: Well, sometimes you are! (both laugh) Sometimes I really don't get what you're saying.

H: Sarah knows. Talk to Sarah about it. (laughs)

AUGUST 9, 1992

Dear Howard,

Between Monday and Thursday I went from being the one who made this whole thing happen to being the Designated Problem. I'm not sure how or why this happened, but I don't like it or especially deserve it. You said I was making you jump through hoops to explain things you think are obvious. You told Melissa that my "constant need for reassurances must come off as irritating to people" and "that this is very undermining" to the process. You and she discussed how "unfortunate" it is that Nita's the one who is out front the most. I walked out feeling it wasn't safe in your office.

I've been confused about integration since day one. I don't know why I don't get it. Maybe it's like being on that Rocket To Mars. Maybe I have to land it and see for myself. Or, maybe you know enough about Mars that I'd be foolish not to know what you know before I try it. Since it's probably the most significant event of my life, I owe it to myself to keep asking until I do get it. Why you take my lack of understanding personally is way beyond me.

You've acknowledged my writing skills many times. Why are you suddenly convinced I can't understand a figurative term? Why tell me repeatedly to have Sarah explain it? Beyond being really insulting, you forget Sarah and I have been inseparable best friends for 35 years. If she could help, she would have before I even asked the question.

Maybe it's true that Nita "laughs and smiles" while she whines and seeks constant reassurances. But Nita never asked to be out front all the time, and being Nita has been hell. Even so, Nita held it together well enough to get to the point of seeing you, and it's Nita who had the courage to endure this last year. This happened despite the fact that Nita's scared out of her mind, a circumstance which might well give rise to the need for constant reassurances.

I want integration, even if I don't get it as a concept yet, and we seem close to it. Even if I am "just another alter," I'm doing the work. I'm writing this letter — not Sarah. I'm the one who shows up to see you. It's very disheartening to know that no matter what I say or do, it can and will be trivialized down to "That's Nita talking!"

Nothing in nine months has brought me closer to tears than the thought that we might have a problem, and now of all times. There's a wonderful old poem, which I didn't write, that has this line: "I love you, because you are making of the lumber of my life not a tavern but a temple." As Melissa said, your "imperfections" are not seen as such when all votes are tallied. Nobody expects you to be perfect, except maybe you.

But we're at too critical a stage for me to stop expressing myself on any topic! I need your latitude if I ask things that seem obvious. Nothing seems obvious to me now except my fear.

AUGUST 12, 1992

H: As always, I liked your letter a lot. I think you were offended by me.

N: ***(shrugs) I was totally offended.***

H: (laughs) You don't want to talk about it.

N: ***I'm glad you picked that up.***

H: Oh, yeah. I'm quick. My apologies. I'm talking to Nita today, maybe exclusively. In this process, I don't want to leave any stone unturned. I've got feelers going out in a million different directions, and it can get confusing, even for me. I can cross certain areas, maybe crudely, without knowing what the impact will be later. That's why your input is always good. Whatever I do, nothing bad is ever intended, but it doesn't mean it doesn't have a bad effect. So my apology is for not being on it as well as I wanted to be.

N: ***Yeah?***

H: (laughs) Let's see if I can do more. I get a lot from you of "You're the expert here." And "Just because you know what you're doing, doesn't mean I know. I have a right to know more, and be reassured. If I don't quite get it, I need to get it. You're not talking to an idiot. If I say I didn't get it, there's a good reason why." I agree with that. There was never an intent to dismiss or talk down to you. Even when using words like "undermine." I didn't mean in the sense that you're being difficult. If anything, you're incredibly cooperative. I get a profound sense that Nita very much is intrigued and fascinated by the subtleties of life.

N: ***Yes.***

H: And that this is to be taken seriously. Otherwise, it would certainly be insulting to you, because these are the great questions of life.

N: ***I was particularly insulted that you kept saying to talk to Sarah. I thought, "No! You talk to Sarah!" (both laugh)***

H: That's just my own ineptitude with certain aspects of what's going on. I think you already forgive me in advance. At the same time, you don't want to just let me off the hook.

N: ***Well, I want to move forward.***

H: You know what it is? You demand what you should demand.

N: ***Not too much, huh?***

H: No, I'm up to it. I never want to disappoint you. Transference is the feelings you have for me. Countertransference is the feelings I have for you. I have to be in touch with all that, hopefully to a greater extent than I have been. I will just try to recuperate from each blunder. Here's another extreme that sounds contradictory, but the subtlety is where we will talk about it. On the one hand, I understand exactly what's going on, the processes, and all the terminology I throw around. I'll go so far as to call myself an "expert," even though it's not my specialty, because I pay close attention to global and specific issues. On the other hand, I don't know anything about what I'm doing.

N: ***(alarmed) Oh, don't say that! Tell me you know what you're doing.***

H: *Understand the subtleties.*

N: ***It's a good thing you didn't say that a year ago.***

H: *I even debated saying it now. No, I have complete confidence about how we'll proceed. But because it's you, and you're unique, as all people are, I never did it with you, so it's uncharted. I'm still left with anxiety about the specific unknown all of us must live with. I play to the expertise more than to the uncharted, because I know it's there. But I'll always be honest with you. If I don't know, I'll tell you. Which could make you wonder, "Well, hell! If you don't, who does?! What am I doing here?" (she nods) What Nita doesn't have that I'm hoping can be developed is a willingness to take certain leaps of faith without having specificity that there is enough substance and track record. That the unknown is exactly where we want to be. The best way to get into it is to do your step work and research, your real knowledge work. Then the part that's unknown, you don't have anxiety about because you recognize it has to be unknown, and you jump.*

N: ***Seems like a lot to ask from the endless why person.***

H: *She demands a lot of me; I demand back. If it's an issue, she has to make some peace with it because I don't believe her way of resolving it is to continue to ask why. At some point, if it is endless, a leap must be taken based on "I have enough information now. I'm not bothered by the gap that exists." Why does that make you feel so down? (she shrugs) Maybe the gap isn't little enough to make the leap. Maybe you do need to ask more why's. A time will come when, even though you could ask a million more, you still aren't going to get any better information.*

N: ***I guess it's just the whole thing is too weird. Nita exists by committee.***

H: *Why do you suppose? Why her?*

N: ***Nita was anyone who would be called Nita. It just happens to be me. Nita was manufactured to fill the need to have someone there instead of Anita.***

H: *Is she real?*

N: ***(laughs) I'm here! What does that mean?***

H: *I don't know if that scares you.*

N: ***Even if I am just another alter, it still all comes down to me to do whatever needs to be done.***

H: The reason I asked if she is real — okay, yes, she's real. You're Nita. But when the committee conferred, did they take a little of this, a little that?

N: No, it could have been anybody. And Sarah came into the picture because she's Nita's opposite number. Where Nita's afraid to try new things, Sarah will. Nita needs things in black and white, Sarah sees shades of gray. They realized that Nita by herself would look too abnormal. She'd be too paranoid; too scared.

H: Sarah balances it?

N: Yeah, and hopefully Sarah's the one they see.

H: Your splitting off may also have been an act of integration. Balance exists in these alters like a distortion of a real person. We all need some kind of balancing. What makes this particularly tricky, is that the very thing that created balance in you is having these alters. Now we're saying, they won't be out anymore. You'll be one person. It's getting to the point where everything you do, I call it an act of integration. "What's integration, if everything is? Then nothing's integration." (she nods) There's something else that transcends anything I can say or do. Like it or not, within you operates a great wisdom. These people existed for a specific reason. Probably a good one. There's a great utility to your why's. I haven't played that up enough. The problem is, I become aware of something, and deal with it, hopefully effectively enough that you will, too. But I wonder what else we ignore since we can't run with all these balls and hold them at the same time.

N: I don't know how to say this. I think you get led to where you need to go, whether I want you to go there, anyway.

H: I think you're right. I wouldn't have changed any of the interactions we've had for anything, because they all bore fruit. I've got good instincts.

N: I don't trust my own.

H: So when I'm operating on mine, even if there's logic connected to them — they aren't just out there in some void — you must wonder where in the hell I'm coming from. "Come on! It's my life we're talking about. You can't go on gut feelings here." (she nods) I can't tell you why I talk to specific people, but I know I've always talked to the right ones. I don't even make a game plan. I'm aware of a competition to express. At the same time, there are others who probably just want to lay low, by choice. Others could be greatly amused. Others might say, "Wait, wait! Warm! Cold!" Like we're playing that game. Do you have the most credibility about warm/cold?

N: I don't think so.

H: I was thinking the same thing. Yet, I felt you'd be insulted if I deferred to other people.

N: ***Lynn is probably better at that.***

H: What do you think about forcing you to speak about what the others think or feel, without hearing from them directly? We'll just say Nita understands what's going on and has the credibility. Nita got us here to begin with, and acted with great courage. Nita's paying for this. Not only you are central, but you are the credible one.

N: ***I don't know enough to be credible.***

H: Well, maybe you do. Don't defer it.

N: ***(sighs) Maybe I'm tired of being central, and doing all the work. I'm not the right person for this. I feel like I'm not good enough.***

H: How many times can I say you are? There's a point where it's plain stupid not to relinquish the way you act and deal with things. You look at me, dejected, saying, "That's just the way it is. I'm not good enough." All that rap. I'm not going to debate your worthiness. You honestly don't know that you're okay; that you're worth it?

N: ***No.***

H: You don't know better? I'm amazed. I can't get fancy. I can't get you from your blind side, and have you say, "Ah, I guess I am worth a lot. I'm a good person."

N: ***I felt especially not good enough after listening to all those people talk. None of them like me. They say it's just too bad Nita's out front. Yeah, it's too bad. I didn't volunteer for this assignment. And I wasn't good enough to start with, or Sarah wouldn't have been necessary.***

H: I want you to develop patience, and have some resilience. You see it in me. You criticize me for insulting and offending you, and not for a moment do I think, "She doesn't respect me. She isn't being helped by this process." You knew I was acting in your best interests. I say you're impatient, which doesn't mean you're not good.

N: ***I think I'm pretty resilient already, or I wouldn't be here.***

H: I'm not talking about the resilience you have, I'm talking about the resilience you don't have. If I want you to be better, it doesn't mean you're not good.

N: ***You want me to be more resilient; more patient. Fine.***

H: I feel like you don't believe we're making connections today.

N: ***I keep kind of...flipping in and out.***

H: I'm reluctant to talk to anyone else because I don't want it to play back to you as, "You see? He can't get the information from me; he's got to talk to somebody else."

N: ***I'd rather you talked to somebody else.***

H: Oh? You don't like this anymore.

N: ***Not particularly. But, I just think it moves faster.***

H: That was sort of the rationale, and you were offended by it. (laughs)

N: You should put Lynn in charge.

H: Okay. But you say that defeated; dejected.

N: Probably everything we discuss will make me feel like that.

H: Are you giving me permission to put Lynn in charge? (she laughs) You see it like committing suicide?

N: From what she just said? "Do whatever you think is best, Howard?"

H: You're cynical. I wish your life could be easier.

[Later, talking to Lynn]

H: This letter Nita wrote, she was really pissed off. This could have been her very astute way of shaking the whole system up, and saying, "Look. I did your work for you. Get someone else to kick around. You have no idea how wonderful I made things for everybody." Only she could never say a thing like that. She had to find a way to get to me for the next important step. You know how I say I'm always pleased to get the letters? They're really positive and insightful. I was just as pleased to get this one. I didn't mean to hurt her feelings, but I felt like, wow, something happened here.

L: You didn't see the first draft, either. She was really mad. And hurt. She felt if she's just another alter, she's nothing. Like the whole last year didn't count for anything.

H: She knows better. I will take her dissatisfaction to a point, and then I won't anymore. She'll just have to trust me. There's another obvious thing I didn't pick up. Why were these letters so positive, but whenever I saw her it was like, "Wait! What about the letter?! You said all these good things!" (laughs) She will never tell me anything positive.

Nita worked incessantly toward integration till she reached a point of mental exhaustion and depletion. She acknowledged that her negativity was holding back the process to which she was so firmly committed. In the following segment, fighting her fear, she agreed with Howard to bring Lynn outside continuously.

AUGUST 12, 1992

H: How are you feeling? Other than weird? You're more like Lynn than you may know.

N: Depressed. Why? I'm not more like Lynn.

H: I'd expect you to say that. When you hear this, you'll get real pissed off.

N: I'm so predictable.

H: If you'll notice, you're going full form now. I'm not worried about that, if it's what you do. You've brought this to the place which illuminates all the significance and essence of the issues involved here. Growing up issues, self-esteem, survival. Not to mention intellectual, emotional, and creative functioning. It's really amazing. But you never hear stuff like that 'cause you can't.

N: ***It feels like a failure.***

H: I'm going to say something you need to understand. You've become — I don't mean to insult you — more of a caricature of the traits we're talking about. Which indicates that as we speak you're allowing Lynn to take her place. You've done some incredible work. There's a reason why you don't cry, by the way. Nita thinks she's not worth anything. However bad she feels, she can't cry about it. If she was worth something, it would be something she could consider sad. That's how bad it is for her. She doesn't think she is worth the tear. It's not going to be a problem anymore.

N: ***'Cause Nita's not going to be anymore.***

H: The best of Nita will survive. The stuff that's not so great won't have an overwhelming influence. We're not getting rid of you.

N: ***That's what it feels like. I know it's for the best.***

H: You trust me, don't you?

N: ***Yes. It's just kind of upsetting.***

H: I imagine it would be. Do you know how Lynn feels about it?

N: ***She's happy. (going numb) It'll go faster. But I don't get to see the end of it.***

H: It's like running a race, and wanting to be at the end to see the triumph. But the parts of you that hold you back are enough of a detractor from the end goal that it's really impossible for you to be there in the way you're talking about. In a way, none of you can be there. I talked to Lynn, not like she's the end product, but it's her turn to take the baton in this race.

N: ***Will I lose me?***

H: No, it's something different about you, but it's not a loss. I recognize it feels like one.

N: ***It feels like I'm giving up, never to be heard from again.***

H: This may be something you put in the category of "Don't worry about it." You won't be unhappy.

N: ***I guess not many people are offered the opportunity to be somebody else.***

H: That's right. But bear in mind, you're not becoming anyone different. You are all these people. "Is that really not integration because we're just switching one for another, and we've still basically got the problem?" Yes, but it isn't the same problem. We're selecting an alter who is conducive to the issues in your life now, which will allow a greater degree of access to the others. So there's enhancement and enrichment to look forward to. It's not just a substitute. It truly is integration because it's calling on the better parts of you to operate out there.

N: ***It's like dying.***

H: I understand that you feel that way. But it's the most negative way of putting it, which is what we're trying to cope with here. This switch makes it very concrete why you should think things will be better. An alter is being tapped who operates on all the things you were trying to change. You wanted to feel and function differently.

N: ***You would never talk to me again?***

H: No, I most definitely will.

N: ***I have a real helpless feeling about it.***

H: One of the problems is that I can't alleviate all the feelings you have because part and parcel of what you do is to come from negativity. I can't expect you to say, "Go for it. For the first time I feel I have a real shot at solving this problem." You don't talk that way.

N: ***(sinking deeper) If I want to say something, I'll never be able to.***

H: Tell me if this is true: you don't want to talk.

N: ***At all? I wouldn't have any control over it.***

H: You're saying it's all or nothing?

N: ***I'd only be able to talk when you wanted to talk to me.***

H: My thinking is that the need to switch over and talk to various alters goes away. Something less than that kind of integration would be that if Nita were to talk, I'd bring her out. Nobody else would think to do it unless they actually understand the dynamics. It could be, in some unconscious way you were aware it was coming to this, and it was sad to you.

N: ***I did think about this.***

H: You wanted me to pursue it, but couldn't actively get me to do it.

N: ***It was sort of like "What if?" You don't know if things can actually work.***

H: I'm feeling very strong and positive about this move.

N: ***And it's forever?***

H: If you mean, is it forever good to do this, yes. Is Lynn the end product? I really don't know. It's more complicated in the long run than just who gets to be you. I thought you'd find that amusing.

N: ***That's what I've always said to you. I was afraid I wasn't going to be me. And I'm not.***

H: What if I said, "Yes, you are right. It comes down to that."

N: ***I have no choice. (He looks skeptical) It's always been my goal to get this over with as quickly as possible. If this is the way to do it, then it must be done.***

H: The essence of you will still exist.

N: In a way, it's a relief.

H: I sense that, too.

N: And in a way, it's just a big failure.

H: I can tell you how it's not a failure, but you won't buy it. Maybe in some deep way, you're with me, and not saying anything. But if it comes down to you saying "I failed," so what? You're going to triumph in the ultimate of your existence anyway.

N: You believe that?

H: Oh, yeah. No hesitation at all. Are you going to get used to the idea? Do you want time with it, first?

N: No! I want to do it. But it's like being sent on a secret space mission, and you can't tell anybody that you might never come back.

H: The most Lynn will probably say is, "I feel better. We've resolved a lot of issues and integration has occurred. I feel more positive; more upbeat; I have more energy." Everyone will say that Nita, who changed her name to Sarah, finally got the therapy she needed. They will all wonder, and no one will really be wise that Lynn has become central.

N: By then I won't care anyway, will I?

H: No, you won't. I think you have a right to fuss, but it's about something that won't matter.

N: So what if you could just switch to Ernie right now? Would you do it? You said Ernie is your strength.

H: I'd go with it! Are you kidding? Who needs to be Howard? I'm not making fun of it. You're asking if there's a way I can be my best without steroids? I'd do it (snaps fingers).

N: Then I guess I'll do it, too.

H: Okay!...I want to make sure you get prepped for it emotionally.

N: This isn't even the ultimate dangerous act, is it?

H: I don't believe so.

N: Great. (sighs) If we did it tonight, what would happen?

H: We want to look for good physiological signs, like the ability to see and focus. I don't want you to have headaches. You'll walk out of here feeling good. But you've got to be okay with, "God, that was weird!"

N: If I'm Lynn will I think that way?

H: You'll think, "That was weird, but it makes sense. We should have done this before." There should be fluidity, and a sense of completion. Certainly there will be all kinds of detail work to be done. But you'll have the tools now, with peak performance operating for you.

N: And when I'm Lynn, then what?

H: That's too broad a question. We'll talk; we'll reflect. We'll get a program started.

N: I want to say yes, but I'm scared.

H: I don't think there's any way you can do this without being scared. You want to go for it now?

N: (sighs)....Sure.

H: Do you have as much confidence as you can muster, in this moment?

N: (terrified, becoming increasingly disoriented) I think so.

H: Do you trust what's going on?

N: Yes.

H: Do you believe it's a good move?

N: This is all on tape for later if it goes horribly wrong?

H: Yeah, you're covered.

N: No, you're covered. (he laughs) I'm serious!

H: I'm sorry. I feel a deep sense of responsibility about this. There's no way I can be here otherwise.

N: These are questions they ask people when they sign their wills.

H: Are you of sound mind? (laughs) Look, I could play this real safe, and talk psychobabble to you forever. Or I can have the guts — cause I am deeply affected by this. I don't wish any bad thing to happen to you. Forget even professionally; personally, I don't want it to happen. So if you haven't detected it, I've been talking extremely carefully. I think once we've uncovered this as the direction, anything less is just bullshit. That's the problem. Every time we uncover something, we have no choice but to walk through it. Right?

N: Yeah.

H: This whole process tonight is going to be successful.

N: (anxiety building) That's good.

H: But I need Nita. She has another role to play here. You'll see, this will work out just fine.

So Nita went inside permanently, while Lynn made her debut as the central figure in my life. Five days later, Howard again met with us, and was eager to learn how Nita had fared "on the inside."

AUGUST 17, 1992

H: How have you been the last week?

N: Kind of weird.

H: (laughs) It's real weird.

N: Kind of like having an out of body experience. Sort of not being there, but being there?

H: Would you have ever guessed we'd go this far?

*N: **I've got to the point where I believe anything is possible.***

H: Did you feel like you died?

*N: **No, just sort of like being left at the train station.***

H: Is there any way you can feel part of the triumph?

*N: **What's the triumph?***

H: Oh, give me a break. You see what's going on. Do you feel like I've killed you off?

*N: **No, I figure it was necessary. It must have taken some grit on your part to do all this. Which isn't bad.***

H: It's a good way of putting it. I wish you could be happy.

*N: **Gee, don't we all? A lot of things are moving and working out.***

H: Will you get to come to the party?

*N: **Am I invited?***

H: Oh, God. Don't you know better by now?

*N: **I doubt there'll be a choice. If it's like what you said, you won't be able to talk to us anyway if we integrate.***

H: What about the idea of not integrating in the way we first understood it, so you can always tap into this?

*N: **How is it integrated, if you can go to different people?***

H: Integration speaks more to an access to all of who you are, with ease and complete control, as opposed to making all of you one. I'm not modifying my notion of what integration is. It's always based on the essence of who you are. But integration for one person can be different for another.

*N: **I guess we won't know till it happens, will we?***

H: We're actually more in control, so our ability to predict should be increased.

*N: **Yeah, but I think Charyse is gone.***

H: Well, not in any way that's distressing to her.

*N: **I don't think the process cared whether she was distressed.***

H: The process is very dependent on how the alters feel. Integration may automatically cause some to become what we would consider one. Let's say there's a hundred, and in one fell swoop it condensed down to twenty-five. There may be this final core number of alters who, from then on, are always accessible.

*N: **Is that normal?***

H: No, that isn't normal. (laughs) Statistically speaking.

*N: **Then you're just making it up.***

H: Oh, geez. This is so negative. That's even insulting.

N: When people integrate, do they normally keep people to talk to?

H: Oh, that is normal. Integration occurs in many ways. It's not uncommon, and may be completely desirable by all central enough core alters to keep the others around. Not in a freak way, but more in a helpful way.

N: But I'm not very helpful, am I?

H: Well...(laughs) you negative person, you. You've reached a point where certain parts of you are a hindrance to what you say you want to accomplish.

N: I won't be a hindrance anymore.

H: It doesn't mean you need to be eradicated. I've considered the possibility that we could do psychotherapy with the goal to feel better as Nita. (noting her grimace) Well, there it is! You just threw it out the window!

N: Isn't that working at cross-purposes to our total goal?

H: No! Why should any alter feel distressed? Why should I make Erin feel good? Why don't I just say, "She's a little kid, she'll get over it?"

N: Because she has something you want. I don't.

H: Here's where psychotherapy comes in. I'm going to get real tough with you. If you maintain negativity, you're absolutely correct that your usefulness goes away. But if you are something more than a negative person, I want Nita's other attributes. With what we've been through, how can you maintain a negative posture? How can you tell me things aren't possible anymore? Maybe I need to talk to Peter, too.

N: He thinks you scored a coup, putting Lynn out front. Brilliant move. Check. Not quite check-mate.

H: Wouldn't Peter admit that what he called a coup, without you, would never have happened? I've got to get you to stop feeling sorry for yourself.

N: I feel like I'm holding my breath until I go zooming off into space like Charyse.

H: You won't.

N: How do you know?

H: Would Charyse, if she were here, have any regret, or was she pleased?

N: I think she was pleased.

H: There's no good reason why you should integrate in the way Charyse did. But if you did, it would only happen if you allowed it.

N: Why?

H: Because you matter. It can't be done without you. It would ultimately be what you wanted. Did Charyse commit suicide?

N: No. But I don't see that she had a choice.

H: She definitely had one. Nothing will happen against your will. Do you believe that? What's it take?

N: It's pretty scary inside, if you want to know the truth.

H: I appreciate that. I don't know if your fear is part of your negativity.

N: If this is what I am, how does therapy work on it?

H: Don't you believe people can improve things they don't like about themselves? You've never had more reason to be positive than these days. You won't lose yourself; you'll be more of who you are; the best of who you are. You've seen things happen you probably never could have dreamed before. And you were pivotal in it. You have cause to rejoice.

Howard never spoke to Nita again. Later that evening, events forced by Anita created a pathway to partial integration for the majority of my alters. Nita joined them. I believe she traveled that path willingly. Her hard-fought goal of integration gave her some peace for the first time in her life. I know she is inside me still, because I have moments of pessimism and doubt. I need reassurances occasionally. But my integrated "self" points to my progress and knows Nita does, in fact, share in my triumph.

17

Lynn

My mother was a stupid, bitter woman who thought letting me lick the spoon every Friday when she made chocolate chip cookies would somehow make up for all this crap.

—Lynn, June 1992

Lynn was my internal drill sergeant who kept chaos at bay. Nita was her external counterpart, and often they acted in tandem, although Nita did not realize this till quite late in the process. As a result, they had ongoing tensions. Lynn thought Nita was a bit stupid, but understood once she was "out front" what a limitation it placed upon whoever was the central person. Nita feared Lynn wanted to take over completely, and wasn't too far off base.

May 20, 1992

N: Who are you?

L: I'm the one who made Charlotte stop. She was telling him how bad you are.

N: Why did she do that?

L: You know all the answers already. She was afraid you would tell.

N: I was always going to tell.

L: This was much, much later. You were seven.

N: It was over by then?

L: It stopped but it wasn't over. He never really left. He still came around with his wife to play cards with mother and father.

N: But he couldn't hurt us after that.

L: He didn't have to touch you to hurt you. When he came in the bedroom you pretended to be asleep but you saw him. We all saw him. He ensured our silence. He stood in the door, laughing softly so mother and father could not hear, opening and closing his knife.

N: Did Charlotte see him?

L: Of course! And you were going to tell all over again. You were going to make them believe you, and he would never come back. But Charlotte wouldn't let you. She said you were a liar, so you fought with her. A very physical fight.

N: We did that a lot.

L: But you think about this one sometimes. I make you think about it. You pushed her and she fell onto the metal trash can. Mother gave you hell.

N: I remember that, but not what we were fighting about. Who are you?

L: I am the loudest. I wake you up without a clock. Mother was irritated beyond belief when I did that. She really hated you. And I wake you up now. You used to have such a hard time waking up, even with two alarm clocks. Did you really think you were sleeping?

N: You're waking me up? Why?

L: You need to do more things. You sleep and we worry. You might not wake up again. Like Charlotte.

N: I don't think that's possible now.

L: (sarcastic) Right. I know why Charlotte wouldn't let you tell. She thought it was over. She thought it was nap time.

N: We never talked about it again. And I forgot I was going to tell.

L: Very good! And what did Charlotte do?

N: Charlotte never got mad again.

L: Charlotte took a real long nap.

JUNE 24,1992

N: I'd like to know what you think I can do to control Lynn.

H: What's your worst fear?

N: That she'll take over again, and I won't come back.

H: Ever.

N: If nobody knows it's her. You said it's like riding a bicycle, and that frustrated me terribly. It's saying, "You've done this before. So do it now." I don't know that I've done it before.

H: I don't want you to fight with her, okay? Her intention is just to get things on an even keel. She understands subtlety and balance. Her greatest injury is probably fairness. She gets no credit for anything, and she suffers the abuses. So instead of repressing her, or overcoming her, or putting her aside, she's fine.

N: That's how I control her?

H: You control her by getting into dialogue with her. She needs to express that this is unfair, and you have to sympathize with her. If you do, she'll have no reason to take over. The reason you can't get back — if you ever feel you can't — is she's saying, "Hey, I've got the podium now. You're always pushing me aside. I'm going to say what I've got to say." Don't give her a reason to feel she must take over, and she won't. She's very pragmatic. She understands this very well.

N: Thank goodness somebody does.

H: (laughs) All the others understand pretty well, too.

AUGUST 5, 1992

H: Tell me what's been going on in the past few weeks.

L: Lots of chaos.

H: More than usual?

L: I don't have as much control over things now. I don't know what to do about it.

H: What happened to make you lose control?

L: When it all starts coming out, there's no controlling it. As long as it was our little secret, nobody knew, and everybody shut up. It's not a secret now.

H: Is there anybody who knows who shouldn't or doesn't need to?

L: It's not the fact that people know. It's the fact that we know people know. The people inside think if everybody outside knows, then it's okay to come out. So everybody wants to come out at once. And I can't stop them.

H: I see. Do you understand what integration means?

L: That it'll stop being parts, and start being a whole.

H: Right. If it integrates, then they all will be out.

L: That's not my understanding of it. If it integrates, the traits of the people who want to come out will come out, but the people themselves won't come out.

H: Let me say it another way. Do they, in some way, feel they will die if it integrates? They'll cease to be?

L: Some of them think that. Sometimes I wonder.

H: Do you think if it is demonstrated that when the ones inside integrate, and they don't die, really, the others will be impressed favorably?

L: You told Sarah that Charyse was gone, but she's not really.

H: None of them will ever be gone. That's what I'm getting at.

On August 12, 1992, Nita and Howard jointly concluded that she was holding the process back with her negativity and depression. Despite her fear, Nita agreed to switch places with Lynn as the central figure. Howard then discussed the ramifications of making a switch with Lynn.

L: ***I think I understand integration better than Nita, but that doesn't mean I really, truly understand it. I agree with it in spirit; it doesn't mean I have to know every little detail. But if you want me to lead you somewhere, I'm not sure how or where you would be led.***

H: *Why do you suppose Nita was the person by committee who was the central person?*

L: ***How shall I put this? Like, she was the next one off the assembly line?***

H: *What would your life have been like if you'd been out front? Would you have been in the same career? Married the same person?*

L: ***I never would have married that man!***

H: *So your life would have been completely different. Did you ever want to be the central one?*

L: ***That wasn't how it was supposed to be. I would have done things differently, I think. But who knows? Maybe I would have made wrong choices, too.***

H: *Do you think Nita ever feels like, "I don't want to be the central one"?*

L: ***If she could have gotten out of it, she would have long ago. She's hated it.***

H: *I don't know how dangerous this is, but what do you think about the idea of doing a switch here?*

L: ***I get to be out front all the time? (laughs) Is that possible?***

H: *Well, why not?*

L: ***I'd be out front pretending to be Sarah, who's really Nita? Oh, dear! That would be...interesting.***

H: *I want to know if you think there's any danger in it. Some kind of mental collapse.*

L: ***Only one person can be out front at a time. Obviously there were times when others were out, and Nita always came back.***

H: *I'm wondering if...you're the central one?*

L: ***What does that do?***

H: *You express yourself with more confidence. Your recovery time seems to be very quick. You don't have any more insights, and you're not a better person, than Nita. It's just your characteristics are conducive to at least a therapeutic working through. Maybe that's very practical. Nita has no more claim to being central than you.*

L: ***For how long?***

H: *Is there a problem? What if it was forever?*

L: ***Forever? Most people who know Nita would see a difference right away.***

H: You'll want people to say, "Gee, you've changed. You seem great. You're up." Part of integration is that, yes, there is a change.

L: But how is that helping integration? How does that make it go faster?

H: You're a vehicle for change that moves quicker and more positively than Nita. Nita may have gone as far as she can. She got you here; she did it. Maybe she can rest from the worrying.

L: She'll worry whether she's out front or not.

H: So maybe it's not in your best interest that she be out front, although I am validating that wherever she does worry, there can be a legitimacy to it that's worth exploring. But for the purpose of super-accelerating, maybe we shouldn't be stupid about this. We could figure you're right in position. I don't know that there is a better person.

L; I don't think there is.

h: A little ego, that's great. Exactly what I'm looking for. Why don't we have you leave the office today, and be the central one for the rest of what we do here?

L: (laughs) Oh, my God! It's so strange. Is that normally done?

H: I don't know if the textbook says, "Never, ever allow the other person to leave." I have an instinct about it, whatever the textbook says.

L: But I don't know what the deal is, because there's a lot of concentration in doing this. Focusing on an object helps. For some reason.

H: This is good. I like what I'm hearing.

L: Like this cup.

H: Oh! And when you don't have the object. . .

L: It scatters.

H: I noticed with each person that the cup is very much a prop.

L: Yes. It makes me wonder though, if I really could learn how to do this. I could try it.

H: What you're demonstrating, and how you're talking, isn't really far from how Nita sounds. Did you know that? There's the same sense of humor. Same intonations and intellectual level. Maybe you're more alike than not. The troublesome part is the negativity and bitterness. The difference between Nita and Lynn may be very subtle. I don't know if that's disconcerting to hear.

L: I prefer to think I am the good things of Nita, and not any of the crap. What does that have to do with the cup?

H: Didn't we talk about Dumbo's feather before? That's the focus. But as you've been talking to me, you're more integrated than you may be aware. You moved in and out of these alters with no difficulty whatsoever.

L: ***That was just her basic freaking out. But now she's kind of accepted it. That's why it moves faster.***

H: *I want to try something with you. You've looked at me a few times.*

L: ***Yeah, but it's just like a real quick break.***

H: *Does it ever threaten the — what do we call it — connection?*

L: ***It can. It gets kind of indistinct.***

H: *Let's test it, okay? I think you're up to it. I'm not worried.*

L: ***You're going to take my cup.***

H: *Yeah, I want you to give it to me. We'll both learn something. (he takes it)*

L: ***(instantly disoriented) It's like spinning.***

H: *All right. Here, take the cup back. Take it back.*

L: ***Oh, God....Wow, everything's going around. (he puts the cup in her hand)***

H: *I want to talk to Lynn. I gave it back without any problem, right?*

L: ***(dizzy) Yeah, you did.***

H: *I'm not tossing you out into the world. Have you noticed, when we get together, we test a new thing all the time? If that isn't accelerating, I don't know what is. We don't do much that's safe, meaning, we've never been there before. We always go to another place.*

L: ***(sighs) Yeah. Interesting.***

H: *I believe we can mechanically manipulate these boundaries. The better parts of you will operate unimpeded by the parts that aren't so great. You're going to get peak performance.*

L: ***By doing what? Like giving you the cup?***

H: *The cup is just a demonstration that this boundary truly exists between alters. You can feel the switchover. That's why your head is spinning.*

L: ***Do you think if you took the cup longer, it'll go away?***

H: *Yeah. We'll increase the time so you can exist as Lynn. But understand, it isn't like there's Lynn, and then all these others. These are all you. The idea is to bring the best out in you. Lynn has some qualities we want operating out in the world. It isn't like Nita went away and her usefulness is gone. It's more that she's done her work. It's the simplest way to create improvement. From what everyone says, Nita didn't have any real claim to being central, other than her number was up.*

L: ***True.***

H: *Then why not choose it, instead of on chance, on what's required now? You have good ego strength. You're saying, "Just give me a chance! Someone's got to do it." That's healthy and positive. It does not represent a failure on Nita's part.*

*L: **I don't understand how we get past this dizzy part.***

H: Do you believe doing a switch is a viable direction?

L: Yes.

H: Then let's play with the boundaries, and see how you do with it. Nita and I get along because the others have some way of expressing themselves through her. My feeling, quite strongly, is they can be accessed through anybody. These alters are all very distinct, and their place for being has real purpose. So it wouldn't make any difference who is central. You're on the second leg of the relay race.

*L: **I agree with what you say in principle, but that little demonstration took me aback. I didn't think there'd be that much of a problem.***

H: I wasn't surprised at all. It confirmed that the switchover can happen. It's not just a minor, subtle thing. It's a real shift if Lynn walks out of this office and functions in a more positive, progressive, and ego-strength manner. I say we try that one again.

*L: **Try the cup thing again? (groans)***

H: How bad was it?

*L: **It was spinning pretty well. There was an after-effect that sort of echoed.***

H: Are you completely better?

*L: **Right now I am.***

H: So you did recover. What if you give me the cup and look at me?

*L: **I don't think I can do that for very long. If the switch is made...there are some of us who don't need to be called to come out, but I don't know how this affects the whole thing.***

H: That's what I was asking before: does Nita somehow provide a channel for the others to come out? My hunch is, quite confidently, we won't lose anything, and we'll gain everything. There is no good reason for Nita to be central; it just happened. Her value is still important, but peak performance cannot be accomplished with negative thinking. Lynn now demonstrates the person who provides the mindset for peak performance. This, of course, does not mean we're going to change your name.

*L: **And when they say, "What happened to you, Sarah?" (laughs) I'll say, "Oh, Howard's wonderful!"***

H: You'll say, "If anyone tells you therapy's a bunch of shit, they don't know what they're talking about."

*L: **And they all lived happily ever after.***

H: Don't get cynical on me now! But, as a matter of fact, they did.

*L: **(laughs) That's what I want!***

H: This seems to be the direction I asked you for, and got it. I'm really grateful.

Virtually all the alters experienced dizziness and blurred vision when trying to focus on something other than the cup, or their fingers. The following conversation details the efforts Lynn and Howard made to bring Lynn literally into Nita's focus, to enable Lynn to drive home that same evening.

H: I'm feeling really confident about this now.

L: I can tell! You've done this before?

H: (laughs) Yes and no. I've never done it with you.

L: But with other people? Okay.

H: All situations are different. I think there's the expectation that you won't be able to focus, and it's not true. You've just become accustomed to talking with me without other distractions. But there are times you integrate the rest of me and the world around you and your environment.

L: Not very often.

H: Don't play to the "not very often" — the point is, you do it.

L: (with resolve) Yes, I've done it a couple of times. But it's very quick, almost a blur.

H: I want you to look at that lampshade to your right.

L: (tries to turn her gaze) I feel like I'm glued to the spot.

H: That's just a feeling. Take a deep breath....You're real close to it. You haven't lost your consciousness. Keep your eyes closed, and turn your head toward the lampshade.

L: Keeping my eyes closed is not a real good idea, either.

H: That hurts? You're still here.

L: (sighs) It's better than taking the cup away.

H: What we're doing, so you'll know? We're finding the place where you have a little discomfort, but not a lot. That's just anxiety.

L: Is that what it is? It's not real?

H: Well, "just" doesn't mean it isn't real. You deal with anxiety by taking deep breaths. Don't stop breathing during this process. What are you doing?

L: I'm trying to make myself turn toward the lamp! (laughs)

H: See if you can tilt your head back. Don't turn it, there you go, you've got it. That worked.

L: (mutters) Yeah, no problem. I can't keep my eyes closed forever.

H: Open your eyes. Look straight ahead at the wall. Very good!

L: I'm going cross-eyed. Oh, it's hard!

H: Bring your eyes down at the moment you feel it's too much. Wow! You're increasing it all the time. You're very gutsy. I love it. It's just what we're looking for here.

L: ***(smiles) You're just saying that.***

H: Ah, come on! I'm impressed! I'll go out on a limb and say it. This is so neat!

L: ***Oh, geez. It's doubling.***

H: You would have had more anxiety if we hadn't done this tonight. You're going to be so happy.

L: ***Oh, God.***

H: I want you to look at the wall without closing your eyes.

L: ***That's so hard!***

H: It's just a reflex action. What's the feeling?

L: ***Like I can't breathe.***

H: You're there....You knew this was going to happen.

L: ***It's like the wall is so white, it almost hurts.***

H: We probably could have done something less stressful. But you're so far into mastering this, I don't think we need to try it. I've never seen you so healthy.

L: ***Lynn?***

H: It's you, don't get it confused. I've never seen you, the embodiment of you, so healthy. So positive. You look like the long jumper who's psyched himself up, and is getting ready to take the jump. You look great! You were bold and courageous enough to say, "Okay, let's do the switchover tonight." You didn't want to live with it for a week.

L: ***That would have been hard for Nita.***

H: I didn't want to put her through that. Where you're at now, you've been before, and you'll be able to go home just fine.

L: ***Oh, gosh. A small victory.***

H: Ah, such enormous triumph. This is really wonderful. Think of all the breakthroughs we've been through. Lots, right? So many that it's like...

L: ***Ripley's Believe It Or Not.***

H: Now this one on top of it.

L: ***It's a little weird, don't you think?***

H: Well, sure! (laughs) It's very weird. But it just never ceases to amaze me.

L: ***That I can top myself weirdly?***

H: Oh, yeah! Imagine the next time we get together!

L: ***(laughs) What will it be like? I will be too happy, I'm sure.***

H: You will bounce in here. (laughs) Wearing a jogging suit.

L: ***I'll have so much to tell you.***

H: You know what it is? Whatever it takes to bring about the full scale com-

pletion of what you attempted from the moment we met each other, is going to take place. It'll all be legal, too.

L: ***(laughs) It better be. I know some good lawyers.***

H: *You know how you were feeling before? "This doesn't feel right. This isn't life?" What you're having now is what was meant to be. Lynn comes with that peak performance. Nita always found a way to see the worst in it. There was a need to do that before, but not now. Would you mind giving me the cup? (she groans) Dumbo's feather, remember? (he takes it)*

L: ***(dizzy) Oh, God!***

H: *You can fly! All around the tent. And you can make fun of all those people.*

L: ***Oh, geez.***

H: *This switch is not as fancy a trick as you may think. This is a real important moment, and yet, it's also very predictable, and obvious.*

L: ***(having trouble focusing) What is? That I would take over?***

H: *I've avoided the word "takeover." It makes it sound like an uprising; a coup.*

L: ***She's not in this place anymore.***

H: *You know what I would like to do? But I don't think it's wise. I was thinking of talking to Nita, and asking her "How is it?" So she could confirm it wasn't that bad.*

L: ***So you'll sleep better tonight?***

H: *Thank you for knowing me very well.(both laugh)*

L: ***You can sleep better just on general principles.***

H: *I will talk with her again another time. How do you feel?*

L: ***I'm dizzy....(gives a mock scream) I'm fine.***

H: *You see? You're okay. Sense of humor intact.*

L: ***But I still can't see. It just goes — whoa! — out of focus.***

H: *I think you're dizzy because you're saying "This isn't me, anymore. This is like I switched my brain."*

L: ***I did switch my brain! (groans) Oh, God!***

H: *"How do I get you to understand?!" (she laughs) It is a switch.*

L: ***It's the weirdest feeling! You don't feel like Frankenstein?***

H: *A little bit.*

L: ***(laughs) I knew it! It's got to be pretty neat for you, to see this happening in front of your eyes.***

H: *I can't deny it....It's really bright in here. (walks back and forth in front of her) Am I in your field of vision?*

L: ***(laughs) You look like a duck. Howard the Duck.***

H: My kid says that to me all the time.

L: Don't take it personally! I'm just reveling in my freedom here.

H: I will accept the slings and arrows that Lynn hurls at me. I asked for it, after all.

L: (laughs) Yes, you did! I'll remind you of that.

H: Yes, every time you do a zinger. You know what? You're going to find you have a different body image. How you walk, or whatever you do, you'll do it differently. Probably more healthy, with more flair. Don't be thrown by it. You might find you like different foods, or have different interests in TV and music.

L: (laughs) It's just like Alakazam!

H: You might like different colors.

L: You are Frankenstein! And I am your monster!

H: Nita liked gray. All of a sudden you'll start dressing in yellows. (laughs)

L: (still dizzy) Oh, God!...This isn't like a pill that wears off, right? I'm not going to wake up and be Nita tomorrow?

H: It's not likely. But if it happens, and you discover you're Nita? Five deep breaths, focus on an object, and bring you back. Don't ever be dissuaded — imprint this in your mind — if you find yourself being Nita. Don't say "It didn't work."

L: I can always come back.

H: If you can't do it, I can. But, you'll be able to. It'll be the first thing you think about when you wake up tomorrow.

L: Who I am?

H: Sure, did it work? Was it a dream? You'll do all that. We're going to wire this thing in. It could happen that you'll wake up and say, "Lynn!" Best thing. I'd love it. But if it doesn't, don't worry one bit. Of course, if it's Nita, she'll make a big deal about it. I want to get through to Nita on this, too. Be cool with it. Look what we're doing here. It's a big deal. We're looking for acceleration, and we've done it.

AUGUST 13, 1992

I am Lynn. I'm out front now instead of Nita. It's very strange. I don't know how many times I've thought, "If I were her, I wouldn't do that." Suddenly, there are no limitations. The freedom is overwhelming. I'll get used to it. Everything looks a little different now. I feel an energy which may be nerves; this just happened a few hours ago. I can't sleep; not because I'm worried about anything. I could make this endless list of things I want to do.

Howard is great! I can't imagine what Nita was so worried about. I figure it couldn't get any worse than it already was, so what's the big deal about trying something new? Life is too short to screw around like we've been doing. No more!

AUGUST 17, 1992

L: ***I talked to Nita on the computer this morning. I took the chance to see if anybody talked back to me.***

H: *How's she doing?*

L: ***Depressed. I think she felt not good enough.***

H: *In certain ways, I suppose that's true.*

L: ***Despite all her limitations, she did a hell of a lot.***

H: *Yeah, she's a hero. With all she had to deal with, she did the very best with it, above and beyond whatever could have been expected. She saved all of your lives. I ended up feeling sad, too. You do that, and then discard the person, like they did their job.*

L: ***That's what worried me about it, because she said she'd never talk to you again. I thought, oh, my God, what happened if they're all gone, and she was right?***

H: *You can shrug that off, or I can tell you the practicalities if that were to happen. You want to know something? So what? Not that you should be worried. . .*

L: ***(incensed) Easy for you to say!***

H: *If, in your being central, the need for the others goes away, or in some subtle but profound way they trickle into the central part without having to split off in such profound ways that might be integration, in and of itself. You've already experienced something like that. If it's not integration, even then, so what? If the central person is carrying on in a way that brings about the greatest productivity in your personal purpose in life, so what? If there's a casualty — or casualties — experienced, so what?*

L: ***That's very callous. You've been dealing with Nita for the last year, and to say, "So what?" if she's a casualty — it's pretty cold.***

H: *I don't mean it that way. We're not killing her off. Even if that happened, isn't it better than what was? If you had to go with the highest possibility for the greatest productivity, isn't it better this way?*

L: ***Yes.***

H: *I think I misspoke when I said "So what?" Because I like everyone. And it's all really neat. Isn't it?*

L: ***(laughs) What were you thinking about when you went home last Wednesday night?!***

H: *I was thinking it was neat. That's as profound as it gets for me. (both laugh) I thought you and Nita were incredibly courageous. I think you're all wonderful!*

Throughout this session, Howard spoke to several alters, returning to Lynn each time, and finding her increasingly disoriented and dizzy. He saw two possibilities. Either she just needed time to adjust to the switching; or, the integrative process was closing up access between alters, resulting in her distress. Two opposite possibilities, both of which required time to verify.

H: What do you think of this idea? I said I'd talk to the others. What if I didn't?

L: Forever?

H: Don't get into forevers. I don't know yet. What if doing this back and forth between alters is not where it's at?

L: What's the work, if it's not that?

H: The work may be done. "This isn't done! This is not what I want!" No, but the basic work may have really been done. The problem with what I'm telling you right now is you're still coming back into focus.

L: I'm fine. I don't look like it, probably. My head is still sort of circling the planet.

H: The work is life. You said your experiences with people you talked to outside were rather good.

L: Yeah. Everyone said, "What happened to you?" It was all positive. I stuck with the analogy of the relay race, and everyone thought it made good sense. Everyone was happy, and thought it was a good move.

H: Did that make Nita feel worse?

L: Not worse, because she wants this. But, just like, "Why don't they tell me this to my face? I'm such a drag, or what?" There was no "Gee, will I ever be able to talk to Nita again?" She wants them to miss her.

H: They can't understand a thing like that unless they're really involved the way we are. At that superficial level they'd say "Oh great! You'll have a nicer personality!" Of course, it's like they just killed off who knows how many people in your existence. I'm glad you shared that. I thought you'd use vague terms, but you were very specific. You've been open about it.

L: We left it kind of up in the air last week, whether we would tell anybody. But the whole thing since day one has been run without secrets. It didn't seem right. Nita had a plan, and it seems to fall out of the plan to start hushing things up.

H: Do you see how Nita lives? You respect where she was trying to take this, and the integrity she had about doing it in a certain way. It doesn't mean there shouldn't or couldn't be a new game plan, but the basic integrity remains. Nita's influence is here with us. They're all here with us.

18

The Inside Sarah

Inside Sarah's decided to be a free person, and to let the feelings be whatever they are, and not be afraid of them. Being afraid prevents you from accessing what would naturally come out. Sarah doesn't worry that if she has the feeling someone will get mad at her. She doesn't keep it to herself. Even if someone did get mad at her for having a feeling, she feels free to have it anyway, and to express it. It's very healthy.

—Howard to Erin, December 10, 1992

There's a part of me
That dances far into the night
Long after the music stops playing
It's the heart of me
Looking past the shadows to the light
No matter what the darkness is saying
There's the best of me
That touches you with this song
You whisper other verses now and then
When the rest of me
Is lonely and not feeling very strong
You know someday I'll sing again

SEO/04/15/88

I presented to Howard with Inside Sarah in tow. She was my best friend since earliest childhood, so I know her well. She was a beautiful child. She was often told as an adult that she could have been a model, even when our body was overweight. Of course, Nita would have died first, so there was never any question of that happening.

Sarah was the brightest, most beloved child. I believed that if my mother just met her, and gave her a chance, all would be redeemed. The catch was, I couldn't afford to be wrong. Sarah's existence would be evidence of insanity, and I believed my mother just waited for some reason to get rid of me. So she never knew Sarah. My father, however, saw more of her because he doted on me when I was very young.

As I grew older, I had only to think of Sarah to feel better. When I went out with friends, I took her along. She was socially at ease and adept. My hair is thin and mousy; hers held the curls and looked good. She understood makeup in ways I never did, which caused a stir when people saw Nita all done up. She seldom concerned herself with what anyone else thought about her, while Nita obsessed about blending in, and fading out.

Sarah brought good things out in me, and encouraged me to participate in ways I never otherwise would have tried. She insisted that I submit a poem to my school's creative arts magazine, which won first prize. I was convinced it would not be published, much less win. She was the creative force behind a dance group I led in high school which auditioned for the annual spring show. I choreographed the majority of a dance for twelve Raggedy Ann's and Andy's. We did not win the audition, but I was complimented. And I've always said I don't know how to dance.

JULY 20, 1990

Dear Hank,

On July 16th you met the real Sarah, who wants to have fun; who doesn't analyze things to death; who acts instead of reacts. I think she surprised you. Don't you like her better? I do! And everything's been so boring and un-fun since. So why can't it be like that always?[1]

My vision of Inside Sarah is a vibrant, beautiful woman, creative and innovative, gracious, desirable, and loved. She took care of herself when no one else wanted to. She found humor in situations no one else would have tried. She worked hard at her art, and played equally hard. She bought beautiful clothes which fit her self-image, but not our body. Only Inside Sarah could believe in possibilities becoming reality.

MARCH 12, 1985 *[letter to friend]*

I have so much to tell you! Sarah is becoming a very big deal in my life, and she's explaining a lot to me. I got out my Board of Directors, and was surprised to discover she's not even on it. How can that be? She's all the positive voices combined. She is everything that is good about me.

Sarah's the one who takes risks. She knows she deserves good things, and is willing to fight for them. Sylvia said, "Sarah knows she deserves good things, while Nita makes sure she doesn't get them." That's true. I went into her office in a burst of energy — totally Sarah — and midway, before her eyes, I turned into Nita, almost crying. Our group assignment was, "What kind of shoe are you? What kind of shoe would you like to be?" I described myself as very functional, colorless, old, and rundown. What I'd like to be is a pastel pink dancing shoe, very frivolous, expensive but sophisticated. Sylvia said, "Go out and buy those shoes." It was like a shadow crossed my face. I thought, "Sarah is the one who wears shoes like that — not me." I felt this overwhelming sadness! It was so strange.

Since I was young, Sarah was always getting herself into situations where she had to be rescued. When I was very young, she was rescued by QuickDraw McGraw! Mary said I must give up the idea that I have to be in a situation where I need to be rescued to get positive attention from people.

Last summer you said, "Until you figure out your role in your disasters, you will keep having them." I think Sarah's intentions have always been good. Rescue is synonymous with love. Somebody cares. I am only beginning to accept and feel how much more healthy I am when I don't perceive myself as needing to be rescued. Isn't this great? I feel like I've discovered the key that sets me free.

MARCH 27, 1985 — GROUP THERAPY NOTES:

How am I going to get these shoes? By creating experiences where I know I am worthy of all that pink dancing shoes connote. The fun, fantasy, acceptance, and love. By allowing myself to believe in the Sarah in me — and to know that all things are possible, if I want them badly enough.

APRIL, 1985, NOTE TO MYSELF:

Negative things we hold on to are a security blanket, too. GET YOUR SOUL OUT OF THE BODY OF NITA. Take the tape out and burn it. Emotionally still there. Rationally, you know you're Sarah. You're worth it. It's possible.

JANUARY 4, 1995

Dear Howard,

I've found letters written in 1985, six years before we met! I cannot convey how lost these writings made me feel. Not that I am lost now, but how lost I was then. It was right there out in the open, everyone could see it, and nothing was done. Two therapists openly acknowledged the existence of Sarah, and accurately described her. So they had seen her. Never once did we talk about dissociation or MPD. And the statement that "since I was young I needed to be rescued." (major sigh) Nobody followed up on that, either. Sometimes, Howard....

AUGUST 11, 1992

H: I'd like to talk to the inside Sarah. Tell me something about you.

S: I write poems, and I like to make people happy, and I like games. I like birthday parties. Fun things.

H: How old are you?

S: Sometimes I feel real young, sometimes real old.

H: You must be a very attractive person to the others. They think well of you.

S: I never cause trouble.

H: Do you want to have some influence? I think everyone's struggling. There are some who are frightened, some confused. They've all acted with courage, but they need help and guidance.

S: ***But you have Lynn.***

H: *Are you jealous?*

S: ***No. Lynn's a good leader.***

H: *She certainly has been.*

S: ***I don't think I'm supposed to lead. Sometimes I write poems and they make people think about things, and that's sort of like leading, but not directly.***

H: *I wonder if there's a way to magnify your influence.*

S: ***there aren't very many of us who are really happy. Nobody else, all the time. I'm happy most of the time, but sometimes my poems are really sad.***

H: *Why do you suppose your poems are sad?*

S: ***It's like I write it down and then I'm not sad anymore.***

H: *That's really healthy. It means you're very in touch with your feelings, and understand them well.*

S: ***Sometimes my poems make the others not as sad, too. Sometimes they just don't like it. And I don't care, because it's my poem.***

H: *You're very free, then. Why wouldn't they like it?*

S: ***Because it makes them feel bad. They don't want to know what's happening. Sometimes you've got to write about what's happening, even if they don't want to hear it.***

H: *That's right.*

S: ***I write my poems whether they don't like them or not.***

H: *Are there many more that aren't happy?*

S: ***Oh, lots more unhappy. It gets boring sometimes. Maybe you can't have fun all the time, but you can't have fun at all if you don't try.***

H: *You're right. I get the feeling I'm able to appeal to some of them. Do you think that would be productive?*

S: ***This does seem different. I don't know if it is different, really. But maybe that's why they go along with you.***

H: *I'm interested in anyone who is resistant or skeptical.*

S: ***If we do this thing you want to do? Am I not going to write poems anymore?***

H: *Are you frightened about that? Do you think I'd ever want it so you can't write poems anymore?*

S: ***I don't know that you want it, but is it going to happen?***

H: *Of course not. You'll write poems better than you do now.*

S: ***(excited) Really?***

H: *Sure. You'll be getting help from everybody, so the resistance will be removed. The thing that's very healthy about you is you haven't let them get you down.*

*S: **There's no point! It won't change anything to get down.***

H: Sure. But while you've been able to maintain positive productivity in your own life, it can go further once you sense they are now on your side, they help each other and, thanks to their perspective, they add more depth to your writing. Who knows? We might have discovered where the skepticism is.

*S: **(very curious) Where is that?***

H: Could it be you? If you fear it's going to have a bad effect on your writing, you could say, "Listen, don't tamper with this because at least I can do my writing."

*S: **(cheerfully) But, it's not me. I don't get involved in that kind of stuff. It's too stupid to argue about.***

H: You really are healthy.

OCTOBER 15, 1992

Dear Howard,

Sometimes I'm really slow! You said this at least six months ago, but I didn't get it then: In many ways, I'm still waiting for the inside people to show up and help me out now. I also really don't have a clue how to deal with and relate to outside people. This has probably been quite obvious to you all along, but it's a revelation to me. I need to unlearn a lifetime of bad habits and problematic behavior, and then learn a bunch of new good ones to replace them. It's totally overwhelming.

This also explains a very empty, ongoing feeling, which I've been denying exists. With her integration, Inside Sarah's not talking to me anymore. It was one thing to lose the voice that constantly said "I hate my life." But Sarah was my lifelong best friend. She was real to me. She was more reliable and there for me than most outside people I've ever known. I know she didn't really die, but I don't know how to deal with it.

This part isn't as scary as the Twilight Zone part, but it's a lot harder. It hurts so much more when it's just me left here to feel it and somehow deal with it. That's part of it, too, isn't it? Feeling anything other than fear, so completely.

OCTOBER 19, 1992

H: You want to talk about Inside Sarah? What would she say to you now?

*S: **It was never this conscious thing, like I had to think about what was said.***

H: I'm giving you a push-start. Make a comment about her. Say something you feel about her.

*S: **She was always there.***

H: She's sitting right there (points to her left). What would she say in response? Don't search, or you won't find it.

S: ***(laughs) I know what you're getting at. She's not there.***

H: *Don't fight me.*

S: ***I'm not fighting you. I'm fighting myself.***

H: *You know her well. You know exactly what she would say.*

S: ***I understand all that.***

H: *(laughs) I don't care if you give me a hard time.*

S: ***I'm just testing it. (he laughs) I know what you want me to say.***

H: *I know that! And you really hate it.*

S: ***(loudly) You want me to say she'd say, "I'm still here."***

H: *That's exactly what I was thinking. Amazing.*

S: ***But she's not still here, so I don't want to say that.***

H: *You're pouting. Out of all the alters, who pouted?*

S: ***Nita. So? Nita's not here, either.***

H: *You're able to have all the parts operate, and you know just what they say and do. Sarah said, "I'm here." She'd be right, too.*

S: ***In the poem "Thirty Years On," she says, "Do you wonder where I am tonight, or does my silence comfort you?" Her silence never comforted me.***

H: *Why do you suppose she asked that?*

S: ***'Cause even though it was like breathing, it was also a sign that I was crazy, because here was this voice. Silence might confirm my sanity. But it's just as crazy to wonder where she is.***

H: *The ultimate message is positive. There's silence because there aren't voices in your head. You're you. Those are just your thoughts. She was saying, "I'm Sarah. You're Sarah. I've never gone away; I never will."*

S: ***Whether I thought I was crazy, or not, the silence was not good. Because there was some (gasps) I was going to say "healthy" (both laugh). . .***

H: *Oh, how dare you!*

S: ***Some positive benefit from Sarah being there that made me feel more okay than not. So the silence was never a comfort. I felt I lost my confidence, or my ability to laugh when she was silent.***

H: *That puts all the emphasis on the aspect of you to be taken up by Sarah. "I gotta do all the emotions?" I say, "Yeah. Don't worry; you'll like it. You'll get to feel what you thought Sarah felt, but as you."*

S: ***You said I have to not think of Sarah as a loss. It seems like a big loss to me.***

H: *You think of it as a loss because something's different. But it's not a loss because she's still with you. You are her. Your feelings are her feelings. You know this very well. In a sense, you haven't lost anything.*

S: ***I haven't had any urges to buy wild clothes lately.***

H: It's not time, that's all. Everything's being balanced out. If Sarah operated all the time, you wouldn't be doing what you need to do. If any alters operate by themselves all the time, they distort what's supposed to be happening. If they're blended together, the balance is exactly what you should be doing. You had a lot of complaints before about out of control things in your life. Balance means you'll buy clothes when you can. If the grief is, "Why can't Sarah be there all the time?" — you don't want that to happen. Sarah doesn't even want it.

JANUARY 21, 1992

Dearest Sarah,

You're turning out to be one tough cookie. I've known your pretty, funny, smart side for so long I take those qualities for granted. But you're courageous! You're a fighter, a survivor. The rewards are manifesting in every direction. A million lonely-night fantasies posed that someday they'll see. And it's happening! You never gave up hope that somehow, someday, they'd all listen to you. You've got so many dreams to make happen now. The past can serve as nothing more than a reminder of how far you've brought us, in spite of the evil of our childhood. You are not tainted by that evil.

19

Erin Elisabeth

Erin? Are you there still? Have we missed you again? No one will be mad if you stayed behind. All it means is you weren't ready to go inside yet. Sweetie, tell me if you're there, please.

—OUTSIDE SARAH, APRIL 19, 1993

JUNE 29, 1992

H: Erin, it isn't good to feel frightened all the time, is it? You must hate it.

E: ***That's how it is.***

H: Would you be surprised to know it is in your control?

E: ***That's just brainwash. Grownups want you to believe stuff all the time that's not true.***

H: Would you be surprised to know grownups are scared, too? They have problems, which makes it scary for a kid to be around them. A lot of times that's why grownups say things that aren't true.

E: ***Grownups are just mean. They don't care who they hurt.***

H: Could it be you don't know enough grownups yet, and if you knew more, you'd feel different?

E: ***Too many grownups already.***

H: That makes sense. What do you feel about me? So far?

E: ***(grumbling) You ask a lot of questions.***

H: (amused) I do, don't I? Do you have any questions for me?

E: ***Why are you doing this?***

H: That's a really good question. I see you hurting. I talk to kids in serious situations, and I'm pleased to see they do much better. They have control of their lives, they feel good about themselves, and they're not frightened anymore. I thought maybe if I talk with you about your hurts, you could feel better, too.

E: ***I won't feel better.***

H: I wish you could. I don't think little kids should hurt like you hurt. It's not right.

E: *You're just saying that.*

H: *Well, you don't know why I'm saying it. But I think you will, as soon as you want to.*

E: ***That's like a brainwash if I ever heard one. Why would I know when I know? I already know what I know. To say I'll know later is like what all grownups say.***

H: *You don't know whether you can trust me, or if I'm just saying nonsense. That's okay. Sooner or later, you can know. Unless we talk, you won't know.*

E: ***That's big brainwash stuff. Why can't I know now?***

H: *You can. It means you'd have to take a chance with me. Now, your Mommy? You'd never take a chance with her. You'd figure she'd do the wrong thing. You don't know whether I would mistreat you. You just figure I might. If you took a chance, and then I don't hurt you, you'd know then.*

E: ***It's a trick. If I take a chance, then you'll do it.***

H: *That's what I mean. I could hurt you in the worst way you've ever been hurt (she flinches) but if I didn't hurt you when I could. . .*

E: ***Then you'll do it when it's a better time.***

H: *You'd feel more confident to take another chance.*

E: ***That's too many chances.***

H: *But that's what trust is. You've talked with me, and that was taking a chance, wasn't it? Did I hurt you?*

E: *Not yet.*

H: *If I ever hurt you, will you tell me?*

E: ***You'll just do it again for sure if you know it hurts me.***

H: *Don't you think I could have hurt you by now, if that's what I wanted to do?*

E: ***(scared) I guess.***

H: *I want you to trust your feelings first. If you don't trust me, your feelings are the important thing. Not what I do or say. You don't have to doubt your feelings, or think they are wrong.*

E: ***Well, I don't like it when you talk all this talk about how you could hurt me.***

H: *Does that scare you? (she flinches) I won't hurt you, you know.*

E: ***I don't know.***

H: *I won't talk about hurting you anymore. I think you're brave for talking to me.*

JULY 1, 1992

Dear Howard,

The experience with Erin was much more real to me than what happened with Lynn. I felt Erin's terror. Even listening to the tape now makes me hyperventilate. The best and worst parts happened simultaneously. When you (endlessly) went on about how you could hurt her, I know you were helping her distinguish that you aren't doing it. But did you realize you were doing "Ron-speak?" For awhile we thought you might actually be Ron. Erin thought if she didn't look, she wouldn't know for sure. I thought, "If I can make things appear on my walls, I can make his face look like Ron."

At the end of the session, I wasn't sure of anything. I felt so helpless because it's true, you could hurt me badly if you wanted to. (Knowing you don't want to was not great comfort.) And out of control, because I believed that if she looked at you, you were going to be Ron, no matter how irrational that is.

The best part was, she still has enough spunk left to tell you she didn't like it. She isn't so far gone into the terror that she's folding now. It was a start on trusting you to admit her fear, especially since neither of us were sure who she was talking to. It confirms that even in the scariest moments with Ron, I really did tell him to stop, in spite of my fear.

JULY 7, 1992

Dear Howard,

I think you are nice but I feel bad cause you want to be friends and sometime I don't want to. So I will give you chances cause you are nice so far but I can't tell you if it's a chance or you will know so that doesn't count as a real chance. You tell good stories could you please not say scary ones. Erin Elisabeth p.s. You know lots about cats.

AUGUST 11, 1992

E: We were at the hospital forever, and nobody cared.

H: When you're by yourself, and you don't think anyone understands, think of me.

E: That's hard sometimes.

H: You could think I'm holding your hand, and I feel what you feel, and understand what you understand. If you do that, you won't be alone again. That's what I do. Plus, I want you to know, it's not going to be like this forever.

DECEMBER 10, 1992

S: My initial response to Erin's reappearance was that this is a major step backwards. I know it's a step forward because she would have been there whether I knew about her or not. Better to take care of things now. But even more so, it feels crazy to talk to her on my computer. I'm resisting it.

H: Don't, okay?

S: (irritated) Well, I knew you'd say "don't."

H: What's your reason for resisting?

S: ***It seems like a sign of sickness, not health. In the last month, I've had little lightshows. I thought I'd lost time, and talked myself out of it. "There's no way this is happening again."***

H: *I was so glad when you called. Not only did you say, "Guess who's there?" But I knew you knew you had integrated.*

S: ***I never questioned it.***

H: *I was really pleased. Not only does it look clean from the outside, but the inside, too. You would say, by definition, it's not, because she's there. (she nods) Even just by the numbers game, I'd say, "We left one person in there on purpose, just to close the door behind them." Yep! It's clean! You did it. That was really powerful. Not only is there a person to report this, but one who can deal with the most tragic incident of your life. This could not have been planned, scripted, played out any better.*

S: ***That's why I think it's crazy. (sighs) I'm not going to argue crazy with you again. But it feels too neat. Driving here tonight I thought, "What if she's really not there? What if you can't talk to her? Oh, geez, I'm losing my mind all over again." I came up with some possibly textbook reasons why I could make this up. Part of it is for your attention. As if I didn't have enough already.***

H: *What does my attention give you?*

S: ***Charlotte and I talked awhile ago about having sexual feelings for therapists. She asked if I had any towards you. I said, "No, I just want him to adopt me." (both laugh)***

H: *That's as profound as the sexual feeling, isn't it?*

S: ***It's just as nutty as anything else.***

H: *Ah, come on. You want to be intimate in my life. You want me to be your father, and play games with you, and do things good fathers do.*

S: ***Yeah.***

H: *Isn't that a neat thing? Particularly if you haven't had it?*

S: ***But isn't that kind of weird?***

H: *Really? So if I told you it's natural and normal, and exactly what happens? It's a very delicate area. If it isn't handled with skill, it can be badly botched. But that it happens is common, and many times even very desirable. Many people's difficulty is to emote and relate in a primitive way. Wanting to be taken care of, or wanting sex, or to be loved by the therapist is common, if not universal. I'm surprised you think it's weird.*

S: ***I always said something happened at six that caused my father to become alienated from me. But Erin's saying "That's what they all say, especially daddy grownups." I realized I pulled away from my father, because I didn't want to know if he was like the other daddy grownups I was meeting.***

H: It's good you're so empathized with that feeling, which is what Erin's all about. So I come into your life, and I think I'm up to every one of your challenges. I've never flinched with any of your stuff.

S: Not outwardly.

H: (laughs) Not even inwardly. I rise to the occasion as a father would to deal with what presents. Showing wisdom, strength, courage, empathy, love, devotion, caring. Erin would say, "Yeah, looks good, I don't believe it. Daddy grownups don't do that." Her integration occurs when she says, "Fathers can be trusted." You trust me as an adult. You need to trust me as a child.

S: That's kind of hard to do.

H: You want me to help you? I always will be good to you.

S: I told her that. (shrugs) I don't feel like I'm her. If I know that, she doesn't.

H: When you write, you're on the cutting edge of the sophisticated understanding of your situation. When you're with me, you kind of regress.

S: I thought I just gave you this wonderful insight! Too bad, huh? (both laugh)

H: That's what you get for laying an insight on me!

S: Yes. I regress.

H: That wasn't a put-down. The regression is like you want me to draw it out, as opposed to, when I read your stuff, I can see you're drawing it out. You want me to do the work. You want me to take care of you. Does that ring a bell? As more of your good adjustment, you need the ability to feel like a child feels. Open and free. Not closed, guarded, and fearful.

S: I think I'm going nuts again. Is it more sane to wish she's there, or not? I can't figure it out.

H: It's probably mixed. You don't want to have MPD. But you have affection for who she is, what she knows and understands, and how she's a key to your problems.

S: See. . . I know she's there. Because I'm spinning.

Erin appeared and talked about integration issues with Howard. He said he did not know how to talk about bad things with her.

E: I don't want to talk about the bad thing! I told her that! I'll just feel worser, and you'll think I'm a bad person.

H: There's something I don't know about you that I'll think you're a bad person? Honey, do you know what "abuse" means?

E: When Mommy hit me, it was a bad thing, 'cause I wasn't even bad when she hit me lots of times.

H: That's the part I want to talk about, getting hit for no reason.

E: She always said I had one.

H: Do you know there are many ways to abuse somebody? You can hurt their feelings and their bodies.

E: And you could scare them.

H: That's right. There's nothing more terrible than what you're talking about. And your mother did that to you. Today you still feel like you're a bad person, and I don't want you to be mixed up about it. Will you take a chance, and tell me why you think you're bad?

E: (whispers) I can't.

H: Try not to worry, honey. Can I tell you that, whatever you think, it's not your fault? You may feel bad about it, which is normal. But it doesn't make you bad.

E: I'm so scared.

H: I don't want you to hurt anymore. I want it to go away.

E: (anguish) It can't ever go away!

H: Your feeling that it's your fault and you're bad, can go away. That it happened, can't go away, but it's not your fault.

E: They said it was.

H: They were wrong and bad. I also understand that in some way you want to talk about it. That's why I want you to share it. Not because I want to hurt you.

E: (anxious) I can't breathe.

H: Are you with me? I'm Howard. Can you feel me with you?

E: Where would you be?

H: I'm right with you. Sometimes people, in their heads, think about other places.

E: I don't want to think about the other place. But I keep doing it. It's really hard to breathe in here.

H: Erin? Do you want me to talk to you anymore tonight?

E: (nods) Yeah.

H: That's the right feeling. I'm talking with you because you want me to. It'll be better.

E: It can't be better!

H: Wasn't the reason you stayed behind to tell me?

E: I didn't want to disappear.

H: You won't disappear, honey. Inside Sarah didn't disappear. She's good; you're good; all the good didn't disappear. The good is why we even got together. You're going to have the kind of life you wanted, Erin. You're doing wonderful. You made it, you know that? You got through the difficulty. You're strong and brave....Honey, where did this bad thing happen?

E: (anxious) In a real big room. It had big doors.

H: Who was there?

E: I don't know, except for Uncle Ron. They all look the same.

H: What were they saying?

E: Bad things. About me. They call me bitch.

H: Were they saying jokes and laughing?

E: Sometimes. I felt real sick. They talked funny...like slow...like in cartoons.

H: Did they touch you in ways they shouldn't have?

E: (whispers) Yeah.

H: Did you say anything?

E: I was scared. There was nobody to help me. And I couldn't talk real good.

H: Did you cry?

E: Sometime. I try not to. 'Cause they like it.

H: Oh gosh. So they'd do things to make you cry more? (she nods) Why would your mom leave you with Ron?

E: She was real mad. She said I was bad, so (sighs) I had to go to the bad place.

H: Was there ever another girl there?

E: That was...later.

H: Will you please tell me about that?

E: (whispers) I can't. That's really bad.

H: That's what is hurting you, honey....These are very bad men.

E: There was bigger girls later. There was just one, but the next time I came there was another one.

H: You saw something, didn't you? I don't want it to hurt anymore.

E: It's gonna hurt always! You're gonna think I'm bad!

H: I'm telling you, honey, I won't. Did the men make you do anything?

E: I just told you! They touched me and all that kind of bad stuff. It's really bad!

H: It's bad, but it's not you being bad. You know how you say "brainwashed" all the time? You've been brainwashed that you're bad. Honey, you're not. We've got to clear this up.

E: Now you'll know for sure. (whispers) I can't....(louder) Sometimes I...they told me...they said I was bad....Sometimes it felt good...they said I was bad...because it felt good. And they only did it...'cause it made me feel good.

H: I can explain that, honey. You're not bad.

E: It's worser than that! (fearful) I saw a really bad thing.

H: Tell me what you saw, honey.

E: (whispers) I woke up.

H: They thought you were sleeping. But you weren't.

E: (whispers) I woke up and there was an angel all in white.[1] I thought she was an angel. They took pictures of her. But they hurted her like they hurted me. They made her do like the same things...and she liked it too! And then...they hurted her bad. They (whispers) stabbed her. And she screamed. And I pretend I was asleep 'cause I thought they stab me too. I was bad 'cause I should have helped her.

H: How could you?

E: (whispers) I could have told her what to do. 'Cause they never stab me.

H: Honey, you weren't big enough. There were more of them.

E: (louder) I thought I could help her! (crying) She didn't like it anymore. She was tied down like me.

H: Can you hear this? Honey, you're not bad. I want to explain why. You feel bad about it because you're good. They used your goodness, and turned it against you.

E: (crying) But after you think about it you're gonna not like me.

H: No, honey, I could think about this forever, and still not think bad of you. Will you please believe me?

E: (whispers) I can't.

H: Let me help you. A bad person wouldn't feel bad about this. What you've told me is horrible, but it's not you. It's them. You are a good person.

E: (crying) You said I was a brat! So you must just think I deserve this.

H: I don't think you deserved this. I used the word "brat?"

E: It was a bigger word, too, but I remember the brat part.

H: I'm a good person, and I do wrong things sometimes. I'm sorry.

E: My Mommy called me a brat all the time too.

H: I didn't mean to call you that like your mom did. Can you forgive me? (she nods) Not for me. I want you to forgive me for you, so you don't hurt about it anymore. That was a mistake....Now, you're okay. Tell me you believe that I don't think you're bad.

E: It's what you say.

H: Oh, Erin, if I could unzip my inside and you could see my heart, you'd know it. I want you to know it through my words and the way I sound. You like me. You care about how I feel toward you. (she nods) That's good. But you don't have to worry about it. There's nothing you can say or do that's going to change it.

E: I feel so sad! (crying) Are they gonna put me in jail now?

H: No way that'll ever happen! See, you know right from wrong.

E: ***Will you come see me?***

H: Yeah. You and I are going to know each other forever. Oh, what? See you in jail?

E: ***People visit people in jail.***

H: No, no, no. I'll see you in good places. You're not going to jail. Now stop it. You did the right thing. You should not have screamed. We wouldn't be talking today if you did.

E: ***There was more girls than the first one and I should have told so they wouldn't come. That's my fault, too!***

H: You told your mother, who didn't help you. You did your job. You would have been killed if you did anything more. And you did tell me, a person you can trust.

E: ***It's a long time has gone. It's way too late.***

H: I don't want you to worry about that. But this is very important. This is the part that can be confusing to a little girl. When two adults care for each other, and they want to feel good together physically. . .

E: ***Like a mommy and a daddy?***

H: Yes. They hold each other and it feels good to touch each other. Sometimes they wear clothes, sometimes they don't. But that's because they want to, and they agree to it. Have you ever held somebody's hand, and it felt good? Even in your private areas, sometimes it feels good. That's normal. It's a very special thing, and only happens with adults who agree to do it. When these bad men touched you, you felt confused, scared, and hurt. But it was also mixed with touching the areas that feel good. They're supposed to feel good. That confused you. When you liked it, you felt there was something wrong with it. That's how they abused you.

E: ***I didn't want them to, but they said I made them.***

H: They did every bad thing they could. I don't want you brainwashed anymore. Enough of that nonsense! Do you understand me? You're a terrific kid. You did good. I want you to take a deep breath.

E: (fearful) Why?

H: You'll feel good. Do that again. I'll talk with you another time. Thank you very much for telling me. I want to speak to Sarah.

S: ***(gasps) Oh, God. I've got a headache.***

H: You're on the other side of it. Erin had ambivalence, but she still needed to talk. She's better.

S: ***She's so scared. Oh, God.***

H: She's less scared than she was.

S: ***(laughs) How about me?***

H: That's residual stuff. You're a lot better off than you were, too. You just haven't been feeling the things you should have. Erin needed to tell, and was willing to relive it, just to process it. She needed some education, and to understand she was in grave danger of being killed. Her definitions of good and bad are screwy, even though in her core, she has a sense of it. She knew she couldn't bear to live with this all by herself. What Erin must do first, is give up this idea that she's bad.

DECEMBER 12, 1992

Dearest Erin,

I understand something about you now that I never knew before. You've been on a rampage the last few weeks — and rightly so — because you knew these horrible memories were coming out. It must terrify you. When you don't want to think of bad things, you eat.

You've feared all these years that if this story ever came out, you would be blamed, even though you were helpless and barely survived. Look who's first in line to blame you? Me. I grew up feeling I was a fraud and that everything was my fault. You were always there, holding your breath, begging me not to tell anyone why. That's another reason why we forgot about these bad things for so long. We were sure we'd get in big trouble because we didn't tell sooner, and maybe some girls wouldn't have died. Then we felt bad because we forgot, and couldn't remember what the real thing was that we should feel bad about. We've always known we did something bad.

I wish you could see that you're really the hero, but I can't even make myself believe it, so why should you? Those girls were going to die no matter what you did. Nothing you do to yourself will bring them back, or can even be seen as a punishment, because you weren't bad. You punished yourself for surviving. And I am contributing to it.

I'm so sorry I've blamed you all these years. I believed I didn't deserve to be happy, and now I understand why. Our life has been so unfair, to have made us believe we were bad because bad things were done to us.

DECEMBER 15, 1992

Dear Howard,

I think I get it! You get to be the good, strong father. I get to be the hopefully much better in all categories mother. Erin gets to feel like a normal child, and then she'll want to integrate. But I'm not sure I want my role. I have trouble just taking so-so care of myself. What will I do with a traumatized little kid? I need Mommy lessons. (Thinking of expanding your repertoire?) Maybe this is just denial because of how terrible the things were that happened to her. Maybe I don't want to integrate that. Maybe I don't want to internalize that much pain and degradation. Maybe I'm afraid it will be me crying in your office, feeling so out of control, and like there's no hope.

DECEMBER 20, 1992[2]

E: Maybe if Howard really knew me he'd be mean now.

S: Do you really believe that?

E: He makes me confused 'cause I like him but he's gonna be mean sometime. They're always nice first. They say it just like he did. They say you're a good girl I wish you were my little girl. And they want to help you. They say this won't hurt this'll feel good and it hurts lots and they laugh when you cry. And they tell their daddy friends to do it too!

S: Howard isn't like that. He promised he wouldn't hurt you. We've known him a long time now.

E: Maybe he's waiting for a little girl. Maybe he's waiting for me.

S: Erin. Think about it, okay? You said you like how he laughs. Did you ever like how the bad men laughed?

E: They laughed mean.

S: That's one way you can tell. When he laughs he makes you feel good.

E: Yeah. (whispers in my ear) But what if he is bad?

S: We'll make a plan. This isn't like before. If anyone is ever bad to you, lots of people will listen this time for sure. You know how I was saying that I'm not really Nita, or Inside Sarah, or Lynn? I'm all the inside people all mixed up now. They're still there, but I can't talk to them like I can to you. All of us together are a much stronger, better person than we were apart. We're going to make good choices now, so we don't get into trouble. You're safe, Erin.

APRIL 19, 1993

H: If the whole of who you are is healthier and more in control if you go inside, then you're absolutely right. It's a good thing. I think you saw this coming. I think you're sad about it, and so is Sarah.

E: I am sad. (crying)

H: Do you think it's like being in a really neat kindergarten class where you learn a lot, and really liked your teacher? It seemed like your whole existence, good things happened, and you were always safe. All of a sudden, it's the end of the year, and you're going into first grade. There's an anticipation, even excitement, that it's vacation time. But it's like, "Gee, will I ever see my teacher again?"

E: I never saw Miss Hart ever again.

H: I want to give you a clue about life, okay? I realized, early in my life, that if I held on too tightly to what was ending, I wouldn't grow happy. It would be like instead of my best day is coming ahead, I'd already lived it. Happy adults move rapidly through certain parts of development of their life. They have an energy from feeling good about today and tomorrow. The past becomes an important memory. It's worked for me to put more energy into living ahead, than holding on so tightly to what was in the past. And I've always felt like I'm a kid. Maybe one who has more control over his life 'cause I get to do what I want.

E: ***(sad) You're kind of a teacher.***

H: *Like this is kindergarten?*

E: ***No, this is better than kindergarten. 'Cause it's just me. (crying) And that makes me real sad.***

H: *Like you won't see me anymore? (she nods, crying) Have you liked me? Can you keep me in your heart?*

E: ***I don't know how it works.***

H: *I can always be with you, even if we never talk again.*

E: ***(crying) How do you know?***

H: *'Cause I live that way, too.*

E: ***But you're not just like a teacher. It's so unfair!***

H: *I know how hard it is. But I'm going to remember you forever.*

E: ***(crying) Why can't Sarah go inside, and I could stay outside?***

H: *In a way, it is like coming outside. You're not going away. Who you are is very important, and always will be. It's hard to imagine, but you're going to be happy.*

E: ***But I won't be special anymore.***

H: *That's not true. You're part of Sarah forever. You've always been special, and will continue to be. It might seem like you're going away, but you're not. It's like growing up....In fact, it's exactly that.*

E: ***Sarah said I wouldn't grow up if I went inside. She said I would be the little kid inside of her.***

H: *I don't believe I'd be a good adult if I wasn't able to feel the feelings I relate to as a child. That's what Sarah is talking about. The growing up part has more to do with taking on day-to-day responsibilities in a confident way. When you do that, you get to be more of a kid, without restrictions, and without anyone telling you what to do. Adults who don't think enough about feeling like a child aren't very happy adults. Do you believe me when I say you won't be sad anymore? You'll feel good. You won't have to worry about anything. You'll be free.*

E: ***Promise?***

H: *Yes. That's what it feels like, because I experience it just like that myself. And no one will ever hurt you. You made it. You got through all the bad things. And I'm so happy that we knew each other.*

E: ***(crying) I have a secret. You're gonna make fun of me if I tell you.***

H: Why don't you take a chance?

E: ***I thought you would be a good daddy.***

H: I'm not as good a daddy as I'd like to be. But I think I'm a pretty good one. It's okay for you to think of it that way.

E: ***No, it's not! 'Cause that's what kind of idea, thinking you're like a good daddy, and then I go away!***

H: I can't think of a stronger relationship. A good mommy and daddy is anyone who shows that they care. And I do care. But because certain experiences came before you, it means they also move on. When they do, you keep in your heart what they are to you. Part of being a good mommy or daddy is to help the child have enough strength when they're not there, physically.

E: ***So you think it's a good idea to go inside?***

H: Yes, because you told me you're ready. Keep me with you. Think of what we've talked about, and meant to each other. I hope you feel the trust you had for me was worth it. Sometimes you didn't trust me, but you took a chance anyway. There are other people who can be trusted, too, and you'll know who they are now. You've been very courageous and strong. Can you sense all the things Sarah's going to do in her life? That's all because of you. And every good thing that a child could want to have is going to happen. You're going to be there to enjoy it. You can be proud of it.

E: ***I don't feel so sad now.***

H: I figured you'd feel a lot better....Honey, I want you to take a deep breath, okay? And you'll remember me. You'll always have me with you.

E: ***(crying hard) I love you!***

H: I love you, too....We'll always be together. I want to thank you for helping me. You'll be okay. Take a deep breath, honey. It's all right... Sarah.... Are you okay?

S: ***(crying) No, I'm not okay!***

H: Oh, you're sad, but you're okay....You've handled this real well, from the moment I met you.

S: ***As opposed to what?***

H: Handling it lousy. (smiles) Making it real difficult. You've taught me a lot.

S: ***(whispers) I don't know what you're talking about.***

H: You can't hear me, anyway. You're going to feel sad today.

S: ***Is she gone?***

H: I'm leaning toward yes. You can't help but feel sad, but it was particularly good that she wasn't pushed one bit. I'd always wondered when she would bring it up, on her own, and in what context. The way this whole thing has proceeded and evolved is really noteworthy. You more than survived it; you didn't just get by. You've triumphed. Your writing goes beyond what you say in here, which tells me you have more than a handle on childhood and family dynamics, and MPD, to say the least. There's a depth of understanding of what it really means, clinically. You clearly understand it better than most people who profess to understand it. I've read your stuff and thought, "What a really good way of putting that." You take me on with all kinds of strength and wisdom. I think most people in your situation go to their graves unresolved and split off, and the best they get is they sort of manage their lives. The experiences that define their existence are nuisances. It challenges them forever.

S: ***I feel better knowing she'll be all right.***

As happens occasionally in DID patients, alters we believe to have integrated merely go into hiding for their own good reasons. Erin did this vanishing act three times. I maintained a steady ambivalence, wanting this child who expressed herself so freely in my life, yet wanting to be "normal."

AUGUST 19, 1993

Dear Erin,

I miss you so much. I know you're happier now, we all are. I just miss talking to you. I miss your innocence. It would be okay if you're still there, sweetie. No matter why. I'm wondering now, because I feel you so strongly, if you held back but made it possible somehow for me to feel as if you were gone, so I'd feel the loss and you'd suffer alone in silence forever. You don't have to be silent ever again! You don't have to go anywhere just to make us happy. I'm not sure how happy I am without you, anyway. The last thing I want is for you to suffer. Your life now is about good things and good people in it. Please say something. It'll be okay. I can feel the spinning. You're there, aren't you?

E: *You weren't supposed to find out.*

S: *Oh, Erin! God, I love you so much!*

E: *Now everyone's going to be mad at me again.*

S: *No, you were only supposed to go if you were really ready.*

E: *It made you happy I thought. And now you're crying.*

S: *I'm crying because I felt the pain of a little girl who is trying so hard one more time to please people she wants so much to love her.*

E: *I wish I could make one wish in the whole world. I wish I could belong to someone.*

S: *Honey! You belong to me! I'll take good care of you.*

E: *(silence and spinning)*

Erin and I developed a "sister" kind of relationship over the next year. She learned to play, and began to cooperate with our dietary goals. She spoke to Howard regularly. During this time frame, we believed she integrated yet again, but rediscovered her when I became increasingly involved with the man who would eventually become my second husband.

AUGUST 30, 1994

Dear Howard,

Erin called Dan tonight and they talked for three hours. I was not "there." Dan told me she never actually relaxed. They talked about babies, and yucky stuff (sex), why she doesn't like the sun, bad people, and scary things like moving far away. He said he wants to be friends, if she wants. She told him you said she had to take chances to find out if people were good. They talked about how he and Sarah realized they might be happier together than apart, and that it would be scary to meet and find out if it was true. He promised to give her hugs without any yucky stuff ever.

Howard, this alarms me because I had no warning she was going to call. I realize she knew Dan wanted to talk to her, and it was brave of her. I am not mad, which she was worried about. (And, that you will be, too.)

Dan was pretty freaked out and tense the first hour, but gradually got into it. He felt a heavy responsibility to choose his words extremely carefully. He also was unprepared for my disorientation when he asked to speak to me. But he swears none of this dissuades him from following through on our plans. He wants all of us, him and me, and whoever else is inside, to be happy.

SEPTEMBER 10, 1994

Some issue of urgency arises, and Erin pops up from nowhere, in dramatic fashion. She sends faxes to Howard at 3 a.m. Or calls him. I don't even know she contacted him till he tells me. Since I think she's integrated, when she appears again (after months of silence) it's very unsettling. But she always appears when I need to look at something that would frighten a small child (particularly a small abused child) but perhaps be viewed as not a big deal by a functioning adult. Howard says she is an excellent barometer of my level of denial about any aspect of me. When I stop the denial, she will have no need to appear. Easier said than done!

What I truly love and value about Erin is that I get to be six. I get the proper attention, love, and guidance for that age — which never happened when I was really six. I get to feel that innocence and purity in me, which otherwise I have a hard time doing.

The potential for upheaval currently (and the reason for her appearance) is high. I'm not used to having good things happen without some disaster following shortly behind. Yet, I don't have that sense at all now. I feel I am on the right course. But, just the stress of it all now — writing under deadline; meeting an important someone; possibly moving across country. Can I deal with success and stability?

I've not been in a sexual relationship for years — not since before my memories began surfacing. I thought sex was highly overrated and didn't care for it. (Other alters indulged themselves.) Now I look at it differently, but have no recent experience. Dan and I recently discussed some serious subjects, including sex and babies. (This was, for the first time, with the sense that these things could really happen, and relatively soon. Well, the sex part, anyway.)

Erin was triggered, and came out a few days later in a session with Howard. She sees all sex as "yucky stuff." She's stated many times that she would never grow up because grownups have babies, and bad things happen to babies. It's been a long road trying to help her see that this is not true of all sex and all babies. Her childhood experience is real and won't be discounted. Yet, if she "comes out" when I am sexually active, in essence, she will be molested again. Erin likes Dan, and her phone call indicates a level of trust, but she doesn't know what to do with it. She thought Howard was the only good grownup in the universe.

So things with Erin are in a big swirl, which is perhaps the microcosm for my life generally. But it's a good, hopeful swirl. The fear is borne not from terror, but from the unknown. I feel as though things are coming full circle. Howard's message, since day one, was that I am entitled to love, happiness, hope, dreams, success. All these things are sitting right in front of me, a product of my years of hard work. I am dazzled, and I think Erin is, too.

September 12, 1994

Dear Howard,

Erin called Dan again. She was confused because he and I say we hug each other on the phone, but it's not "really hugs." He explained that make-believe hugs feel almost as good as real ones. She worked up all her courage and asked if he would make-believe hug her, which he did. She told me later that she couldn't breathe, but it was sort of okay, and he let go when she said she didn't want to do it anymore. He felt honored by her trust and courage.

But Dan only told me they'd talked about hugs, in general. I didn't know she'd asked him to hug her till she told me. He said he's trying to build trust with her, so he didn't know if it would be okay with her if he told me. I felt sort of like Alice in Wonderland discussing this with him. I recognize he wants very much for Erin to be happy. But how do I work on what's happening with Erin if I don't know what's happening?

Dear howard

hi I hugged that dan man is that okay. It was scary he hugs like you but you were scary too long time ago. love from Erin Elisabeth we are making a kite with a butterfly.

SEPTEMBER 27, 1994

Erin is progressing by leaps and bounds in her trust of Dan. Although he's never had children, he's a natural. Not to mention how weird it must be for him to be talking to "me," but not really. I have never been more happy in my life. It's an amazing new feeling. I am not used to good things happening and "sticking." I want so much to believe that these good things aren't going to be taken away at the last moment. (Very old tapes playing that tune.)

OCTOBER 2, 1994

Erin's laughing like I've never heard before. Dan says he'd forgotten what fun it is to be a child till he met her. They make animal sounds, and play a game called "Nice kitty" where she pretends to be a cat and purrs for him. She's sung most of the soundtrack of "The Sound of Music" to him, her favorite movie (whereas I am too shy to sing). She isn't afraid to ask for (or receive) make-believe hugs now.

Dan expressed concern that if he does something fun with Erin, he is neglecting me. I don't see it that way. Erin's "thing" all along has been that she's just a little kid and nobody listens to her except in crisis. Howard's told her repeatedly that, with integration, she doesn't have to wait for a crisis to be heard. She's starting to get a real taste now of what it's like to just "be" a child. I think it's a good transition to her wanting to "be" me. The safer Erin feels, the happier she is, the more she laughs, the safer I feel, the more I laugh, the happier I am, which makes her feel safer.

Erin integrated as a happy, safe, beloved child on July 25, 1995.[3]

20

Peter and Rational Suicide

JULY 14, 1992

Dear Howard,

Something truly scary happened. On Friday night, I was cooking, and everything was fine, then I blinked, and the entire apartment was full of dense smoke. I had to run into the worst of it to turn the oven off. There wasn't a fire, but it was close. I figured my cough was like asthma. By Saturday, I was barely breathing, and went to the emergency room. They put me on oxygen for four hours. Lots of tests.

How could I not have noticed so much smoke sooner? The answer is very disturbing. I think one of my people took over, and Lynn or Erin brought me back. (The person didn't cause the smoke — I was stupid — but the person prevented me from responding sooner.)

JULY 17, 1992

Someone woke me up around 3 a.m. last night. I went through a repetitious cycle of people seeing things in my apartment differently, going through all kinds of changes looking at the same object. Sometimes it was me again, wondering what I was doing. It took a few cycles to get that I was seeing through the eyes of the people inside, in some kind of sequence. I kept thinking I should write this stuff down, but I couldn't make my fingers do it, so it became unclear if I was really me even when I thought I was me. Everything was so surreal.

The one who wanted me to die is Peter, who thought it was a fine opportunity to check out. He's the one who wants me to jump in front of buses. This is never going to end! I'm always going to struggle; to flip out in uncontrollable ways. I'll never know peace. I hate feeling this way! I hate feeling so out of control. I feel like such a mess.

JULY 20, 1992

H: Peter, what do you think about this whole thing?

P: I'm glad to talk to you. You're very logical and it's pretty clear this is going nowhere.

H: So you don't have a lot of hope.

P: It's very illogical to have hope. Don't you believe we've been through enough already?

H: *You're aware that some really do have hope, even though they've been through all this.*

P: ***They all have hope in their own little way. It won't amount to anything. It never has, never will. I want to appeal to your sense of reason.***

H: *You want to convince me it's a waste of time to even attempt different ways of finding resolution?*

P: ***Resolution is a rather arbitrary term.***

H: *True. You could make a case for doing yourself in as resolving. You can also make a case for living what you consider as satisfying and productive — you're smiling. Even you, Peter, know what that means.*

P: ***It's not a reality for this life. It's rather cruel to perpetuate the myth that everything's going to be okay.***

H: *Why do you suppose you've been cursed? Why should you have a lousy existence?*

P: ***I have no idea, but it's gone on so long, why ask?***

H: *Out of curiosity.*

P: ***Why is there evil? Why is there dark and light? It just is.***

H: *Some people are lucky, some aren't?*

P: ***It's more than luck. I believe there are forces at work that create situations.***

H: *What's the most compelling force at work here?*

P: ***Once tainted with evil, always tainted with evil.***

H: *Does that mean you became evil, or that you were touched by evil?*

P: ***Touched by evil.***

H: *So you're basically good, touched by evil.*

P: ***The presumption is we're basically good. We didn't have much chance to find out.***

H: *No, you didn't. You asked, what's the point of working this out? Could it be there are effective untried things you've never experienced?*

P: ***I pay attention. I read. Been listening to you all this time. I'm not ill-informed as to how this ideally should work. I just don't think — as the younger ones do — that you're going to snap your fingers and make it all better.***

H: *They believe in magic. That's how young people think. In a sense, that's what it is. I don't have a problem with it. Santa Claus is whatever one wants to believe he is.*

P: ***(sighs) Yeah.***

H: *Peter, I'm not trying to make a case. You're presenting the angles by which you see your world. I've never had a chance to talk about things which concern you.*

P: *I'm concerned about perpetuating this existence for another 40 years.*

H: *You shouldn't perpetuate it, unless you believe it can feel better. Since you don't believe that, you don't want to perpetuate it. You've got this vicious cycle. Have you ever, in your whole life, had hope? Have you ever entertained it?*

P: *It's hard to measure hope empirically. You're a scientist. You should know that.*

H: *(pausing) I didn't know if that was a ridicule or a challenge. I'm still thinking about an empiric relation to hope. Let's not be so scientific. Whatever feeling can emerge that has a glimmer of hope — have you ever experienced that?*

P: *I wouldn't allow it. It's a real fallacy to believe in that. It captures you....(sighs) There are worse ways to be prisoners than this.*

H: *Define, in a simple way, what hope is. Without cynicism.*

P: *Hope is the belief that through your own actions and incredible good luck, things will get better.*

H: *Right. How'd it feel to say that?*

P: *Like I was reading from a book.*

H: *Have you ever cried, Peter?*

P: *No. It's wasted energy. It doesn't change or help anything.*

H: *You sound rather academic to me.*

P: *Thank you. One must fill one's hours somehow.*

H: *You like the idea that you think in rational terms.*

P: *Nobody else does.*

H: *Have you tried to appeal to these people? Not about giving up, but about being rational. Although, you may see that as one and the same.*

P: *It's a very fine line, isn't it?*

H: *Yes. What if you were just completely wrong?*

P: *I guess I would be devastated. But I'm not. So why even mention that?*

H: *Hold on now. If you're truly academic, it means you're not operating with prejudice.*

P: *There's 38 years of experience telling me I am not wrong.*

H: *Do you know who the great academic, Johannes Keppler, was? Astronomer. He worked for Tico Braghe, another astronomer famous in his time, but not good at math. Keppler was, so they worked together. Keppler had these wonderful, elegant conceptualizations of how matter moved in the universe. When you get an idea, and it's really beautiful to you, you like that you thought of it. Its simplicity and elegance have form. His idea was rather brilliant. But when he tested it mathematically, it didn't hold up. It was a great credit to his academic spirit that he never professed this elegant idea to actually exist, because it was never proven. You don't see that a lot in the academic world, 'cause there's a tendency for people's egos to get in the way, and they operate with certain prejudices. So they fudge the reality.*

P: ***To make it work. And so, the point?***

H: *I want to entertain the idea that you have this elegant notion that there's no such thing as hope in your life. The evidence you see may point to it, but the problem is, you're wrong, and you've never applied the mathematics, as it were, to truly test it out. Because, Peter, you do have a self-destructive side to your nature.*

P: ***It's only self-destructive because it's the best solution.***

H: *The best one you've been able to come up with.*

P: ***You don't have any way to prove I'm right or wrong.***

H: *You haven't asked for proof. You've just proclaimed what is, without having a full academic open discussion about it.*

P: ***It's been formulated over years of intense experience.***

H: *I understand how hard it is to give up an idea. But it's not impossible.*

P: ***Why should I? 'Cause you want me to? That's rational.***

H: *I admit it. I want it.*

P: ***I want things, too. So we're at an impasse.***

H: *Wait, wait — say what you want.*

P: ***I'd like an end to this meaningless existence.***

H: *You want your life to come to an end. Which you see as at odds with what I'd like. (he nods) The reason you want it to end — which makes sense — is that you don't believe there's anything worth fighting for. It's just a lot of suffering for nothing. That's because the track record is bad.*

P: ***If you run the same race 100 times, and you lose 100 times, your track record is pretty clear.***

H: *What if you're running the wrong race?*

P: ***It's the only race we've got. So that's totally off point.***

H: *You keep making everything air-tight, don't you?*

P: ***Maybe it really is air-tight.***

H: *Maybe it is. I don't have any problem entertaining your way of thinking. But you won't entertain my way at all.*

P: ***I disagree. I have been all along.***

H: *I'm surprised to hear this.*

P: ***I admire you. You're logical and have great insights regarding human nature. But it won't ultimately make much difference. I'm sorry to tell you that.***

H: I'm sorry to hear it, but it's important to know how you feel, deep down. Are you also sorry to know that the others won't let you take matters into your hands?

P: You never know what the future will bring.

H: Would it surprise you to know they're on guard, and when the opportunities come, they will undermine your efforts?

P: It recently came pretty close to their not succeeding. Doesn't mean it can't be closer next time.

H: What if it gets so close you disable yourself, but don't die? You'll be living in some suspended way which brings you even more torment.

P: I don't know how there could be more torment. I'm already living a suspended life. This isn't living.

H: You may not know what real torment exists even beyond whatever you have experienced.

P: (laughs) So what are we talking? The difference between 99 and 100? It's negligible.

H: What's the difference between a 6.9 and a 7.0 earthquake?

P: That has an exponential quality to it.

H: This is exponential. Don't push it.

P: I don't create these opportunities. They just happen. I thought an appeal to reason might affect your position.

H: That's putting a lot of responsibility into my hands, isn't it? Would you like me to advise the others that I will now stop trying to bring about any benefit because it's gone as far as it can go?

P: It would be a shock, wouldn't it? The truth is really tough for some of these people.

H: Well, that's your truth. I'm not blind to what you're saying. I'm trying to entertain and feel what you feel as best I can. But, it's unimaginable that I'll say to the others, "Listen, Peter's convinced me in a very logical and correct manner. You have my condolences, but you're really better off not being." I get the feeling that while you wanted to make this appeal, you haven't really thought beyond what I was supposed to do with it, as far as the others are concerned.

P: What difference would it make?

H: Compassion. I think it counts. I don't believe you think compassion's a bad thing in life.

P: It numbs the pain a bit.

H: It also gets us closer to the pain, and may make us feel it more. Do you think we'd do well without compassion in life?

P: *There are people who didn't endure everything we endured, so compassion is great for them. Again, that notion of being touched by evil. How much effect can compassion have?*

H: *All the difference in the world. Night and day.*

P: *I suppose that's what you believe. I think it's like water rolling off a table. You can't stop it. Drip, drip, drip. Compassion on top of all of this crap just rolls right off.*

H: *Are you weak or strong?*

P: *Oh, I'm strong. I didn't get here by being weak.*

H: *Your strength is in your...?*

P: *My intellect. My reason. And in my willingness to examine the truth, no matter how hard it is.*

H: *That is to your credit. The truth frees you.*

P: *(amused) The truth frees you to go for the smoke.*

H: *You're 100% correct that when the truth presents itself, the "what to do" becomes obvious.*

P: *They're like little kids waiting for daddy to come home, and it's not going to happen.*

H: *So we can assume they really want something different than what you want. You stand alone.*

P: *Of course I stand alone! Except Anita. We just haven't been out in tandem, unfortunately.*

H: *What if you were?*

P: *(laughs) It would be more than Lynn could handle.*

H: *It's really a battle, the way you talk about it.*

P: *It doesn't stop being a battle just because you "grow up." I guess we both know how we feel about it now.*

H: *You're everything that can be characterized as defeatist, fatalistic, and hopeless.*

P: *You make it sound so horrible.*

H: *(laughs) Listen to you!*

P: *It's putting them out of their misery sooner, rather than later. That's all it amounts to.*

H: *I think I understand completely the sense of hopelessness you feel. But because we've only talked once, less than a thread's width of your existence, if you consider the length of the universe, it hasn't been much chance to talk about possibilities. Here's a challenge for truth. If there were nothing else that could be done, and you've seen it all, heard it all, know it all. . .*

P: *I know a lot.*

H: (laughs) Well, how arrogant of you. But if with all that, one could say, "You know something? You make a good, valid case. But in only a thread's width of all of your experience, you're now discussing this directly with a person who appreciates what you say. Even if you don't agree, you've admired him." Doesn't it make more rational sense to turn your head, look back, and say, "What does this guy have to offer that I haven't heard?"

P: There comes a point where we have divergent opinions about what is best.

H: Why don't you suspend your opinion for a bit? I haven't much liked it.

P: Well, so what? It really doesn't matter whether you like my opinion or not.

H: Don't get nasty now.

P: I'm stating a fact. I didn't come here seeking approval. I sought your rationality in disposing of the situation.

H: I'm offering a rational way through this.

P: It's actually just prolonging it.

H: I'm willing to attempt to prove it, but I want you to at least look while I do it. You're saying, "I've already made up my mind. There's no hope." Of the two of us, I am the least prejudiced. I've had the benefit of not experiencing what you've experienced. I wouldn't want to, okay?

P: I don't think anyone should have to. That's my point!

H: You've lived through hell, and triumphed over it. You understand things we need to know. You could provide a piece of the puzzle. If you could ever feel like "these things didn't happen in vain or without some good resulting." Could that be a way you find meaning in your life? To provide that degree of insight to the rest of us, because you've paid so close attention to what happened, how and why, and the solution? Could you be that generous? If, paradoxically, you feel not only it might be a life you like and might even cherish — give me this little poetic license. I couldn't help myself! (laughs) But it would be a different feeling, and you'll emerge triumphant, even stronger.

P: That's certainly not what will happen.

H: Prejudice.

P: You're equally prejudiced.

H: Oh, I don't think equally. Maybe not at all. I've been more willing to entertain what you've talked about as a solution than you've been willing to entertain the opposite. I don't think you should just get through this with as few scars as you can. You should emerge healed.

P: (laughs) Healed? Where is the reality in that comment?

H: Today it doesn't exist.

P: How many thousands of days have passed already where it did not exist?

H: That was the length of the universe vs. the thread of: something different entered your life. There's no denying this. I'm curious. If the first time we met, by some insightful inspiration, I looked at you, and said, "Peter, I want to speak with you." Would you have said, "There ain't no hope?" Or would you have been blown away?

P: A year ago none of this was public, so it's a pointless question.

H: Follow the logic, if you will. I'm talking to a very hopeless person. I understand why you feel that way. You've had such anguish in your life that a logical resolution would be to say, "Hey, you know something? A no life would be better than a life." Got you. Entertained it.

P: Rejected it thoroughly.

H: I haven't rejected one thing you've said. Come on! I've been very intellectually consistent with you. Anyway, that's your case; it's a good case. Say a year ago, when we first met, somehow I sensed you, your name, your issues, all of that.

P: Like magic? Without any revelations from Charlotte? Or anyone else? That's logical.

H: I didn't say logical. You would have been blown away, wouldn't you?

P: I would have been a little amazed, yes. Do you think you are magic, too?

H: This isn't about me.

P: On what basis would you suddenly know I was there?

H: Let me take that leap, if you don't mind.

P: I'm supposed to give you a definitive answer based on a totally ephemeral premise.

H: Sometimes you have to do that to come up with the essence of logic. Leaps must be taken. It's how things are discovered. Do you believe in imagination?

P: I'm not into creation. There are others much better suited for that avenue.

H: While logic is your strength, I'm hoping you understand how it becomes a weakness, too. It's important to bring features of logic together with those of imagination. They balance each other in a way that you come up with maybe a greater truth than you'd derive by only using logic. For example, at the end of the baseball season, the writers decide who's the most valuable player. All you have to do is look at the stats to figure it out. But more typically, they weigh the numbers with other factors that can't be written down.

P: Such as?

H: Leadership. Sportsmanship. Inspiration. Things that are more of heart, passion, feelings.

P: ***One of the beauties of baseball is you don't really need subjectivity to pick the MVP.***

H: *Listen to you! (laughs) But you know the subjective stuff is factored in.*

P: ***You want me to say all these years of objective study and analysis will be put on hold for however long it takes you to convince me you're right.***

H: *You only have a part of the picture. Just the stats.*

P: ***The stats are the only meaningful part of the picture.***

H: *Do you know you're not even being logical anymore? The thing you value? The form of truth you've looked at is very skewed. While your system of thinking may be very elegant, it doesn't hold up yet to all the factors still to be measured. You're being too much the intellectual snob.*

P: ***What if I am?***

H: *Be the intellectual. Balance it with what the others have to say, because they are you, too. Suspend your destructive activities for awhile. Give us your intellectual prowess, your insights. Give us the stats. We'll need to add them up.*

P: ***If I do all this for you, then do I get to self-destruct?***

H: *Is that your prize? Want me to push you off a building and reward you?*

P: ***I doubt that's how you'll make this work.***

H: *I'm being very sarcastic, I'm sorry. I won't push you off a building, but I'm curious if you want me to. I'm wondering if you actually did it, in the moment before, you might have a lot of regrets and fear. I take you seriously, but I wonder if you're talking a tough talk. That even you, in your heart of hearts, would like somebody to demonstrate it in a logical way, consistent with your personal integrity. Almost a plea, only that person has to work through the defensive mechanisms you've created so diligently. It's an enormous challenge on your part to say, "Penetrate this. I can't help you with it, you're on your own. But penetrate it, please. Find a door. Find a way."*

P: ***Or, it could be exactly what I've said. This is not a life worth living. There is no meaning.***

H: *So that's the challenge. It has to be different, because it's not a life worth living. It's not balanced, productive, or healthy enough. By a long shot.*

P: ***At all.***

H: *I've been reading what Sarah writes. She's very gifted. Do you like her?*

P: ***She's totally lost.***

H: *She's in the forest, trying to find her way out. Are you pulling for her? If you're watching your team, and it's behind. . .*

P: ***I'm not on anyone's team. I'm exclusively in this by myself.***

H: *You don't root for anybody?*

P: ***There's no point. Howard, let's play the tape back. Why would I root for her? For any of them?***

H: *You're watching a movie. There's the guy in the jungle, and he steps in quicksand, sinking down to his knees. Do you say, "Whoever he is, he's a goner." Or do you say, "Grab the branch! Call your friends! Don't move!"*

P: ***This unfortunate person usually has some noble cause like saving the world. In which case, he definitely should grab a branch. We're not out to save the world here.***

H: *You may underestimate your importance.*

P: ***Then don't bullshit me.***

H: *I haven't yet.*

P: ***You value these intellectual excursions as much as you value Sarah's poetry?***

H: *I can't compare them. These "intellectual excursions" are important. They're insightful; they tell me something about who you are; what you know; what matters to you. I'm not here to fight about anything, but they are, nonetheless, a challenge. Sarah's poetry is brilliant and captures her moods. She understands the essence of poetry and emotion. What are you going to do, tell me those things aren't valuable? And then claim you're logical? I admit this is an appeal to logic, not to give up the essence of who you are, but to discover more of that essence. Despite the fact that the people inside are too compartmentalized, you would be an intellectual liar if you didn't admit to the extraordinary productivity and value harbored in all of you. It's a gift to be given to the world.*

P: ***The world doesn't want any part of us.***

H: *I can only speak for myself. If I'm the only one in the world, then it's a valuable gift worth giving. If you have water, and I don't, and I'm thirsty, no matter how lousy your life is, and you've got the water to give, it's evil for you to not. In that moment, there's nothing more valuable. Whatever was or ever will be, I defy you or anybody to argue that point with me.*

JULY 23, 1992

Dear Howard,

I'm trying to go with your suggestion that this is like an endless "E" ticket. To view this as an opportunity to be relished, and met with wonder and excitement. It's a big leap. Peter's power seems very real and scary. Perhaps it diminishes just because he's in the open now. Maybe I make it so just by saying it. I guess that's one way to leap.

It really pisses me off that he characterizes Nita as a monument to mediocrity! I understand why he's correct, but geez! If Peter could learn that reason without civility or compassion is the cornerstone of a meaningless existence — so he's really doing it to himself now — maybe even

he'd see things differently. Maybe he'd have some friends. Maybe he'd get a life, instead of trying to dump the one he has. I like saying this! It feels good.

AUGUST 3, 1992

L: I'm watching Peter, 'cause I don't trust him. He's more devious than he presented to you. He hides behind big words and has no one's best interests at heart, except his own.

H: Is he the most isolated?

L: No, Anita is. She's dangerous when she gets out, but she hardly ever does. Peter gets out all the time, so in a way, he's more dangerous.

H: Any suggestions for me, with Anita and Peter? Why'd you laugh?

L: I don't know what to tell you. I thought you knew!

H: I know what I know. I want to put it all together so whatever we do, it makes the most sense. Do you feel it's hopeless to make an appeal to them, that integration means they'll work together to be more of who they are, in a positive way? There are all kinds of opportunities for positive intelligence. And positive aggression, for Anita. They all can channel the essence of their core self into something healthy, productive, and gratifying.

L: Do you really think that's possible?

H: It has to be possible. I don't want to be negative and say everything's just a waste of time. I can't believe that. Is Anita the most difficult and troublesome of all?

L: She's like a little child having a constant tantrum, but she's got butcher knives in her hands while she does it.

H: Oh dear. I just had a thought that I want to talk to her.

L: Nobody wants you to.

H: Even Peter?

L: (sarcastic) I'm sure Peter would welcome the occasion. Maybe he'd come out, too.

H: I'll respect what everyone's saying. I'd like to talk to Peter.

P: Hello, Howard.

H: So you've been listening in?

P: Yes. You said you could demonstrate proof that there is hope. I'm waiting to see it.

H: Oh, there it is. When you see it, then what?

P: Then I evaluate. I will show you that I don't operate from prejudice. It doesn't mean, necessarily, that I'll agree with your conclusion. But I'll consider it.

H: How would you define hope?

P: The definition we had last time was: "Hope is that through your own actions and/or incredible good luck, things will get better." It's never been true for us. But most people like to believe it.

H: Do you sense that my talking with you is the first real, legitimate effort to have you be a direct influence in ways you never were before?

P: I don't know what direct influence I can have.

H: Why would I bother talking to you if you didn't have direct influence? Why wouldn't I just dismiss you as irrelevant?

P: As a scientist, you would explore all avenues of solution or possible solution.

H: I'm talking to you because you've always been a factor, as is everybody. Nothing can be done without thinking very seriously about each individual. This is different than anything that's ever been done in your life.

P: That's true.

H: Wouldn't that constitute hope?

P: It constitutes "different." We've tried lots of different things over the years. You can call it hope if you want.

H: I'm not playing a word game, Peter. I'm being consistent.

P: I suppose hope would come into play if there were a demonstration that this worked.

H: I may have been trying to accurately describe concepts. When you say "demonstration" do you want me to do a magic trick, or show you something you can touch?

P: That would be nice. (smiles) No, I understand your methods don't involve mathematical equations or things that can be proven in that manner.

H: Maybe you can't feel hope, but would it still be reasonable, if it at least gave an inference of hope?

P: Why is it so important to you that I have hope?

H: Because you won't be a game player unless you have it. Each of you has a desire for something before you'll play. There is an enormous amount of talent contained here, of the highest caliber I've ever seen. By harnessing all of it, there's good reason to believe not only is there hope, but a high probability that integration creates everything productive and healthy, and brings to fulfillment all things desired by this person.

P: How long do we go on with this before we accept that it isn't working?

H: I think something should come of each encounter. You could reasonably expect it even today, if all the elements are in place, and I'm astute enough at any given time to pay attention to them. I recognize the goal here enough to be very humble when I say I need everybody's help. I'm not playing games with you.

P: ***So what would I have to do?***

H: *Give me a sense that maybe this time we will finally conquer all the forces that were against you. In this moment you have someone in your life who is more for you than you've ever had. You know that, without question. We've got to pull together to reach some of these people who are frightened, like Erin, and all the little ones. And there's Anita, who I must talk to.*

P: ***(amused) You must talk to Anita, huh?***

H: *Do you understand that Anita's anger is legitimate?*

P: ***Yes, I understand very well. My hopelessness is legitimate, also. It's all the same thing.***

H: *Fine, but you must have an outlet so it doesn't sustain as hopelessness. She needs an outlet for the anger. Everyone is in an emotional loop that creates more of the same. There's no processing so it diffuses in a more natural and complete way. It's like Anita has this hammer continually coming down on her thumb. There's never any healing, and the pain's always there. All anyone can see is the destruction she causes, as opposed to where it comes from, why it's there, or what can be done about it. Each person will simply explode with their own emotional feeling in that loop.*

P: ***So you believe when all the loops are broken, we'll integrate?***

H: *Yes. Once everyone knows they have an outlet for their legitimate feelings, and that the outlet diffuses into a place of settledness and completeness, the need to compete will be gone. Integration occurs, and the essence of each person actually has a more effective vehicle for its expression. Instead of your anger being destructive, it'll move to another place where it's recognized as the hurt that caused it. Is there any more ultimate triumph, or evidence of hope, than by going through that process, writing your books, losing the weight, and establishing a healthy, romantic, supportive, and loving relationship? Can you think of any better way to get back at those forces? It's a very compelling and powerful drive to live a self-destructive and self-defeating life, but it just doesn't prove it.*

P: ***So what now, Howard?***

H: *Your attempts to be felt and understood, and to flourish in your own life as the intelligent human being you are have always been correct. But it's been channeled in a cop-out. I'm asking you to have a loftier goal. I want your assistance. What's it going to be? Can you sign on, or not?*

P: ***If I sign on, what's the deal? Am I supposed to act as if I really have hope?***

H: *Yeah. Like maybe this could really work.*

P: ***Am I supposed to pretend?***

H: *No. And you can't be a threat to the safety and well-being of the others. You must have a positive attitude about the possibility. If you don't want to have anything to do with writing a brilliant piece on this phenomenon; if you don't want to stake your claim to what you understand about life in a way that the real world will get a chance to see, don't sign on.*

P: ***(wistfully) I would like the real world to see.***

H: *There couldn't be any more hope than exists in this particular situation. There's more depth of understanding, more ability, skill, sincerity, and purpose. If this doesn't bring hope out, I don't know what the hell does.*

P: ***If I sign on for a month, at the end of the month, what happens?***

H: *You feel a sense of satisfaction, direction, and purpose.*

P: ***And if that doesn't happen, then what?***

H: *I guess it's a matter of degree. If it doesn't happen at all, you're screwed. If it happens 90%, you'd be stupid to say, "Well, I'm screwed." You could say, "All right, we're getting there."*

P: ***Okay. For a month.***

H: *That's generous of you. Thank you. Got any ideas?*

P: ***I'm supposed to give you ideas?***

H: *Come on! I've asked everybody, and they all look at me like, "Who, me?" Here they are, wanting to express themselves. I ask their opinions, and they withdraw and retreat.*

P: ***You're the one who wants all this! You're the one orchestrating this whole thing.***

H: *You guys are so passive! (laughs)*

P: ***That's a learned behavior, you realize. Sticking one's neck out can be dangerous.***

H: *Where do you believe should be our point of entry this time? I have to convince everybody.*

P: ***And you believe I'm going to tell you how to do that. You didn't say I had to like. . .***

H: *What? Do anything?*

P: ***I thought I was doing a lot, actually. I presume I am refraining from what you term destructive behavior.***

H: *Right! I've got this very difficult task, and the way help is defined is by not stepping in the way of it. (laughs)*

P: ***You ask for a lot.***

H: *I want it all. You've watched this thing for so long on the inside, it's not like you don't know what could happen. I want you to think about strategies and approaches. You know what I'm trying to do here. I want to talk to Lynn....*

L: ***I'm glad Peter is not being so obstinate.***

H: He's a very reasonable sort.

L: I think it's like having rats in a cage. And, excuse this, but you're the rat, Howard. He wants to see how you'll perform. I think that's what's holding his interest.

H: I'm kind of checking that out, myself. Looking at myself as the rat. Seeing if I can pull this thing off.

L: Oh, please! You can't have those questions. That would be very bad.

H: (laughs) It's like this. I've hit a lot of home runs, and just come to the plate again. The track record's real good. I try to be very honest about what can and cannot be guaranteed. What we've discussed is completely attainable. Exactly how to go about it is something that evolves and unfolds. I have a high degree of confidence. Frankly, I'm more confident each time I talk with you.

AUGUST 17, 1992

P: So you want to savor your triumph? We're all grateful.

H: Now I'll hear from the chorus!

P: No, really, it was a brilliant move, putting Lynn in control. I didn't anticipate that.

H: Do you wish it hadn't happened? Are you upset?

P: It's just a variable in the experiment. There's nothing to be upset about, or not.

H: You don't have any emotional valance about it.

P: Naaa.

H: (laughs) And this is gratitude.

P: Oh! Let's see if I can muster gratitude. I congratulate you on a fine move. Well, it's acknowledgment, not gratitude.

H: Can you be of any help as far as where we go from here?

P: You've got me at check, and want me to tell you how to make it checkmate? It seems to me you were attempting to create a world where we have a life worth living. That was the real experiment. Scientists don't always know where their experiments will lead them.

H: I see exactly where it's going. I may take it for granted that everyone else does, too.

P: I don't think anybody has a clue.

H: Ah, come on! Lynn doesn't? (Peter laughs) Every time we get together we get a real indication of integration, but then there's still "is it soup yet?" Well, no, add the carrots. You want to tell me what you would find minimally acceptable?

P: Some kind of integration that could be felt as such.

H: Lynn just told me about Charyse. That was felt.

P: By Charyse, I'm sure.

H: Oh. You mean, you included?

P: (laughs) Why do you think I'm in this? I want to feel something. Something different. I'll be the first to admit, there have been changes in the last few weeks, perceived as positive.

H: You doubt it still?

P: There are ripple effects to everything. You have to let it all calm down a bit before you make that kind of judgment.

Peter integrated later that evening in the collective fight against Anita's hostile takeover.

21

Anita and the Ultimate Dangerous Act

Howard spoke often of "the ultimate dangerous act," and that we would probably find it sooner than later. Danger lay closest to the surface in my alter Anita. I'd feared her all my life without knowing why. No one wanted Howard to call her out, yet it seemed inevitable. We had no idea what might happen were she unleashed. The events of August 17, 1992, forced the issue. Marianne, a hysterical, hyperventilating, blind woman came forward to reveal Anita's plan to kill us in our car that evening. Lynn and Howard agreed it was necessary to intervene.

H: Anita, do you know I'm attempting to help? Am I for you, or against you?

A: (coldly) Nobody is for me.

H: I know how badly you were abused. I felt bad for you.

A: Nobody cares.

H: It's a difficult thing to explain. When you were little, before you were abused, you were perfect. You were a person someone could love and care about and want to be around.

A: Whatever I was before is irrelevant to what I am.

H: Is there anything that's valuable to you?

A: My pain. It's all I've got.

H: If you let go of it, would you be surprised to be filled up with joy and fulfillment?

A: (sarcastic) Yes, I would be amazed.

H: Do you know why it would surprise you?

A: Because it would be different.

H: Bingo. You've never experienced it.

A: And I never will.

H: The reason why it never will be is it's your way of proving it never should have been. You bought into what was said about you.

A: And done to me, and over me, and around me. I didn't have much choice.

H: *That's why you split off. You had great wisdom that knew you had to have choices. You're going to catch that line at the end of all this tribulation, and regain the hope you wanted.*

A: ***It's not going to happen like that, Howard. Just a flick of the steering wheel. Maybe not tonight, but sometime.***

H: *Maybe not in fifty years. All you're doing is using fear to make your point.*

A: ***It works.***

H: *No, it doesn't. You could have lived out your whole life, and died of natural causes.*

A: ***I doubt Erin will let us go that way. "Sniveling brat" that she is. She's going to eat her little face out. Even Peter dies of natural causes, sooner or later.***

H: *This isn't a test of wills. I'm not here to see what happens.*

A: ***No? Really, Howard?***

H: *You deserve better than what you have, is all. These things should never have happened.*

A: ***And they cannot be taken away.***

H: *I can't take away what has already happened. But, what will happen from here on out, is within everybody's power.*

A: ***Just like that.***

H: *That's how it works. What do you think of me?*

A: ***I think you're on your toes.***

H: *Do you like me?*

A: ***I don't like anyone, Howard.***

H: *I'm a nice guy. I'm wondering why you don't like me.*

A: ***Nice guys are especially troubling. They don't end up nice. Everyone's got a chink in their armor.***

H: *I suppose, if I could be someone with fewer chinks, or who operates in a way that the chinks aren't problematic, it means you should like me. 'Cause I'm a decent guy.*

A: ***The world is full of decent guys, and I don't like any of them, either. You're in good company.***

H: *The hardest thing to hear is someone saying they don't care about anything anymore.*

A: ***(exasperated) What do you think you're doing here, Howard? You want to pick my brain to figure out the most expedient way to destroy me.***

H: *There's a part of you that wants to be destroyed. Did you hear me compliment you a few days ago?*

A: ***The one with violins playing, and everyone takes a share of justifiable rage?***

H: *Yeah, I gave you great credit for existing.*

A: ***That was amusing. Do you think psychologists are by nature just dreamers?***

H: *No. Most of them are assholes.*

A: ***(laughs) So here we have this nice guy psychologist going against the grain of his profession. Putting forth his dreams for Anita. What can we make of that? I'd say he's going to be very disappointed.***

H: *I only have one obligation here, which is to understand you. That's all I ever ask of myself. I don't help; I don't save; I don't cure.*

A: ***I guess I don't get it.***

H: *'Cause you don't understand. I have the understanding I want. If you do anything destructive, my day will go on as always.*

A: ***I'm quite certain of that. But the chink in your armor is that you'll think about it for a long time. "Could have done this; maybe if I'd done that."***

H: *You don't know me, then.*

A: ***Oh, I think I do.***

H: *You can certainly take that chance. If there's any satisfaction in doing something destructive, you won't be around to know one way or the other. The bottom line here is, I don't have any investment in it. I can't even prevent you from doing it. That's presumptuous, and a distortion of whatever I can, or even should, do.*

A: ***The fact we're talking belies that statement. You could have let her drive off into the sunset.***

H: *And the reason you think I didn't?*

A: ***Because you care.***

H: *I never said I didn't care.*

A: ***Your obligation, maybe not as a nice guy psychologist, but just as a nice guy, is to not let something very bad happen to her.***

H: *That's it. But it has nothing to do with whether I can effect any change in you. If I had that power I would have done it long ago.*

A: ***So if you don't have this power, where is all this strength you keep talking about?***

H: *It lies in the knowledge that within you is a strength to overcome what you've been through. I have faith in that. I've seen it happen in you, repeatedly.*

A: ***Not in me.***

H: *Well, I was talking about you, that the rage was justifiable, and comes from the understanding that this should never be forgotten. In a pro-*

found way, you've kept this whole system alive. You've probably had more of a productive than destructive role. There's energy and strength in what you do. But, it's a backwards strength now. It's building a lot of confusion.

A: ***I do well with confusion.***

H: *I do, too. I can look at it and make sense.*

A: ***Round Two! Round One was a draw, I think.***

H: *Did you want to talk to me?*

A: ***It doesn't make any difference whether I want to or not. Nobody else wants you to. The poor little things are so afraid.***

H: *You make it sound like your strength lies in their fear.*

A: ***(grins) They do hop to it, when they hear my name.***

H: *They're doing the best they can.*

A: ***That's the problem our whole life. "The best you can" is shit.***

H: *If the better part of you could come out, the best they could do is to accentuate it.*

A: ***(incredulous) The better part?***

H: *I think something has to be destroyed here. The negativity, bleakness, callousness, non-caring. Your power trip.*

A: ***What would I do without my toys?***

H: *Well, think about it. You could energize all the others.*

A: ***Like I do now.***

H: *No, it's a negative energy which needs adjustment. They could be thankful you had the wisdom to split off, and still keep the appropriate rage, which was always a statement of the atrocities that occurred.*

A: ***(coldly) There will never be enough rage to make a statement of the atrocities that occurred.***

H: *That's the strongest thing you've said that I have to agree with. Unfortunately, you turned all that rage against you. I want you to understand this clearly. Whatever happened to you, is nothing compared to what you're doing to yourself.*

A: ***Oh, please. You do not have the slightest inkling where to begin imagining whatever was done to me. So it's pretty, as you might say, lame to compare it to what I have done since. I'm a novice compared to these people.***

H: *Why would you take out justified rage on innocent people?*

A: ***(coldly) Nobody is innocent here.***

H: *How do you define innocent?*

A: ***Pure. Untouched. Clean.***

H: Try this definition. Innocence is the condition of not deserving a bad thing to happen to you.

A: I'm saying you don't have to have an ax held over your head to prove you're innocent. Whether or not bad things are there, you just are.

H: I think you just made my point. No one deserves those things. That they happened, still means it should not have happened to you.

A: (exasperated) I am not making your point. You have Child A and Child B, both of whom are innocent. Child B has this thing he doesn't deserve to have happen hanging over his head like a dark cloud. Child A is in sunlight and never saw the cloud. We're all Child B, and nothing less than Child A is acceptable.

H: Do you think it's just luck of the draw, which category you're in?

A: The alternative is a beneficent God making it possible for us all to be in Category B land?

H: I'm saying there's a good life, and a shit life. Is it just luck of the draw?

A: I was barely born alive, and my life would have been much better if they had let me die.

H: So far, that might be true. But from this moment on, you can triumph.

A: Triumph?

H: Whatever brings on the good life will be a reason for you to be born. We're only talking about possibilities which you never experienced. But you did some incredibly clever things by splitting off, which says there's a strength in you for survival that counters your self-destructive tendencies. You could have died by sheer will years ago. You could have gone to sleep, and simply never awakened. I contend to you there's a reason why it didn't happen. You were casting a line into hope, only you had to split off to let someone else live out the possibility.

A: I've been fighting against that act my entire life. It was a stupid thing to do.

H: That remains to be seen. It can't be proven. Your premise is faulty.

A: You're not talking to Peter. I don't care if my premise is faulty! I don't care if any of this fits with your nice guy philosophy! I don't care about anything! I may have once, which resulted in this extremely foolish thing. My life has been about rectifying it.

H: Why haven't you been successful?

A: (shrugs) Bad luck, I guess.

H: So you can't win. If it's so easy, with the flick of a steering wheel, you're telling me it's just bad luck.

A: Bad timing.

H: How many chances have you had?

A: You want to challenge me, Howard?

H: If it's the right thing to do, then yeah (laughs), I'll challenge you.

A: How will you know until after you get a call from the coroner's office?

H: You've got this lofty idea you can prove some point here.

A: I can arrange it really easily.

H: And the thing that will make it happen now is my saying, "Make it happen?"

A: You have everyone aligned in a certain way. The chaos inside stopped me before. Now I know exactly where they are, what they'll do.

H: Is it completely orderly now? Enough to make this prediction that you can dance your way through to the end?

A: Lynn has described it as pretty quiet lately. You're helping me make it possible now. (smirks) How do you like that?

H: I don't like it. And who's challenging who?

A: (laughs) Well, I don't know anymore, Howard.

H: If you do yourself in, I will cry. If you're wondering whether I care, or if it would be a source of upset.

A: You made your little speech about how much stronger everyone is now. You say all the time that somebody's strength can also be their weakness. (gleefully) Howard, everybody is tucked away in a neat little corner with you! I'm home free! Round Two is mine. Round Three.

H: You called it early. So how are you going to do this?

A: Why would I tell you? Wouldn't that make it a little too easy for you to stop me?

H: I can't.

A: What? You're doing it by not even letting me drive off!

H: You want to get in the car and go? Here are the keys.

A: Oh, right. I don't think so.

H: Ding! Round Three, I won.

A: Watch it, Howard, your nice guy is slipping.

H: If this is the way you've described, then you should appreciate my influence more. You know I've wanted gratitude from everybody.

A: And you're getting it from me. Isn't that amazing? (graciously) Thank you, Howard, for making this all possible.

H: You know what I've noticed, Anita? You have a nice sense of humor. You're very pleasant. I heard bad things about you.

A: Where are we going with all this, Howard?

H: Are you impatient?

A: You wanted so badly to talk to me. You were so fascinated.

H: Are you being unkind?

A: ***You thought you'd snap your fingers, and make me into this nice little girl.***

H: *You're being insulting. I think much more of you than that. You have a lot of integrity, which means you have a right to your rage and anger.*

A: ***(innocently) I thought you were going to destroy me.***

H: *You don't need much more stress. I want to help you get through it.*

A: ***Have you got a different story, Howard? Let's do it.***

H: *I didn't see all the destructive things everyone talks about. You didn't show me the rage; I'm glad, I don't need to see it. You don't need to see mine, either. So we're both normal. What of it? You seem a nice enough person.*

A: ***(sarcastically) Yes, I'm your typical upstanding citizen.***

H: *I'm a little sick of your cynicism, but it doesn't matter.*

A: ***Want to know what Lynn is saying? (Lynn's voice, panicked) "Don't believe her! Howard, stop this right now!"***

H: *Stop talking to her? Why?*

A: ***(Lynn's voice) "She's fooling you! She's making you believe she's normal. She's not normal!"***

H: *Okay, she's nuts. Say it to me. Are you nuts?*

A: ***In a nice guy psychological way? Probably. If I say yes, are you going to lock me up?***

H: *I can't.*

A: ***(grins) Did I know that already?***

H: *Why don't you leave the others alone? Why pick on them?*

A: ***Why not? Why take it out on me 35 years ago?***

H: *It should not have happened to you, either.*

A: ***Well, so what? It did.***

H: *But, it stops.*

A: ***Yes, it stops. Then it continues in every relationship possible, so it's like it doesn't stop.***

H: *Does it continue in this relationship?*

A: ***I don't know you well enough yet. I know you talk about sniveling brats behind their back.***

H: *You know what I meant by it. Don't pervert it!*

A: ***I'm sure Erin didn't know. (softly) Are these your true colors, Howard? Is that what you really think of Erin?***

H: *You don't have any compelling reason to believe the opposite?*

A: ***In many ways, Erin is a sniveling brat.***

H: *Ah, I wonder why I said it?*

A: ***(laughs) Truth is not a defense in this case! You're trying to help these people, are you not?***

H: *God. You just twisted that into a million different knots.*

A: ***She doesn't think she's a brat, any more than Lynn thinks she's a bitch; and Nita thinks she's manic-depressive; and Sarah thinks she's a ditsy artistic type. They all think they're very normal, except a little nuts. So what's the big deal if I am a lot nuts?***

H: *You're also, in many ways, normal.*

A: ***(exasperated) We're not normal! Believe Lynn. She's easier.***

H: *Then leave them alone. Unless you can be productive. . .*

A: ***Well, screw that! Screw all of you!***

H: *Find a universal truth, a cosmic law that justifies "screw all of us." One thing that's important to you is the truth.*

A: ***Screw all of you! Because two wrongs do not make a right. You want us all to live in fantasyland.***

H: *That's an over-interpretation. I only talk about possibilities, not guarantees. I talk about chances, which are a result of building ego-strength and self-esteem. Those are real things that operate and exist in the world. You've seen them. You've wanted it for yourself, and haven't developed it, that's all.*

A: ***I say again, screw all of you. I don't care if it's connected in any cosmic way. The truth is, nobody cares.***

H: *That's a lie, and you know it.*

A: ***Nobody has ever cared, and nobody ever will. "I know what you want, and you can't have it."***

H: *Here I sit. Everything you've said goes against the reality. And what do you think I want, that I can't have? It's like, you're doing something to me?*

A: ***Not you, per se; everyone of us.***

H: *I say to you, they're innocent; stop picking on them. I say what your father should have said if he'd opened his eyes. I don't care if it's late in the game. You're not going to become the "them" that caused all this.*

A: ***This will never be rectified with the right people. So it really doesn't matter who you rectify it with.***

H: *I can appreciate that. If you go about it efficiently, you can have a very sweeping effect.*

A: ***I don't know that many child molesters and torturers are reading pop psychology these days. Or the three-year-olds they're ripping apart, either. The little book is just another pipe dream, and a pointless one, at that. It's more an epitaph than anything.***

H: *Maybe so. But leave them alone. It's a reasonable request.*

A: ***Why should I? What's in it for me?***

H: *There's nothing in it for you!*

A: ***You drive a hard bargain, Howard.***

H: *There's no bargain here. You want to be pathetic and rageful, do it. You want to destroy, you destroy you.*

A: ***We're all kind of connected.***

H: *Leave the others alone. There's no magic in any of this.*

A: ***And if I don't?***

H: *(exasperated) Then you'll fuck them, and yourself. Those are the alternatives.*

A: ***(pleased) You're getting it, Howard.***

H: *I've always had it. If you can be part of this in a productive way, fine. If you can't, leave them alone.*

A: ***Unfortunately, that's not what I'm all about, Howard.***

H: *It's too relevant, what you're all about.*

A: ***It's the point, what I'm all about.***

H: *What you're all about, be it elsewhere, in a non-destructive way to others. You can torment yourself in your head forever. That could be the legacy of the abuse, the tyranny, the strife. But leave the others alone.*

A: ***It can't go down like that, Howard. It's all or nothing.***

H: *Do you want to join the party, then?*

A: ***It's not my scene.***

H: *You've never in your life had an opportunity to deal with this in a confident, creative, straight-forward, forceful, productive, truthful way. If this is your last chance, you hit pay dirt. That's why you've hung around. It isn't because the chaos prevented you from doing yourself in. Twisting it and making it sound like all the pieces are standing up while you do your deed, I ain't buying it. And that's not a challenge.*

A: ***Then what is it?***

H: *It's just not true. I'd like you to be part of the team now. I have no magic. I'm not powerful in the slightest. I don't presume to understand things better than you do. I've shared with you what I see, know, and understand.*

A: ***(Lynn's voice) "If she agrees with you, it's a trick! She'll never go away! She'll come back!"***

H: *So I don't have to ask if you agree. Does Lynn understand you can't be destroyed because it's an all or nothing thing?*

A: ***(chiding) You've misunderstood me completely, Howard.***

H: *Well, just enlighten me.*

A: ***It's all or nothing with me. It's not that if you destroy me, they all disappear. They all disappear if you don't destroy me.***

H: *What if you were made central?*

A: ***(incredulous) That's how you plan to destroy me? What a concept. (laughs)***

H: *What do you think? We'll just — keep you here.*

A: ***Out in the open, where you can see me.***

H: *Out in the open, where you can do what you want.*

A: ***I can do what I want regardless.***

H: *So no pretenses then. It isn't about whether you're out, or not. We'll just throw away that facade.*

A: ***(smiles) Do you know what chaos you've created at the thought of making me central?***

H: *Talk to me. What's the chaos about?*

A: ***(Lynn, yelling) "Howard, stop it!"***

H: *What's the harm in talking to you?*

A: ***She doesn't understand what you're doing.***

H: *Has she got any better ideas?*

A: ***(laughs) I think Lynn is about tapped out of better ideas. Only you, in your violin fantasy, want me to be central. It won't quite follow the course you envisioned if I am.***

H: *Is that a warning? A plea? You want to live, don't you? And live well.*

A: ***Is it me or you? I actually want to die. I'm inviting you to destroy me. I'm giving you every reason to do it.***

H: *You can be destroyed when you realize there's a reason to live well. When you have hope, you are no longer a threat to yourself or anyone else. The worst things taken away were your dignity and hope. I'm sorry that happened. I'm hearing and sensing that you want to live....I want to talk to Lynn.*

A: ***(reflective) Is it good-bye, Howard?***

H: *(surprised) I don't know, but I wish you well. I'm pulling for you, for the best that you are. That's not a pipe dream. That's what should have been, it's what we live. I'll say good-bye. I want to speak with Lynn. (30 seconds pass)*

A: ***Interesting, isn't it? Maybe you'll only hear from Lynn through me. Wouldn't that be something?***

H: *So be it. (30 seconds pass)*

A: ***Power is a strange thing.What now, Howard?***

H: *Nothing. (60 seconds pass)*

Suddenly, I was Lynn again (or so I believed then), gasping for air, trembling, my voice full of fear and anxiety.

L: ***She's an evil woman.***

H: *Evil feeds on fear. One can say to evil, "Back off!"*

L: ***(Trying to recover) She was playing with me.***

H: *I'm not surprised at all by how it went. I knew she would hold on. It was to provoke fear in me.*

L: ***Did it work? Say no!***

H: *Of course it didn't work. I'm not putting up with that. It was all very calculated.*

L: ***I don't think I'll ever be strong enough up against her.***

H: *She's all talk.*

L: ***Why do you think we all keep her down? She's not all talk.***

H: *You're closer to dealing with it than you were before.*

L: ***It seems like she's closer to dealing with it.***

H: *You sure are giving in on this.*

L: ***When we've restrained her, I've had tons of people helping me, but it was like there was nobody.***

I later described this event as three people (Howard, Lynn, and Anita) standing on a vast nothingness, with light emanating from nowhere...spinning out into the universe. Making Anita central was, in effect, fighting words for everyone inside. I watched inner cubicles collapse into themselves as inside people united to fight against Anita's takeover. When Howard told Lynn to search for Anita, she said, "I can't see her." Howard didn't ask if Lynn saw anyone else. She wondered if the others were taken by Anita. She didn't realize she actually had lots of help. It was in my knowing this, and knowing Lynn didn't know this, that I understood a few days later that I could no longer be Lynn. I was someone new, an amalgam of the many who had united. Meanwhile, Anita disappeared for a year following this session.

In March 1993, Erin disclosed more of what happened to her at "the bad place," including her forced group participation in killing a man who threatened to expose Ron to the police.

MARCH 25, 1993

H: *It's simply understanding things in the most correct perspective. And it's critical that you don't resist. You know that people are a spectrum of things, good and bad. Anybody who thinks they're not capable of doing certain things is fooling themselves. So what you did, any decent, compassionate person who operates by the golden rule is also capable of doing, and worse. This makes a stronger explanation for the emergence of Anita.*

S: ***There wasn't enough already?***

H: There was plenty. Being forced to participate was anathema to you; you could not do it. You actually held to your convictions, even as a youngster — a most powerful, heroic thing. It's an attractive notion that we'd surrender our own lives, rather than do a despicable thing. The reality is, most people would probably do the despicable thing to save their life. A good case could be made that you would have allowed yourself to die rather than do anything you considered despicable. Then Anita emerged.

S: But it was Erin doing it. She has the memories.

H: Erin is the symbol of a scary, distrusting youth. It doesn't necessarily mean she did the act, but in her memories she's the only one who is a little girl. The sophistication isn't developed enough for her to consider that this happened when you were a little girl. We have strong reason to believe Anita has a conscience. She emerges to do the despicable thing, and then knows she must be punished, because she is a very self-destructive individual.

MARCH 27, 1993

Dear Howard,

I've been reviewing the Anita tapes in light of recent discoveries. Here are some of my observations:

A: Nobody is innocent here.

This goes to the heart of why we think we're so bad, and why it's true that Anita had a conscience. She is unwilling to give anyone the benefit of a doubt or any excuse, no matter how victimized they were. That nobody is innocent indicated I must have participated in some way.

A: No, you don't want to know, Howard, because you might think about your children and not want something like that to happen to them.

I saw this as her most despicable act. It shows the magnitude of her lost innocence, that anyone is now fair game.

A: Nobody has ever cared, and nobody ever will care. "I know what you want, and you can't have it."

FLASH: It's caring that I want and think I can't have.

A: This will never be rectified with the right people. So it really doesn't matter who you rectify it with.

She acknowledges some kind of atonement is possible, albeit with the wrong people. If Anita participated in hurting live people, they were random victims, too. If she "relished" hurting them as a proxy for hurting Ron, the same logic applies to hurting anyone randomly now to "rectify" it.

A: It's all or nothing.

Anita must see things as all or nothing because her survival depended upon it. If she'd known she was no longer under those constraints, she probably would not have seen disappearing as her only option.

A: Do you know he turned out to be a clone of Ron? He was abusive;

alcoholic; he hit me; threatened me with a knife; he taunted me. He left me.

Anita sees Ron leaving her as another terrible act. Her life has no meaning if she isn't defending against him or fearing him. In her mind, he never leaves, because she creates the fear that the others react to. Ron's power trip becomes Anita's power trip.

A: I'm inviting you to destroy me. I'm giving you every reason to do it!

She doesn't understand why you're not doing it. Men don't behave this way in her world. It confuses her.

The next months were a blur. My life fell apart. I was laid off from work and lost my health benefits. My asthma worsened, and I became more reclusive. I experienced many flashbacks. Unbeknownst to me, Erin sent Howard two faxes. Erin, who was theoretically integrated. When I subsequently tried to contact Erin, instead I met twelve year old Samantha, who was news to me. She claimed Anita was terrorizing Erin inside.

MAY 26, 1994

H: Do you think that Anita — for all the bad things she's done — got that way for some good reason?

E: It's good to be bad?

H: No, but she may have gotten that way by being abused. Do you believe Anita could ever change, to be good or nice?

E: She's never been nice, ever, ever.

H: I wonder if that's because she's been so badly mistreated? (she cries) I'm just asking.

E: I didn't put little kids in a box! Nobody was nice to me when I was little, and I don't go around being mean! So why should she be able to be mean to me?

H: She shouldn't. I'm just wondering if she could be repentant or regretful. I wonder if she could not want to be and do what she's doing? Do you understand that there's good and bad in all people?

E: Uncle Ron was bad! He was good, too?

H: The truth is, I just don't know about Ron. I wouldn't go out on a limb, and say, "Well, there's even some good in him." But one might encounter something about him that was redeeming or good. I don't figure I'll ever know. So I'll always condemn his behavior, because it was evil.

E: (crying) You think Anita's got good stuff in her?

H: Yeah. The part of this little girl that is naughty, unkind, aggressive or abusive got put onto this person called Anita. Everyone is so frightened of her — understandably — and it makes me wonder if she's ever treat-

ed nicely, would Anita overcome her badness and reform?

Howard reassured Erin that Anita would never again be able to terrorize her. Erin stood next to me inside while Howard spoke with Anita.

A: ***(sarcastic) It's good to tell little girls all these lies. It makes them feel so much better.***

H: *What aren't you telling me?*

A: ***You've always been so optimistic, Howard. It's not going to do enough, in the long run.***

H: *How can you say my optimism didn't accomplish anything?*

A: ***(grins) I'm still here!***

H: *Maybe you're supposed to be here. Maybe you're good.*

A: ***(laughs) Yeah, I am good, Howard.***

H: *You've got a lot of power. Maybe you're also good-hearted.*

A: ***Here we go with that again. Seems like only yesterday.***

H: *Did you put Erin in a room?*

A: ***Little girls talk too much crap from childhood.***

H: *It was painful to listen to.*

A: ***Some things are better left unsaid.***

H: *The idea is that you're tough and can take anything. Yet, what this little girl says has the power to distress you terribly because it hurts.*

A: ***No, it has more to do with connections still out there. The world has some very interestingly bad people. Little girls talking too much could maybe get us into really bad trouble.***

H: *Thank goodness you hung around! You have, in some way, kept a presence consistently here. Perhaps it was important that you not integrate completely because there's more story to tell. You're very tenacious, as is Erin.*

A: ***There's lots more story, Howard. That's my point.***

Howard made a deal with Anita. She was free to "harass" him as long as she left everyone else alone. I felt she was capable of causing him great harm, if not merely disruption. After a particularly upsetting session, Howard asked that I not listen to the session tape until I got my bearings again. I agreed, then promptly listened to it that evening. The next time we spoke, rather than explain myself, I lied and told him I'd not listened to it yet. Anita sent Howard a fax reporting my transgression.

JUNE 3, 1994

H: *You are an interesting person, Anita.*

A: ***Thank you. I guess you didn't get my fax?***

H: *The paper jammed.*

A: ***Darn! (laughs) I thought it would be like a stellar event for you.***

H: Tell me what it said.

A: "Dearest Howard."

H: Oh, how nice. Do you feel about me that way?

A: (grins) You're like the dearest Howard I know.

H: You like me, don't you?

A: You want to hear that so bad. Maybe you should ask Desiree.

H: (smiles) No, I'll get in trouble.

A: "Knowing that you worship at the alter of truth, pun intended," (he laughs) "would you be offended to learn that Sarah told you outrageous lies? She listened to the tape all night. And she has the nerve to blame her sleep disturbances on me."

H: You just had to tell me, right?

A: I'm sure it was quite a shock.

H: Well, she confessed. Was she reassured when I said, "Why are you making a big deal over that?"

A: Oh, she understood then, but she sweated it all weekend. That's paragraph two. That I understood now how well I could produce these distant ripple effects. That I could, perhaps, effectively harass others by harassing you. Then I mentioned Linda Blair.[1] (he laughs) What a nice effect, to think of you sitting in your kitchen at midnight, imagining my phone call.

H: That really scared the shit out of me. (laughs)

A: I said, "A deal's a deal, Howard."

H: You've got a flair, don't you?

A: And I wished you a happy weekend. It makes Sarah even nuttier when I'm quiet. Isn't that great?

H: No, it's mean-spirited. So let's tighten up our deal a bit more.

A: I can't control Sarah's paranoia.

H: You'll just manipulate her.

A: It was so easily done.

H: So don't do it. We're adding that to the deal. These people feel pretty negative about whether you can be trusted.

A: Good for them. They've learned well.

H: They've also learned that you can be trusted because you honored your end of the deal.

A: There are always bigger and better ways to scare them. Deal or no deal.

H: Do you think I'm naive?

A: Yes. And so very "hopeful."

H: What should I have said when I first met Nita? "I'm not a very hopeful person, so why don't you just leave?"

A: ***(laughs) Four times or less![2] You could have unloaded the bunch of us! But no!***

H: *I should not have been hopeful? It's naive to be hopeful? Does hope have no place in a person's life?*

A: ***It must get pretty frustrating, Howard, doing this week after week. You want me to make you happy? What will you do for me?***

H: *What do you want?*

A: ***(loudly) I want the world!***

H: *You can have it. I'll give you the world.*

A: ***(disbelief) That's naive!***

H: *I know, I'm sorry! (smiles) I think the world can be yours. If you make me happy.*

A: ***Why should I?***

H: *You'd break my heart? Tell me you don't like me, and you will have gotten all the hope out of me.*

A: ***You have enough adoring audiences elsewhere. Everybody loves you, Howard. That ought to make you happy.***

H: *None of them matter. Only you.*

A: ***You want to be happy...so do I.***

H: *You get the world; I get liked by you. You'll please me.*

A: ***(concedes) That's a trade-off.***

H: *It's cheap.*

A: ***The problem is, I'm pretty sure I can deliver.***

H: *I can do it. Tell me you like me? And mean it.*

A: ***Geez! You want me to mean it, too! I can't do that. The nice guy psychologist wants me to be nice to him. (indignant) Why is it so important to you?***

H: *I can't explain it.*

A: ***Well, do. Try. You explain everything else, Howard.***

H: *I couldn't believe in anything anymore if I didn't know you liked me.*

A: ***I'm sure!***

H: *I try to be very nice, reasonable, and decent. If all that happens, and you still don't like me — because it would naturally bring liking out — I couldn't believe in anything anymore.*

A: ***You don't believe in Erin? Or Sarah?***

H: *Or trees.*

*A: **You're being so facetious.***

H: I'm dead serious. The whole of my existence lies in being a decent person, in the truest sense. And always, to bring out a liking from people around me.

*A: **There are people in the world who aren't going to like you, Howard. No matter what you do.***

H: Tell me I'm not treating you that way.

*A: **Your whole existence can't hinge on whether I like you.***

H: Well, it's come down to it. I never thought when I woke up today (she laughs) that this would happen, but I just realized the total meaning of life.

*A: **You are a liar! You're on tape. Remember that.***

H: Play the tape, I don't care. Broadcast it.

*A: **I just might! So why would this nice guy psychologist try to pump up my ego?***

H: I'm not doing that. I'm asking to be liked. It has nothing to do with your ego. Frankly, it's only my own narcissistic needs. I'm being quite self-centered now. Now, out with it.

*A: **Can't do that. Burst your little bubble.***

H: You just did. You caused a great pain.

*A: **How can I harass you if I like you?***

H: I forbid you to harass me unless you like me first.

*A: **Oh, that's so pathetic! I like the deal we have already. But what would you give me if I agree to this narcissistic deal?***

H: Oh, so the world being yours isn't enough.

*A: **It's always a package deal with you. First, I like you; then I don't harass you; then I wanna be loved by you.***

H: (laughs) You know I do love you, don't you? (she groans) Yes, you do!

*A: **There's that naiveté again. Do you love me when I stick Erin in the box?***

H: No, I don't love that. That's a sick behavior. You need help. You can't make a distinction between you love somebody, but you don't condone their deeds? I couldn't love a bad person.

*A: **I guess you must. But you just said you can't, so you're confusing the hell out of me. I don't think you can give me the world anyway, so it's kind of a bum deal. You are funny. I'll give you that. I like a good sense of humor.***

H: That means you like me!

*A: **No, it doesn't!***

H: (gleefully) Yes, it does! A person is their sense of humor. That's their essence. It's something I like to know most about a person. You have a good sense of humor, too.

A: ***Knowing that will not take away all the crap of my life.***

H: *Nothing will take that away. There's not a therapy on the planet that will make those bad things good. That's irrelevant, of course, to whether you like me.*

A: ***(mock scream) You're torturing me!***

H: *(laughs) I know I am. You hate it. Tell me you like me.*

A: ***And in that moment, the gates of heaven open wide, and there's this bright light. . .***

H: *(sings) Hallelujah! Hallelujah!*

A: ***Or Publisher's Clearinghouse breaks through the door (he laughs) saying, "You have just won $10,000,000 because you like Howard." Well, I don't think that's gonna happen, either.***

H: *You know what? Whether you say it or not, you can't help feeling it, anyway. The point is, you do.*

A: ***You are not only naive, you are relentless.***

H: *It's just the Anita in me putting you through this. I'm being mean. I can put aside my own narcissistic needs to realize that you do like me, anyway.*

A: ***(sarcastic) Darn. I've been unmasked.***

H: *Remember when we talked about making Anita central? Uh oh! Look out, inside! Maybe I should just let you walk out of here. You're not laughing anymore. Why not?*

A: ***I think you're nuts. Is there a point to all this? (he nods) Care to enlighten me?***

H: *You can't figure it out?*

A: ***I'm sorry I disappoint you, Howard. You must not like me anymore.***

H: *You don't disappoint me in the slightest. Would you dislike me if I were less intelligent?*

A: ***I haven't studied psychology for 20 years. I might have missed a few nice guy psychologist's tricks.***

H: *You seem tired.*

A: ***No, I'm never tired. You're not going to tell me the point?***

H: *To what?*

A: ***To this conversation. My perceived lack of intelligence. Brain-deadness. Tiredness. Begging me to say I like you.***

H: *You refuse to do it, and what am I going to do? Beat you up?*

A: ***Well, what happens if I do, exactly?***

H: *You experience the joys of feeling accepted by other people.*

A: ***(wistfully) You don't think I'm gonna be the next female serial killer?***

H: Oh, please. No, I don't think so.

A: Then I'll live an unfulfilled life, won't I?

H: If you're referring to your impulse to become a serial killer, yes, it will be unfulfilled. But, with integration, it won't matter. Until the integration, it will trouble Sarah that such a thought can even exist. There is a great deal for you to gain with integration. You'll be out, with as much control as you want. You'll enjoy respect.

A: (distastefully) Respect. That's a pretty tall order.

H: That's a very tall order. What do you think I'm doin' this for? I want you to take a deep breath. . . Sarah?

A: Missed opportunities. . . .

S: (sighs)

H: Sarah, you don't need to be frightened. This fear is a problem. We've accomplished a great deal, and you're very tired. I was wearing everyone down.

S: (trying to focus) I'm in the middle.

H: I know it's disorienting. You're kind of like in post-op.

S: "Missed opportunities." What does that mean?

H: I suspect she felt integration could happen, but didn't.

S: She wanted it?

H: I think she did, but she's very resistant. It may not be a missed opportunity. Integration could occur away from me.

At this point I experienced an intense flashback that began with what looked like home movies in my head. Pictures of Anita being tortured and abused. She compelled me to watch. The scene acquired a "you are there" quality. I was very small, trying to hide from Ron, whispering to Howard to be quiet to avoid discovery. Howard instructed me to tell Ron that he could not hurt me any more, but I couldn't do it. The pain and fear grew until I whispered a plea to Howard to make Ron go away.

I could not open my eyes out of fear of what I might see. I was exhausted, and barely able to sit up. Anita said inside me, "Tell Howard that I like him." He danced around the room, full of excitement, and frustration, grumbling, "It's not on tape!" (The session tape had finished already.)

On June 11, 1994, I believed I was prepared to attempt complete integration, including Anita. Howard's many sessions with Anita had fatigued her. She was losing her edge and wanting relief. Integration represented escape. Howard spoke with each of my then-known-remaining alters, who agreed to integrate.[3] Anita offered that he was leaving someone behind. Someone no one else knew existed, far, far away in a room of Anita's own making. To Howard's (and my) astonishment, she guided Original Anita, a three-year-old, to the outside. This was the original me, untouched by insanity, cruelty, and pain. Original Anita was a lovely trusting child who asked Howard if he had any coloring books.

Anita split off from Original Anita at the first opportunity when Ron's abuse started. Her purpose in my life was to protect Original Anita from all harm. Unfortunately, Anita skewed this mandate to the extent that she would have killed us all. Anita volunteered to be most hated and feared as a way to keep prying eyes away from her little hideaway. It worked, too.

The existence of Original Anita validated Howard's repeated assessment that I had not lost my goodness despite my history. Integrating her made me feel more complete, yet I could not become her, and start over as a three-year-old. I also subsequently discovered other "integration leftovers."

22

Missy

What would I be thinking and doing if I truly believed I'm not bad and that I've triumphed? What does it feel like to feel whole? Alive? Happy? Safe? Loved?

—SARAH, APRIL 18, 1993

Missy, a terrified four-year-old, presented herself when this book's first draft was nearing completion. Over a two-week period, her voice became insistently louder in my head, saying, "I can't tell." It was accompanied by horrific headaches, blurred vision, and dizziness, which effectively halted my work. Since I've wanted "to tell," in one way or another, since childhood, this voice puzzled me, but also affirmed another point of view from within. She insisted "the bad people" could find her if her name was said out loud. She believed strongly in magic, good and bad. Howard persuaded her that he held enough good magic to shield her from those she feared. She reluctantly told him her name.

JUNE 2, 1995

Dear Howard,

I found a writing from three years ago, written to you. "There's the little one who wants to please you so much and do everything right because you hold so many keys you are magic. You see her even when she is invisible even when she is magic too she's afraid of what will happen if she doesn't do it right every time she's afraid that her magic is gone she's afraid. "

I was so excited when I read this! We've found Missy. I'd made a grand assumption that this described Erin, but you were her teacher, not her wizard. Missy says she never looks out through my eyes, but she must, to know you are magic.

Missy personified the notion that those "interestingly bad people" will get me if I tell my story. Her beliefs derived directly from her participation in cult-like rituals and ritual abuse perpetrated against her. The idea of an evil cult brainwashing and abusing children has been so ridiculed and stereotyped as to create a backlash against any survivor who mentions the term. But seemingly wild accounts of satanic ritual abuse in preschool cases are relatively rare occurrences in the overall scope of cult activities. These stories sell newspapers.

Every day, however, children are ritually abused by their caretakers in much less sensational incidents. It's reported often enough, and with such consistency in terms of psychological impact, as to require examination. A cult mentality effectively exists within a parent who beats a child senseless in the name of Jesus. Brainwashing techniques are regularly used to teach children they are worthless and should never have been born. The secrecy and shame engendered by child sexual abuse is no less damaging than that which might be created in a cult context. Many incestuous abuses are performed within rituals of bath, naptime, or bedtime stories. The psychic damage is enormous, no matter what label we give it.

In my own childhood, I was exposed to ritualized abuse through Ron's covert activities in manufacturing child pornography, and later, snuff films involving teenaged runaways. Within his attempts to make the films seem more ritualized, Ron began to experiment with satanic rituals and sacrifices. Both Erin and Missy suffered as a result. I didn't catch up with all of these memories in one piece, either. There's only so much horror the brain can manage at one time. It began with the realization that I'd known what snuff films were about since I was a small child.

November 28, 1992

Dear Howard,

I don't know how you or anyone can expect me to experience "triumph" with this kind of history. I'm spinning again. I can't breathe. I got spinning so much it scared me. I can't stand it. Erin is still here, and I know about the snuff films. How can I ever be like a normal person? I will carry this burden forever.

March 22, 1993

H: What are Erin's bad dreams about?

S: I know what my dreams were when I was a kid. There was always a man chasing me with a knife. Sometimes I was tied up, and he'd stab me. Sometimes I died, sometimes not. I had these dreams hundreds of times. I relied on QuickDraw McGraw to save me. Sometimes he made it, sometimes not. I was tied up in a room like a cave, with candles. He'd untie me, and we'd gallop off into the sunset. He knew how to get in and out of the cave, somehow.

Later, in the same session, Howard spoke to Erin:

H: Remember you used the word "brainwash" a lot? They made you believe something that wasn't true.

E: They said it was true.

H: They wanted you to be so fearful that you'd do what they told you to do. That's how it works. What did they want you to do?

E: Really bad things.

H: What's a bad thing? To hurt someone?

E: (whispers) Sometimes they wouldn't hurt 'cause they were already dead.

H: Are you afraid you hurt somebody who was alive?

E: I did it! I know I did!

H: This is a horrible thing they did to you, honey. Do you understand whose fault it was?

E: (whispers) It was my fault. (louder) I should have just stabbed myself and then they wouldn't be able to make me do that ever again!

H: That's a terrible thing to have to decide. I want you to know you're okay, and they can't hurt you.

E: They'll come get me.

H: You feel as if they're still going to get you, but they won't.

MARCH *24, 1993*

Dear Howard,

I can look at this objectively — probably because I say Erin did it, not me — and wonder at how many layers of defenses you had to break down to get here. That's the limit of my objectivity, sorry. I'm extremely depressed, almost paralyzed. Everything inside me fights against accepting this. Why was I spared? Nobody believed me? Because getting rid of me at five was too risky for my mother, so she just quietly tried to create my accidental death over the years?

I keep thinking of her saying, "You're the last one I expected to be here," after her stroke. I was crushed, especially when she warmly welcomed Linda. I'm certain she meant to wound, but now I wonder if her comment was also a verification of how badly she treated me. If I'd known the full extent of it then, would I have shown up, at all?

MARCH 30, 1993

E: Those people are gonna come get me. Howard doesn't know how they do things.

S: Erin, they're far away now and can't hurt you.

E: That's what you think. He doesn't have to see you.

S: Who?

E: The God of Darkness.

S: Oh, geez. Who's that?

E: If he sees you from far away he can hurt you just as bad as if he's by you. He sees you when you're sleeping he knows when you're awake he knows when you've been bad or good. . .

S: *That's a Christmas song!*

E: *It's his song and you only sing it at night.*

S: *Was Mommy there when they made you do bad things?*

E: *(whispers) Sometimes. (anxious) That's why I didn't want to see her dead. 'Cause she could for sure get me.*

S: *No, honey, she couldn't do that.*

E: *You don't know! The dead people reach out and grab you and then you're a dead person too. Howard doesn't know how bad they are. They could hurt him and it would be my fault.*

S: *You take on everything, don't you? They can't do anything to Howard. Maybe you still don't realize that no matter how bad you feel, you aren't bad. Nothing will happen to you now.*

E: *(anxious) There was this bad man in the bad place. But they hurted him, too.*

S: *Why did they hurt him?*

E: *(whispers) If I tell....It was like a song.*

S: *How did it go? (Erin enters a trance that is difficult to break.)*

E: *Oh God of Darkness we submit to thy holy power wherever thou art known oh God of Darkness we submit to thy holy power wherever treason lies oh God of Darkness we submit to thy holy power wherever trespassers would mock thee oh God of Darkness we submit to thy holy power a righteous sacrifice to exalt thee oh God of Darkness we submit to thy holy power all earthly distractions from thy glory and sanctification oh God of Darkness we submit to thy holy power a blood sacrifice for thy forgiveness oh God of Darkness we submit to thy holy power wherever thou art. . .*

S: *Erin!*

E: *(screaming) known and we pray for thy guidance in this world of unceasing pain and disillusionment oh God of Darkness we submit to thy holy power. . .*

S: *Erin! Stop! You're not there now! Come out of it!*

E: *(fearful) You're Sarah?*

S: *Yeah, don't do more of the song, okay? I heard enough. Remember where you are.*

E: *I'm in the bad place.*

S: *No, that was a long time ago. What happened to that man?*

E: *It was like the song.*

S: What are you saying? Don't start the song again.

E: He didn't know about the part where they prayed. He came there just to do the bad thing to me so he was mad 'cause it wasn't about Jesus.

S: Great. It was okay to hurt you, but he's arguing religion.

E: They got mad and everybody killed him with the knife while we sang the song.(whispers) I feel icky.

S: It would be kind of confusing. I'd feel icky and bad, but then there's one less person to hurt me. So I'd be happy.

E: It's bad to feel happy 'cause you did something bad.

APRIL 1, 1993

Dear Howard,

I just bought a book on ritual abuse, waiting till after my own experiences were independently documented. I really didn't want to see it. Breaking the Circle of Satanic Ritual Abuse: Recognizing and Recovering from the Hidden Trauma, *Daniel Ryder, C.C.D.C., L.S.W. (1992). I thought it could generally apply to badly abused people who never saw a cult. Then he discussed a patient exposed to cult activities, with "a heavy emphasis on prostitution and the production of pornography, including "snuff films." Snuff films, said to show people literally being tortured and killed, are sold throughout covert networks as part of the pornography industry."* [1] *This shocked me. I thought snuff films weakened the ritual abuse theory because they were so crassly commercial.*

Ryder emphasizes that cults are sophisticated in mind control techniques, and makes a very scary point. He says children are programmed so compulsive suicidal behavior kicks in whenever they get too close to the memories. The programming is subtle — a compulsive person might just slowly eat to death.

The book has checklists for behavioral symptoms and psychological indicators of ritual abuse. I checked dozens of them, including asthma, insomnia, panic attacks, nightmares, migraines, overweight, hypervigilance, exaggerated startle response. You may say, "Of course, we've been looking at these things all along." But I've never seen them applied as a group to ritual abuse, so it's somewhat alarming. And more confirmation.

Maybe my resistance since day one had more to it than pure obstinance. Think how many times and ways you had to say "you're not crazy" before I got it. Think about Anita insisting, "No one is innocent here." Pure cult-speak. If I was programmed, which seems likely since they had years to do it, then saying, "These things aren't true" doesn't dissolve them. I want to aggressively deal with all aspects of it. ("Faster, faster!" I've found Lynn.) I suspect that when I reach the heart of it, I'll be ready to start crying again which, oddly, I'm looking forward to.

APRIL 18, 1993

Maybe the "programming" dies with recognition that it is a program, but I don't know what to replace it with. My whole life has been externally structured and controlled by Ron and Mommy; by MPD; by programmed responses. Take all the controls away, and I might as well be three again. I don't know what to do or how to act. I've gone from no choice to all choice, and it's just as restrictive, as I don't even know what the choices are.

APRIL 19, 1993

E: Sarah's been real scared of those bad people.

H: You mean, like they'll come and get her?

E: More like, they already got her. 'Cause they got this program in her. The bad people make her think bad things.

H: Do you know what the cure for that is?

E: She said we should come out together, 'cause we're two people that's how they do it. Like there's a crack between us and they could slip in there.

H: That's probably how it works, except it didn't happen this time. They planned to cause you all kinds of trouble.

E: They did!

H: I know that, but it failed.

E: No, it didn't!

H: This was supposed to be a lifelong program. Your life is young. Most of it will be happy. You're going to feel whole, and in control, like a healthy adult feels. You're gonna have fun, and be playful. You'll get to use your intelligence, and be creative. You think you won't like it, right? I think the more you've experienced what's going on, the more information you've given Outside Sarah, the more you've realized that going inside is a good thing.

E: I think if there's like one more bad thing then it would be stupid to not get rid of the bad thing. After all this.

MAY 2, 1993

When I (seemingly out of nowhere) mentioned snuff films to Sandy this morning, it struck me hard that I said in my Fantasy Number Nine[2], "And we do the story where he says he'll kill me if I don't do everything he says, and I say please don't kill me I'll do anything." I originally thought it odd syntax that "we do the story." But Ron rehearsed me to respond in certain ways. Sometimes the story was real. The teenaged girl was given the same "story." Same lines, except she really died. This is why Erin, misguidedly, thought she could have helped. Erin didn't understand that the story had changed profoundly.

It then hit me that I saw this girl killed, as it was filmed.[3] There was a round black and white clock on the wall; she died at 10:34. I burned that time stamp into my brain because I had to remember to tell someone and they would want to know when she died. This is why I looked at the clock every morning at 10:34 for six weeks. I remembered other times etched in my mind, too. 7:42 a.m. 3:17 a.m.

The Number Nine Fantasy is the re-enactment of the making of a snuff film. Sometimes I saw myself die in it because I was grown up, and it was the grownups who died. When I was too embarrassed to describe it to Howard, he said, "Does anyone get hurt? Besides you?" It was no stretch to say I could very easily see myself getting killed at one of these group things. I had seen it happen to others.

I feel so empty and like there's never going to be anything inside of me again. I'm not dealing in my feelings because I think if I let go on this I will go someplace I can never get back from again.

During the next two years, I found an uneasy peace in myself with these memories. Erin purposely avoided integration in August 1992 to be able to tell our story, so when I heard "I can't tell," I knew it was not her. The emergence of Missy evidenced a deeply concealed fear that bad people still lurked in the world, just waiting to get me.

JUNE 7, 1995

Dear Howard,

Tonight Dan and I went to the beach for a walk. He brought a bottle of bubbles (the kind with a wand). We made bubbles all over the beach in the wind. Erin asked if Missy could do it, too. The bubbles amazed and fascinated her; they were "magic." Then a police car came by, siren going. She froze, saying, "There's bad people here." Her logic was, police chase bad people, so everyone at the beach became a suspect. She wanted to go home fast. Dan warned that the seat belt would come up across her. She cringed away from him, saying, "Don't tie me down please!" She had a full-blown anxiety attack right in front of him. She kept saying, "Make me go away!" so he called me out. I was still hyperventilating.

JUNE 23, 1995

Dear Howard,

Last night, Missy drew another picture on the computer. It was inside a castle, with a girl lying on a table, obviously dead (flowers on chest). A wizard spread magic colors over her. In the background was a circle of fire. She told Dan that bad people were using bad red magic while the wizard kept the girl safe from the bad magic after she died. Dan tried to get her to believe the girl was really sleeping. She adamantly named the picture "Dead Girl."

I was exceedingly depressed, and told him this image was real. Missy's only means of exerting control was to create magic to protect

the girl after she died, since Missy couldn't help while the girl still lived. This might explain why I was out of focus most of the day yesterday.

Dan and I treated Missy's fears as entirely legitimate. When she balked at looking out the front window, a friend suggested that the wind "paints her invisible" so bad people cannot see her. Dan bought "magic rocks" and let her select the most magic ones to place in each room of the house to protect us. He also bought a wind chime with metallic painted butterflies surrounding a "magic wand." He told her the chimes blew magic throughout the house, and whenever she heard them, she could know she was safe.

We encouraged her to draw pictures of her safe magic oasis. It always (even when drawn in outer space) consisted of a pond surrounded by magic flowers and a rainbow. Howard instructed Missy to "make a rainbow" with her hand by moving it in an arc in front of her whenever she felt afraid. Erin (grudgingly) acted as a helpful big sister when Missy was most fearful. When I completely integrated a month following the beach incident, Missy was internalizing a sense of safety for the first time in her life.

I don't really care what the FBI or anyone with their own agenda says about the "reality" (or lack thereof) of cult activity. I know what I know, and I knew it before I met Howard. I don't believe Ron and my mother were involved in an organized cult; I think they made it up as they went along. One does not need cult organization to create and inflict cult-like cruelty and control. My personal documentation which evidences the reality of their activities is stored in ancient poems; persistent nightmares; phobias shared with Charlotte; and two small children who feared continuously that "the bad people" would find them.

I know now that my lifelong mantra "I know what you want, and you can't have it" was a form of programming. As was my belief for so many years that I was crazy, worthless, and a bad person. Learning to never trust anyone by way of horrendous lessons prevented people from getting close to the real me, and my truth. At least, until I met Howard.

23

Integration and Aftermath

Integration means you are one person who has the happy, excited, life-fulfilling stuff, as well as the sad, tragic, and scary stuff. When you integrate, you won't be flooded with only good stuff. All those parts come together in one person. It isn't just the idealized alter who surfaces and wins out over the others. You are as much the stuff you don't like, as you are the stuff you do like. On top of that, it's irrelevant whether you ever discover other people.

—Howard to Nita, April 13, 1992

Integration is an endlessly scary and intense process. I think I'm doing very well, under the circumstances, but I'm not Wonder Woman.

—Sarah, July 22, 1992

Howard and I encountered no greater mystery, or greater source of frustration, than the concept of "integration." I could not conceive of being anyone other than "me." Everyone has an occasional fantasy about switching places with someone for a day, but what if circumstances required you to make it permanent? Would you switch with someone you'd never met before?

I especially could not envision becoming a composite of all these characters inside. What did integration really mean? Would I talk differently? Would I think like me? Would I be more (or less) intelligent? (My own assessment maintained that some of these people were not very smart.) Would I change my taste in music? Clothes? Men? Would I still write poetry, or was that a function of splitting? Would I feel more alive and less alone? Or would all the confusion and chaos focus on just one instead of many? What would integration feel like? How would I know it had happened?

I philosophically espouse complete integration as a goal for people with DID, although I do not force that belief upon anyone. It's difficult for me to believe I could feel whole without being whole. I am still learning what that really means, and the transition is ongoing. Perhaps that is what "being normal" is about. We are all in a continual state of integration, regardless of our childhood experiences. It's like a lens constantly refocusing, sharpening our image of how we see ourselves and our world. We take in our feelings and thoughts, our interactions with other people, and we reshape who we are in that moment.

People with DID do that, too, but in a slower, more exaggerated fashion. I've yet to meet a multiple who did not integrate in stages. It takes a long time to put all those pieces back together. Early in the process, we don't realize several pieces were deliberately swept under carpets, behind doors, on the back porch. Some pieces are real challenges to find and assimilate.

Even so, I discovered that each time I integrated a part of me, I felt more whole, more capable. The closer I came to complete integration, the less fragmented and frazzled I felt. I discovered a greater sense of control. I became a larger, more distinct "self" with fewer remaining separate smaller parts. Paradoxically, I also felt "not like me." I felt alone and empty till the newer sensations of each partial integration settled in.

The issue for many multiples, and their therapists, is whether everyone internally participated in any integration which might be called "complete." Each time I thought I was "finished," I discovered I wasn't. New issues brought forth new alters in ways not previously addressed. Even now, my sense of "complete integration" is so new I cannot claim it yet. But I feel complete in ways I did not a year ago. Time will tell.

Integration tossed me into a world where people cope and function as one person routinely. I still labor to prioritize my life work in any kind of routine way. I still search for that elusive thing called balance. Dozens of people inside create a certain amount of chaos, but things also get done! I still feel overwhelmed by how much "normal" people do just to run their lives efficiently. I am nowhere near it yet.

I've also had to deal with an intense loneliness inside, vastly different from any sort of loneliness felt externally. The loneliness inside cannot be easily managed, no matter how many good, loving people are now in my life. I grew up believing that everyone heard voices inside and experienced internal chaos. Not hearing those voices is quite a paradigm shift, to which I still must adjust.

But the benefits are breathtaking. Integration made me feel alive for the first time. When I feel things now, I know I feel them. I'm slowly learning it's okay to feel all feelings, even unpleasant ones. The bonus is, I get to feel pleasurable feelings as well. I also don't worry about my sanity anymore.

It's difficult to explain even to people who try to understand what integration means to someone who has been "in parts" for a lifetime. I still talk in a "we" way sometimes. Some of my "before integration" friends assume I can now just get back to being "me" — whatever that is. They don't realize integration is like being three all over again. I don't know how to act in certain situations because "I" never did it before. Or I only know how to respond in a fragmented way. What does "sadness" mean to someone who doesn't feel it continually? I don't know sometimes when I feel sad if I really should. It's confusing and scary being responsible for me all by myself now.

The most comforting aspect of integration for me, and what I especially want other multiples to know is: Nobody died. Nobody left. Everyone's still here inside me, in their correct place to be without controlling my body independently. There was not a scene where everyone left except one. I am a remarkably different, "brand new" person. I've spent months learning how to access my alters' skills and emotions — and they are mine now. I have balance and perspective that never existed before. I'm happy and content. This isn't about dying. It's about celebrating living to the fullest extent possible.

APRIL 13, 1992

H: I want you to be open to the discovery of these parts. Not one of them can hurt you unless you repress knowing it. Then it makes a stand.

N: Why?

H: It only reveals itself as an operation, as opposed to a thought, if you try to repress or deny it. It's like anybody who tries to deny part of themselves, or a feeling, or belief they hold. It manifests in destructive ways: substance abuse, overeating, being a workaholic, dysfunctional relationships. It's irrelevant until something is revealed. Then you take it in as, "Here's something more about myself I didn't know before." That's normal.

N: It doesn't feel real integrated.

H: Sometimes people feel a little crazy. That's also normal. It's not reasonable to expect high level functioning with total integration and confidence in yourself all the time. I understand, you're going for it. But the doubts that slip in aren't supposed to throw you as much as they are if you understand them as processes of normal, natural realizations, when they occur. You have your whole life to find out who you are. What you mean to yourself. What you want to accomplish, and how you're going to get there. You've been terrified over this notion of how many people are there.

N: Wouldn't most people be?

H: Yes. But beyond that sort of primitive thinking it doesn't matter. It'll reveal itself when it happens. Be excited about it. That's what integration is — the flexibility to go back and forth. You're frightened because you're doing it through the metaphor of these people. That's how you functioned in your life. You don't have to use that metaphor, or if it naturally comes up, it's nothing more than someone knowing more about herself. Your wanting to know how many people are in you is like wanting to know how many are in me. I couldn't tell you.

N: (smiles) There are a few.

H: Yeah! See, integration is also not being bothered by it.

N: I feel like if I'm not afraid of it, it's not real.

H: Yeah, well, that's crap. Fear replaces all other feelings, and then you only know things through fear. It's either bad feelings or no feelings —

so I'll go for no feelings. What a horrendous choice to have to make. These discoveries are what normal is like. You need just to translate it without the metaphor. Own yourself as a complete and whole person. As one, not as many.

APRIL 15, 1992

H: Could Charyse be gone? Could she not be needed anymore to cry?

N: Then who else would?

H: (smiles) You?

N: (laughs) Duh! What a novel concept.

H: Right before my eyes, you're integrating.

N: (agitated) What says I'm integrating?

H: Oh, you always do this. You put out such a challenge.

N: I thought I would cry, and that would mean I'm integrating.

H: Maybe you were wrong.

N: (sighs) But I do need to cry.

H: Then cry. The demand is for you to do it. Don't have your parts do it for you anymore. That's a bold challenge, and I do it very advisedly.

N: (hesitates) Don't have my parts do...anything for me anymore?

H: Just the way you say that tells me we're on the right track. There's trepidation about it. Listen, this is where you have all the control. You've gotten used to having the parts do things for you. This is very dangerous.

N: I'm still doing that?

H: I said, "Well, you do the crying." "Whoa! Who are you talking about? Me?" The way you just responded. (she sighs) Yeah, and that whole sigh. It's right there.

N: (agitated) What's right there?

H: Whatever needs to happen that's to your benefit is right there. The difficulty you're having with that kind of command. That's integration. Look how uncomfortable you are.

N: Yes! I don't know why. It really bothers me.

H: That's a sign.

N: A sign, that these other parts are going to come out?

H: Oh, yeah! Integration brings all the parts out, under your control. Wanting, or hoping, that they take care of things keeps them in their places, to come out in their own good time, according to the demands. Then it throws you for a loop. That you are so uncomfortable is more verification that it's on your shoulders. You are integrating. Your struggles will be yours, not someone else's.

N: Or someone else's triumphs.

H: Hey, I like that!

AUGUST 24, 1992

S: There was a book and movie called "I Never Promised You a Rose Garden".[1] *The girl in it was psychotic, self-mutilating, committed to a psychiatric hospital. She got help, she seemed resolved. But she walked out as this timid person into a whole new world. She looked lost, like she really didn't know what to do. The thing was, yes, they never promised it would be easy. But I felt they were throwing her to the wolves. Maybe she wasn't having psychotic episodes anymore, but she didn't seem prepared to live a real life. I want to be prepared! I don't merely want new things throwing me, instead of old things.*

H: Do you see yourself as that person?

S: No! I have more confidence than ever in my life.

H: The whole notion of integration has been talked about in too incomplete a way.

S: About people with MPD not really resolving it? Like maybe they only partially integrated, and learned to live with it? I would have learned to die with it.

H: You had to solve this. There wasn't any half-way process. You dealt with the fear, and acted with courage. I hadn't taken into consideration that what happened with Anita was the most frightening thing to you. And it didn't matter. It had to be done, anyway. (she nods) It's stopping short of taking advantage of that opportunity that keeps it unresolved. You were brave enough to go for it. And you pushed me to push you. People with MPD must demand a lot from their therapist, who can't back down from it, either.

S: Right, but it plays to their limitations if they're not really sure how to handle it. The other side is that the client must be extremely motivated to see all the things they don't really want to see.

OCTOBER 16, 1992

Dear Howard,

This is how it went, in a chain reaction:

I realized Nita had always acted like the alter she was, while the others popped up, unbeknownst to her, to provide balance when needed. This resulted in an acute awareness that nobody's popping up anymore — nothing is automatic now — and I feel alone. Inside Sarah doesn't talk to me anymore after years of having her around, like breathing. The hurt is all in me and can't be deflected on anyone else, which intensified the hurt and my feeling of emptiness. It escalated to where I was assaulted by these intense feelings, with no way to deal with them and nowhere to put them, until I couldn't stand it anymore. I called you.

I've never understood so clearly before what happened with my feelings when I had the others around. It's not really that I miss being in pieces. I just don't know how to deal with it.

December 7, 1992

E: What happened to Lynn?

S: She's here. We're all inside together, except for you.[2] I know it's confusing. I'm kind of everybody all mixed up.

E: You're not really Sarah, either.

S: Inside Sarah's inside, too.

E: But who are you?

S: I don't know how to answer that. I'm someone else. I'm the new improved Sarah.

E: Does Howard know you're different?

S: Of course. It really does get better, and it happens real quick.

E: Does it hurt when you disappear?

S: No, it feels kind of lighter. It's like when...a cloud comes out from in front of the sun and you feel warmer. It doesn't hurt; it just feels different. Better.

DECEMBER 10, 1992

H: You've become very adept at communicating. Your skill indicates your understanding. You articulate the dynamics extremely well. You're truthful, forthright, reassuring, and very in touch. There's another interesting thing you get from this development. With a great sense of confidence, you integrated.

S: I think so.

H: You did it! And from the outside looking in, you'd say, "Wow! That's right! We did it!" This was very clever, because from the inside out, it's like someone was left behind to say, "It's clean in here." With an echo. It's a further verification of the integration.

S: She doesn't know who I am. I'm not any of those people.

H: She doesn't know how to address you. It's a mind-boggling concept, this multiple dynamic. The skill was indicated in how you described it to her. "Well, I'm really all of those people still." It's not about that they went away; they found their real places to be. There was a bit of a lament that you hadn't written like Inside Sarah. Even then, there was a sense of "but it's okay."

S: She might think it's okay; I didn't.

H: In the short term, it doesn't feel like a benefit because you long to write like that. In the long term, which you haven't yet realized, there is a benefit, even if you can't put your finger on it. She's often critical, calls it brainwashing. You're saying it's okay, but feeling, "I do want to write that way, so it isn't okay." That makes it legitimate when she says, "People tell me things to make me feel a certain way, but they really feel differently. That's the adult way, to not be real."

S: ***I told her I was very sad about it. I wasn't lying when I said I felt better much of the time, too.***

H: *But do you feel a tug to put the emphasis on feeling better?*

S: ***Someone has to be the adult in this relationship.***

H: *You wouldn't call it brainwashing, but you could see how she might. It's a rather sophisticated notion. It's not appropriate for kids to be burdened in certain ways. They have to grow and develop so they can take on those burdens at more appropriate times.*

S: ***How can she grow if she's arrested? I understand what you're saying about real people with kids. But Erin's not going to move out of this, is she?***

H: *No, she'll resist it. But we nurture the resistance so when she comes to a place of comfort with it, she's grown to it naturally. You demonstrated the skill; you knew how to talk to her. It's not clean, but this is how you deal with kids. How they get comfortable to take their next steps.*

S: ***If she'd been comfortable, she would have gone inside with everybody else.***

H: *Let's just say she had her good reasons. And she has wisdom that may be beyond our understanding. Let's just say this is great! And before I forget, you will write like Sarah. That this discovery has been made will hasten whatever is supposed to happen. I wondered when you'd start to feel the pieces of integration are more accessible. Sarah should rightly feel the access of those positive parts she loved. Integration ought to have made those things even more accessible. Your "betterness" would increase 100-fold. That's what's supposed to happen.*

S: ***I'm waiting for that!***

H: *Now I know what the missing part is. When you integrate completely, Sarah will write the way she wrote.*

S: ***What if it never integrates completely? You said she didn't have to if she didn't want to.***

H: *She'll want to. We won't force her to do anything. We respect her. We care about her. She has more to tell us than we have to tell her. She's a key. Oh, come on! It's okay.*

MARCH 8, 1993

Dear Howard,

I used to say I was disappearing, more every day (which was probably true for Nita, all things considered). Well, now it seems reversed, and I am appearing more every day! It takes time to let it all sink in. If

the worst I can say is I haven't written a poem lately, then I'm blessed. I have no regrets.

You once told Erin that when she is scared, she should think of you, imagine you are holding her hand, and she wouldn't feel alone. This is the same little girl who gave up reaching out to anyone years ago, but in my mind I see her reaching out to you. She's come so far.

April 19, 1993

S: *There was a point last night where I could almost feel the integration happening, but Erin wanted to talk to you again.*

H: *I thought it wouldn't necessarily take place like before, which was rather dramatic. I thought you might fade into it. I was trying to imagine it. And here you are, verifying that you could feel it fading into an integrated state, but there's still a hanging on.*

S: *It was like I was fighting for it to happen. And then I stopped, 'cause I didn't think it was fair to her. Later, I thought, "Oh, you're making all this up." I say I know this is true, and I don't know if it is.*

H: *Well, you're mourning Erin, aren't you?*

S: *(taken aback) Yeah.(sighs)*

April 20, 1993 4:35 a.m.

Dear Howard,

I can't sleep. If I ever again have trouble crying, all I have to do is listen to this tape. It breaks my heart. I wanted this so much (happy happy joy joy), but I'm feeling so alone, and unmanageable. Everything is running to extremes. I don't know who I am, and this "me" doesn't really feel like me. Sometimes the difference feels subtle, and then suddenly I am a stranger.

Everything seems exaggerated and uncontrolled. I feel kind of nutty, but I know I'm not. Even with a practice run at integration last year, it feels different. It's intense. It feels chaotic, and I don't know if it really is chaotic, or just feels that way due to overload. It looked like the last piece of a jigsaw puzzle, but it really was the piece that makes it look 3-D now, instead of lying flat on the table. The remaining piece is much more than that. My mind keeps racing on and on....

April 25, 1993

Dear Howard,

I'm much better now, although I still have moments of intense sadness. It's hard to explain my thought processes last week. Whenever you've seen Erin's emotions, it was Erin expressing them, not me. But when you said good-bye to her, I felt a searing pain, despite knowing that it was like saying hello to me. Saying good-bye to her seemed like saying it to me. Your comment, in the context of my feeling guilty over "doing this" to Erin, that I must remember I was doing it to me, seemed to indicate that if I am doing this to me, then you are, too.

I had a wild recurring thought — the one that made me feel nutty — that if I'm Erin and me now, then it just makes me a conglomerate alter. The implication is that all alters go inside — like the integrated me must go inside someday, too. I wondered how to convince you that I didn't need to go inside, and what I could do if you were as relentless with me as you were with her. I also knew it wasn't you who was confused here, but I couldn't stop these thoughts.

I understand that any doubt in you would only have created needless doubt in her. The relentlessness probably had to be, but I was increasingly aware of her pain becoming my pain. I thought, "Can't she change her mind?" ("Can't I?") It seemed like you were unaffected by her tears, much like you told Nita before she went inside that her fear was not the compelling factor in whatever happened. I felt that the depth of Erin's (my) crying was an indication of the depth of her (my) pain — but you proceeded anyway. I see how this puts you in a major no-win situation. Your strength has always been a great comfort. So you exercise it, and I say you're relentless and unaffected by the results. Maybe when we're in the middle of the events that bind us it's best that you just do your thing.

I still ache over Erin, but the pain recedes. I no longer think you'll try to make me go inside. My theory is that my ambivalence made integration like landing a little plane, bouncing up and down till it settles. Maybe there were bounces where Erin wasn't really inside, so I felt like her very intensely in those moments, and thought you were trying to make me go inside. Am I even close?

MAY 9, 1993

Dear Howard,

There are many times when I feel like I'm three and have just awakened from my worst nightmare. I don't know how to deal with things still. When you've lived your whole life feeling you're bad, and suddenly you know you're not — and I do know it — all choices are up for grabs. Do I do it because I'm not bad? Is that the same as doing it because I am bad? What would a good person do? Is everything from before tainted, so I should do something new?

MAY 15, 1993

Dear Howard,

I still have moments where I well up with tears when thinking of Erin. The intense pain I felt when she said good-bye was really her stored up pain from a lifetime, juxtaposed against the idea that when Erin finally finds something good in her life, she has to give it up. The depth of her sacrifices are overwhelming, and I felt terrible that I was requiring one more. I haven't yet had a sense of her, like with the others, so I can't really say, "Okay, she's happy."

MAY 22, 1993

Dear Howard,

I still cry frequently over Erin. She's a persistently painful loss because for the first time ever I got to be a child in a safe context. I was uninhibited and naive. There was this nice man saying sweet Daddy things, and sometimes it seemed real. With integration, I lost not only that naiveté, but the wonderful Daddy things, too. I break down at odd moments, over those losses. It's part of Erin's triumph that these people did not completely destroy her naiveté, but I can't sustain it. I can't reclaim it, either, knowing what I know. And you're not my father. So we move on, and it's ultimately good, but my present grief is one more sign of how totally bereft I was as a child.

JUNE 26, 1993

Dear Howard,

A year ago, "integration" was just a word, and your office was a scary place. You had, only weeks earlier, spoken to Lynn for the first time, and my life was a nonstop nightmare. That I now feel so alive, hopeful, and bursting with possibilities is astonishing.

NOVEMBER 24, 1993

Dear Howard,

I always seem to "take stock" with you at Thanksgiving. I'm particularly grateful because it's the first year in my life where I can honestly look back and say, "Wow! This one's so much better than last year." On the surface, that may not look true — being unemployed; sick with asthma; Charlotte not talking to me. But things well below the surface make it so.

I'm so grateful that we rediscovered Erin, and that she was able to see and trust you as a wonderful father. I'm grateful she stuck around to finish the story, because it lets me get on with my life without wondering forever what pieces are missing. I'm grateful that the nightmares have ceased, as have the hallucinations, lost time, power surges, voices, and my prior inner chaos. (Perhaps the outer chaos is an expression of what no longer exists inside? Hmmm.)

I integrated all known alters in April, 1993. Until January, 1994, I'd never before felt such internal freedom. It was scary and exhilarating. There were adjustments to make, and new skills to learn.

The January 1994 earthquake in Los Angeles played a pivotal role in my discovery of remaining alters. It brought to the surface a fear I'd not known in years. I literally believed I was going to die in the darkness that morning. I felt helpless; alone; out of control; hidden; vulnerable for all the wrong reasons. Subsequent aftershocks sent me scurrying back to my anxiety. It took months to recognize these feelings as identical to those experienced when I was a small child, going weeks sometimes without seeing Ron. Then he'd appear, unpredictably and out of my control. Never enough time to prepare.

By June 1994, I felt increasingly out of control, but attributed it to "post-integration anxiety." I ignored a lot of signs. I was stunned when I said to a friend, "Friday seems like it lasted about four hours." It felt too familiar. I tried to contact Erin, and discovered six inside, including her. They'd always been there, but each had reason to not integrate previously, and to not make their presence immediately known. They remained more or less dormant until the earthquake's too familiar fear triggered a "multiple alert."

It's integrative for me to even know this. Even when I presented as "multiple," I had an integrated mindset. At first, I considered this discovery a major step backward. But I made a deal with myself years ago that I would never pretend again.

About this same time, I was increasingly more involved with the man who would become my second husband. When I moved across country to be with him, I knew only of Erin and Desiree left inside. We would eventually discover Missy and Susan as well.

NOVEMBER 7, 1994

Dear Howard,

Dan and I continue to learn about each other and grow. He's content to let me be whoever I am in this moment, with incentives to make changes I wanted anyway. We've become partners with so little transitional angst, it astounds us both. Your plans for me are all coming to sweet fruition. A whole new life. New me. New love. New confidence. New home. (Getting out of my icky apartment finally.) I'm reveling in all that's been accomplished and how big the payoff is now.

Even with all the progress, I still felt unsettled. I still searched for resolution.

JUNE 5, 1995

Dear Howard,

Nothing is getting done, and it doesn't matter how much I want to do it, nothing happens. There's something inside which rebels against all authority, and people saying I "should," which includes me. I'm continually spacing out. Is this an effect of Missy, or is it programming? How to counter it? Someday, Howard, I'd like to know what it's like to just be "me."

JULY 20, 1995

Dear Howard,

We have not met formally. My name is Susan. Dan and I talked last night; I convinced him I am benevolent. I've been around since the early days when Baby Susy decided being a baby was the way to get through life. I thought not. My "job" is to be productively bored. Sometimes that is a great challenge. I read; I play computer games; I crochet; I volunteer for tremendously tedious tasks that other people want done. Everything I do is productive, and all knowledge gained benefits us all.

Dan asked what benefit there could be. I told him Sarah is never bored writing her book. She is fascinated and horrified, condensing a couple years' horrific experience into a few pages. It compresses her feelings in ways that become unmanageable. It's not that she asks me to take over, but some internal mechanism makes it happen.

Dan said (which I find alarming), that he's attached to each of us, and it will be traumatic for him if we completely integrate. The others won't want to integrate if they think it will hurt him. While his greatest desire is for our unification, the fact of his hurt will be an impediment.

I think it's time you got to know me, Howard. I've hung around in the background because I was still needed. But even this is getting boring, if you know what I mean. My mandate is bored productivity. Part of that is helping Sarah to completion. I realized I must step forward if that is to happen. I know things no one else knows. Dan asked good questions, but you might ask ones which finish this.

JULY 25, 1995

I told Howard I had that unsettled, depressed feeling I got each time before when I integrated. I suddenly asked if I were driving this whole thing. He said I have control over my own life, and I could decide this right now. I asked, "Why didn't I do it four years ago?" He said it was like Dorothy in *The Wizard of Oz*. Click your heels, and say, "There's no place like home." She says, "Why didn't you tell me this three hours ago?" He said I wouldn't have believed it, either. He's right.

But something felt different this time. I told him I needed some ceremony of integration (don't know why, never needed one before). He offered to make one then and there. I could feel myself pulling in that direction but knew Dan was not prepared and needed closure. So I held my breath until I knew I was, in effect, saying no. Howard said it was like a marriage. The wedding isn't what happens on the wedding day, and the piece of paper isn't what makes it real. He is not married to the idea of an integration ceremony, or to his being part of it. I grew very sad, almost crying.

JULY 26, 1995 AT 1:00 A.M.

Dear Howard,

I think we had our ceremony last night.

After we said good-bye, I woke Dan up, saying I needed some major hugs. He agreed it was a decision over which I have complete control.

This last weekend, we celebrated my birthday. On Saturday, he bought a gold heart charm for my necklace. It means more than I can say, but Erin and Desiree thought it was neat because we all got to wear it. Sunday, he took Erin out to breakfast, gave her a watercolor set, and homemade certificates for Ben & Jerry's. She was so happy.

While we hugged, he was saying all the sensible things about integration, things we know intellectually, that they aren't dying, they will always be around inside me (I'm crying again). Then he said, at the exact moment I thought it — but it wasn't really me thinking it — "And you can always cash in those Ben & Jerry certificates and take her with us inside." I started crying, because it seemed Erin was saying it was okay. (God I can't stop crying.)

He said, "The bottom line is, whenever you're ready, you do it." I said, "But you wanted to say good-bye." He said, "No, I'd rather remember how happy Erin was on Sunday, how free she is, how special she knows she is, than cry with her when we say good-bye." Desiree told him last night she would love him forever, past integration. So he didn't feel the need to say good-bye to her, either. He hardly knows Susan, and Missy is just beginning to get her bearings. I realized, he was saying good-bye. And started crying again. (I'm typing this with tears rolling down my face.) The pain was so intense, and this thought flashed in my head, "It's happening." I just let go into it.

And now I can't stop crying. I ache inside, Howard. I feel broken. And yet, I'm supposed to feel whole? I know you're here with me spiritually, as you said. And Dan would wake up again if I asked. But I'm feeling so alone inside. (Just typing that started the tears afresh.) I don't know why I would feel this so acutely if it weren't true. I have to stop to try to breathe and see through the tears. It's always hurt before when I thought Erin integrated. This is the first time where I felt an indication from her that she wanted it. Not just that I wanted it.

I feel lost, Howard. The intellect is miles ahead of the feelings. I'm anything but lost, but it sure feels like it. I hope this pain soon gives way to renewed strength and balance and feeling as one.

So while you may not be married to the idea of the ceremony of my integration, I insist on performing a small part of our ritual by recording what is happening to me for you in this fax. Thank you for ceaselessly giving of your time, energy, and love to me, Howard. It is no small thing to be able to say, "I saved a life today."

8:00 A.M.

I cried all night. I've always said, "That's Erin crying, not me." Suddenly, I had this wellspring of pain flooding me, with nowhere to go. I don't think I'm done crying yet. I'm so wiped out that I'm not feeling much of anything but sad now. I also feel, somewhat weirdly, a little lighter?

JULY 31, 1995

Dear Howard,

Dan startled me greatly Friday morning. He calls me Sweetie. Since Friday, he's called me Sweetie Honey Princess, which adds on Desiree's and Erin's endearments. I'd told him how Erin worried she wouldn't be able to talk to anyone. You said, "I'll always be talking to you. You and I are going to know each other forever." So periodically, Dan talks to them. He also bought roses. Pink "for me"; red for "everyone else." It alarms me because it feels like he can't let go. Am I making too big a deal, Howard? I don't want to hurt him anymore. I said a game monster's name in a way that made him grin. He said, "Erin said that!" He looked so happy, so relieved. It was good to see Erin can still express herself.

And how do I feel? Somewhat depressed. Things are different, but it seems so subtle. I don't need proof, but keep looking for it. I know that makes no sense. I can still talk about "we" quite easily; then at times it feels so fake I don't want to come near it. Sometimes I feel I must have been out of my mind to talk that way.

AUGUST 1, 1995

Dear Howard,

This is integration? (sigh) (Sorry.) I've spent most of three days feeling like a shell. Like there's nothing inside of me. I started crying again last night because I don't know who "I" am now. Dan pointed out how I am very sensitive to things now (I am), and how I don't have the same coping mechanisms in place anymore (I don't). I am someone observing me trying to be a person.

My theory is that reading the Erin chapter for the first time after integration made it suddenly "real" to me, and I've numbed myself against feeling it. Meanwhile, the whole inside crew is beginning to feel more like a dream than like it was ever real. Thank God for my computer.

AUGUST 9, 1995

Dear Howard,

Since integration, Dan and I've stopped playing. I need that as much as Erin ever did. He said, "Erin made it totally uncomplicated. I could just be with her." I asked if he is bored with "just me," since he doesn't have direct access to Erin and Desiree, and can't seem to see them in me. He says he is never bored with me.

But I don't feel like Erin or Desiree. If he loved us equally, I suddenly feel like I'm only getting 1/3 of his love. The other 2/3 is going nowhere. He says he doesn't love me any less, but he doesn't love me any more, either. He hasn't been able to transfer the love he had for them to me yet. I know you said it might take a few months to get this all in sync, but I don't want to fuck up the best relationship I've ever had while I wait to feel an integrated feeling.

AUGUST 28, 1995

What a difference a few weeks make. I'm feeling more like me each day. I don't feel lost anymore. I'm gaining a better sense of who I really am, and what I want to accomplish. Dan and I've had some rather intense conversations while we sorted out these changes. We're emerging on the other side stronger and even more committed to each other. The loss and mourning (especially for Erin) continues, but we're able to play again. It's not perfect, but I suspect it will improve over time. I also suspect this is more like what normal is than not.

OCTOBER 5, 1995

We see Erin and the others in many ways now, it's just they express themselves through me. It's like "an inside joke" between me and Dan. Their presence makes us smile when we recognize them. I still miss Erin's (and Desiree's) effortless and unabashed playfulness. I'm playful, but in a more subdued way. The substantial tradeoff is, I feel more focused, more real now, too. I can live with that.

JANUARY 18, 1996

The more distance I get from the integration event, the more I continue to feel "like me." Sometimes I'm depressed and overwhelmed, as there's still so much to learn, to discover, to feel, about "becoming one." I take small steps and try to remember to be gentle with myself. Some days I wish it were easier, but I never wish I could go back.

24

On Forgiveness and Philosophy

But then, don't you have to let go of everything that was wrong in your past?

—NITA, AUGUST 7, 1991

Forgiveness is a frequent topic among survivors. Many believe their healing will never be complete until they reach that state. Others believe the act of forgiveness can forestall their nightmares. (For most people, it's seldom that easy.) Survivors with a religious persuasion are often pressured, from within or without, to forgive as part of their belief system. Some debate whether it is more important to forgive ourselves, instead of, or prior to, forgiving our abusers.

Why do we need to forgive ourselves when we were innocent children caught up in forces not of our making? I once felt I'd done nothing wrong, and to "forgive myself" created a new lie. I figured self-forgiveness indicated I was somehow at fault. But part of healing is recognizing how we have hurt ourselves as a result of the hurts received at the hands of others.

I learned to forgive myself for hating who I was, hurting my body, and hurting others when I lashed out in my pain. I forgave myself for burying my personal truth for thirty years, and for my lost potential during all that time. I forgave myself for not believing in my own goodness.

I don't believe any survivor is capable of truly forgiving before s/he is ready. Pretending to forgive might constitute denial of ongoing issues. I call it "pretending for peace." It's sometimes easier to pretend than to keep up the fight. And it's hard to get pissed off about things that supposedly are forgiven.

AUGUST 7, 1991

H: Some people experience something so bad that for the rest of their lives they will be failures, in some way.

N: To prove this horrible thing happened? To make them right about what happened when they were young?

H: Exactly. They've got to struggle with it. If they become everything they would have become anyway, what do they surmise? It didn't make any difference.

*N: **Why don't they just say it made a difference, but they worked twice as hard to come out even?***

H: That's what a healthy person says. "Isn't it great that I don't let it negatively affect me anymore?" This is where forgiveness comes in. You feel the pain and forgive its source, which doesn't mean it was okay it happened. It means this isn't going to negatively affect me anymore. It caused pain, which is compelling reason enough for it not to have happened. That becomes the new, and I dare say, correct perspective anyone needs to have about childhood abuses.

*N: **But then, don't you have to let go of everything that was wrong in your past?***

H: A very good way of putting it. Don't you?

*N: **And it's gone? Like it never happened?***

H: It happened. You can remember it, tell someone what happened. But you're no longer negatively affected by it. You don't have to grapple with it or deal with it. It's there as a report of your recollection, not as an influence. What color were the walls in your bedroom? Blue. It's just a report. What street did you live on? Elm. It's where you lived, that's all.

MARCH 11, 1992

Howard is saying you feel it and forgive it now, till the next time you feel it. So I could forgive my mother now, then some other trigger presents which must be worked through, and I forgive her again. And no, I haven't come close to forgiving her or Ron. Howard's not talking about me embracing them and acting unaffected by what they did to me.

Howard has a thing about generosity; he thinks there isn't nearly enough of it in the world. (He lives it, too. He's generous beyond belief.) When I've ranted about people who hurt me, and for whom forgiveness is a nonissue, he's said, "Could you be that generous — not to forget what they've done — but to allow yourself to move on from that pain into something from which you will directly benefit?" It's very difficult to look him in the eye, and say, "No! I can't be that generous!" Especially when I am so clearly withholding from me. It becomes me doing it to me, instead of them. This is an often overlooked aspect of forgiveness.

JUNE 1992

H: Have you ever wondered about the purpose of philosophy? (laughs) You're giving me the look now. You've never wondered.

S: No.

H: Here's the meaning of life; what is; how it operates; here's. . .philosophy. You could say it's a lot of fluff, or you could say philosophy may be, of all disciplines of human endeavor, the most important to develop and understand.

S: ***Why? (laughs) The "right" question.***

H: *I don't think anyone can live well, or have a chance to live well, unless they can conceive a purpose in their life. Without philosophy, you can't do that. You've got to have philosophy to get out of bed every day. Without philosophy, how could you pay your taxes and make sense of a thing like that? Or stand in line at the DMV? I'm serious.*

S: ***So I took a purposeful stand, and said, "The reason I'm here is to bug my mother?"***

H: *No, of course not. If a person is in your situation, does it mean this person will be scarred and damaged forever because of it? No, because they'll have a philosophy to work it through so they aren't negatively affected by it. This should not have happened, but it did. I'd hate to think you're just screwed for the rest of your life. The goal has always been that you move beyond this so completely that your life will be whatever it would have been anyway.*

S: ***That concept goes right over my head. I won't have the life it would have been anyway because I didn't live the life I should have had to live it anyway.***

H: *That's why you're in a loop that you can't get out of. Until you can conceive that your life is going to be what it would have been anyway, it'll be impossible for you to move beyond.*

S: ***I think what you're saying is circular. My life can never be the way it would have been anyway.***

H: *Of course it can.*

S: ***It doesn't have the basis for all the stuff that would have happened to make it what it would have been anyway.***

H: *You create the basis. (she sighs) I'll grant you, it's a tall order. But, you've got to create it. What are we going to do with people who grow up like this? Just extinguish them? Put them out of their misery?*

S: ***Some do it for you.***

H: *And what do the others do?*

S: ***(sarcastic) I have to build the foundation for the life I would have had anyway.***

H: *Well, yes, exactly. I will even tolerate your sarcasm, because that's what you do. I have high hopes for you. You're one of the most talented, sensitive, and gifted individuals I know. That is a report and observation; it is not a compliment.*

S: ***Thank you anyway.***

H: *(laughs) However you can receive it, just take it in. You would have been a joy to be with, for any parent, because of the gifts you brought very naturally. If you'd had parents who recognized, nurtured, appreciated, paid attention to, and supported your gifts, do you think your life would have been different?*

S: ***Sure.***

H: *That's exactly the life I want you to have as an adult.*

S: ***I'm saying I can't get it because I didn't have that.***

H: *I'm saying you can. And that's all there is. I don't even want to argue the point. I want you to adopt this philosophy because it's your only way out. Of all the things you ever thought would get you out of this, would it be the law? Psychology? Science? Politics? No, philosophy gets you out. You exist, and you're entitled to good things. You always have been, and always will be.*

AUGUST 3, 1992

P: ***So we're all going to forgive Ron?***

H: *Some things are a lot to ask a person to forgive. I dare say you're in that category. But also know it's not a one-time deal. It's continual. The way someone experiences it is, "Geez, I haven't felt like that in a week. God, that gets me down. Whew!" They go through the whole sensation again. There's no therapy, counseling, input, or even forgiveness, that makes a bad thing good.*

P: ***So it will be like it never happened.***

H: *That is the most profound manifestation of forgiveness, to live like it didn't happen. Not to hide it. It's just not visible to people on the outside looking in.*

SEPTEMBER 21, 1994

Someone once told me that his best definition of forgiveness is giving up your right to get even. To me, the best way to get even (but more likely, ahead) is to live the life I was supposed to live: full, happy, fulfilled. Getting even is finding a life partner who doesn't think abusing me is the best thing he's got going, who cherishes me "just because," and doesn't hesitate to tell or show me. Getting even is following my dreams to successful completion because I believe in myself, no matter what they said or did. It's feeling satisfied that I've done my best for me, and not because I'm afraid of something. I'm not willing to give up any rights to getting even.

If I believed that forgiving Ron and my mother would help me I'd do anything to make it happen. I still believe it would somehow take something away from me. Like it would make everything they did (not just to me) okay. Like we could all forget about it. I'm not willing to let anyone forget about it ever again. Is this vindictive and unforgiving, or a statement of survival? I'm in the latter camp. When I've completely healed and reclaimed all the power in my life still awaiting my discovery, then I'll think about forgiving them. Right now, my focus must remain on me.

I've come almost full circle now. I adopted Howard's philosophy, often grudgingly. But it works! Everything he predicted and planned as the reasonable outcome of my therapy not only occurred, but transcended all my expectations. It didn't happen overnight, but Howard made everything easier to stay with the process. The results are extraordinary. Life is good now. I am at peace with myself and my world today. And I look at tomorrow as a gift to be anticipated and cherished.

Endnotes

Introduction

1. Most names herein were changed to preserve privacy. My childhood terrorist's name, however, was changed to protect my publisher's liability. My various alter names are the originals.
2. Proponents of False Memory Syndrome — who maintain that overeager therapists implant false memories of abuse in their clients — will be unhappy to learn that Howard never once mentioned the subject before I did. He also never hypnotized me, put me on drugs, or age regressed me. He did, rather, what no one else had ever done before: he listened.
3. Dissociative Identity Disorder (Multiple Personality Disorder) specific criteria: 1) The presence of two or more distinct identities or personality states (each with its own relatively enduring pattern of perceiving, relating to, and thinking about the environment and self). 2) At least two of these identities or personality states recurrently take control of the person's behavior. 3) Inability to recall important personal information that is too extensive to be explained by ordinary forgetfulness. NOTE: In children, the symptoms are not attributable to imaginary playmates or other fantasy play.
4. Despite strides made in the last four decades, we still hear daily accounts of children being tortured, mutilated, sexually abused and discarded. Nobody is listening to their stories, either.

Chapter 3

1. The apartment break-in is discussed more fully in Chapter 12.

Chapter 4

1. Statistics provided by President Clinton's Proclamation of April 1995 as National Child Abuse Prevention Month, released by the White House on April 5, 1995.

Chapter 6

1. For a complete list of all known alters, see Appendix .

Chapter 7

1. Jacob Segura made these observations a month in advance of Charlotte's disclosures. At the time, I thought he was stretching a bit, and was per-

plexed by how he determined his observations.

Chapter 8

1. An essential attribute in any good therapist is an extraordinary sense of humor. The laughter is every bit as important as the insights and reality checks.
2. It was not until January 1995, when perusing a review of *When Rabbit Howls* that I noticed mention (with considerable skepticism by the reviewer) that Trudy Chase claimed a similar phenomenon. I have yet to read her book, I suppose because I have enough nightmare fodder of my own. Whether one believes it is possible for DID to alter electrical currents is not the issue here. It was happening to me long before Charlotte mentioned it, and before I knew of the existence of Ms. Chase's book.
3. My mother died six years prior to this occurrence.
4. Howard's philosophy regarding therapy is that many issues can be dealt with on a short-term basis, i.e., four visits or less. Barring that, he sees patients in the fewest sessions necessary to accomplish mutual goals.

Chapter 18

1. Note that this letter, and others in this chapter, were written years before I met Howard.

Chapter 19

1. I first saw actress Amy Irving in "Carrie" when it was released, about 1979. Involuntarily, and loudly, I gasped, "That's the girl!" Then shrank into my seat in acute embarrassment, as patrons shushed me, and my friend stared. I had no idea what girl I was referring to, so this event augmented my list of things that made me feel crazy. When Erin spoke of "seeing an angel," I understood at once that the girl looked similar to Amy Irving, who is alive, of my generation, and obviously not involved.
2. This is an internal conversation between Erin and myself, transcribed onto my computer as it occurred.
3. See Chapter 23.

Chapter 21

1. Referencing the movie, "The Exorcist," and Anita's penchant for scary things.
2. Ibid. Note 4, Chapter 8..

3. Not all of them followed through. See Chapters 22 and 23.

Chapter 22

1. Daniel Ryder, C.C.D.C., L.S.W., *Breaking the Circle of Satanic Ritual Abuse: Recognizing and Recovering from the Hidden Trauma* (Minneapolis: CompCare Publishers, 1992).
2. See Chapter 14.
3. Erin also describes witnessing this in Chapter 19.

Chapter 23

1. Hanna Green, *I Never Promised You A Rose Garden* (New York: Henry Holt, 1964).
2. In December, 1992, we believed Erin to be the lone integration holdout. This was not the case. At least two partial integrations followed of other discovered alters prior to what we now believe was the final integration, which occurred on July 25, 1995.

Appendix

The following is a list of all known named alters. Where followed by a letter in parenthesis, that is the transcript identifier. The term "my age" indicates the alter followed my age chronologically.

Anita (my age) ("A") See Chapter 21
Atina (my age) The good parts of Anita, but looked like her
Baby Susy (6) Decided to survive by remaining a baby
Carol (3) Wanted her Mommy
Carolyn (12) Flirted with teachers; interested in clothes
Charyse Noel (4) (Inside Sarah's arrested twin)
Chrissie (10) Wasn't afraid when fantasizing and pretending
Desiree (19) Sexual purity untainted by memories
Erin Elisabeth (6) ("E") See Chapter 19
Honey (10) Intervened when my parents fought
Inside Sarah (my age) ("IS") See Chapter 18
Jimmy (my age) Denied anything ever happened
Karen (6) The artist
Kathy (5) Good at spelling; worried about everything
Little Girl (4) Came out when Ron called me that
Little Zsazsa (4) Daddy's favorite little girl
Lynn (my age) ("L") See Chapter 17
Marcie (7) Stopped talking when Ron threatened to kill her
Marianne (my age) Blind, terrified of Anita
Mark (6.5) Wanted to run Ron over with a fire truck; the fighter
Melissa (my age) Healthy skepticism
Missy (4) Terrified of the Bad People; See Chapter 22
Nita (aka Outside Sarah) ("N" or "S") See Chapter 16
Original Anita (3) Protected by Anita in high secrecy
Peter (my age) ("P") See Chapter 20
Pretty Sarah; Sarah Princess Sarah (6) Childhood fragments related to Inside Sarah
Samantha (12) Tomboy; wanted to shoot hoops with Howard
Sissy (my age) Responded to Charlotte
Steven (my age) Anita's robotic henchman
Susan (my age) Mandate was bored productivity

Other transcript identifiers:
Howard Asher ("H")
Charlotte ("C")
Linda ("LI")

[illegible]

[illegible] followed by [illegible]

[illegible] See Chapter [illegible]

[illegible] wants [illegible]

[illegible] Played with teachers [illegible]

[illegible] See Chapter [illegible]

[illegible] Chapter [illegible]

[illegible] came out when [illegible] called [illegible]

[illegible] See Chapter 15

[illegible] fire truck, the [illegible]

[illegible] Healthy skeptic [illegible]

[illegible] See Chapter [illegible]

Original [illegible]

Peter [illegible] See Chapter 20

[illegible] fragments

[illegible] Sarah

[illegible] always wanted to [illegible]

[illegible]

Other fragments and entities:

[illegible]

[illegible]

[illegible]

INDEX